Lesbian Lifestyles

Women's Work and the Politics of Sexuality

GILLIAN A. DUNNE

First published 1997 by
MACMILLAN PRESS LTD
Houndmills, Basingstoke, Hampshire RG21 6XS
and London
Companies and representatives
throughout the world

ISBN 0–333–65781–0 hardcover
ISBN 0–333–65782–9 paperback

A catalogue record for this book is available
from the British Library.

10   9   8   7   6   5   4   3   2   1
06 05 04 03 02 01 00 99 98 97

Printed in Hong Kong

To my dear friends, Paula Munro,
Jennifer Jarman and Shirley Prendergast

CONTENTS

═══ ACKNOWLEDGEMENTS ═══

First and foremost, I would like to thank the 60 women who participated in this project. By sharing their wisdom with me they made this research both possible and an extremely enjoyable experience. One of these women died tragically in a car accident. Her hopes for the future are recorded in this study. This book began its life as a doctoral thesis. Consequently, the development of the different stages of the research has involved encouragement and constructive criticism from many people. Henrietta Moore supervised the study. I am greatly indebted to her for her moral and practical support, her intellectual contributions and the continuing contribution she has made to the unfolding of the ideas that spring from this research. I am also grateful to Michelle Stanworth for having given me the courage to embark on the project, and for initial guidance and supervision.

I have also been lucky to have had access to a lively and intellectually stimulating research community. I would like to extend special thanks to members of the 'Groovy Gang' reading group, and Sociological Research Group, as well as occupants of the 'Attic'. They provided both friendship and the opportunity to discuss and clarify ideas. My thanks, then, to Jennifer Jarman, Karen Hughes, Andrea Doucet, Jane Ireland, Ginny Morrow, Shenna Jain, Teresa Brennan, Sharon Dolovich, Anne Marie Goetz, Bob Blackburn, Ken Prandy and Graham White.

A range of social and psychological processes exist to limit the possibility of a thesis coming out as a book. I am greatly indebted to those people who have encouraged and facilitated this process. Worth special mention are Henrietta Moore, Bob Blackburn, Jennifer Jarman, Sarah Green and Shirley Prendergast. The end product has been greatly enhanced by the ideas and insights that I have gained from them. Their comments on the script, as well as those of Wendy Botthero, Nina Hallowell and Kim Perren have been invaluable. My friend Pip Wheldon has been particularly helpful in encouraging clarity of expression. I would also like to thank colleagues at Anglia Polytechnic University who have taught me a great deal about the communication of ideas. A special thanks to Maureen Fitzgerald. While this book has been made possible by the contributions of all these different people, any limitations are ultimately my responsibility.

The research process is a stressful and emotionally draining experience and I am extremely grateful to Shirley Prendergast, Sarah Green, Pip Wheldon and Paula Munro for their generosity in providing the very welcome emotional labour which supported me throughout. Developing the thesis into its book form has also required time. I thank my colleagues Bob Blackburn and Henrietta Moore for letting me turn my attention away from current research so that the summer could be devoted to this book.

GILLIAN A. DUNNE

CHAPTER ONE

Researching 'non-heterosexual' women: theoretical and methodological issues

INTRODUCTION

Central to the feminist enterprise has been the review and re-assessment of the relationship between the public and the private. In this, so called 'private activities', such as household work and sexual relationships, have been shown to connect with the public. The recognition that the conditions of women's association with the private flow from relations of domination rather than the expression of nature allows us to redefine the political to include previously personal activities (Jones, 1988). Thus the 'private' world of sexuality has been included within the realm of the political and can be subject to critical gaze. An important reason for this inclusion is the knowledge that sexual meanings are socially produced rather than the natural outcome of some essential sexual nature. Given that hetero-sexuality is usually produced, the social mechanisms which construct sexuality are deeply implicated in the production of gender inequality. While most feminists would agree that sexuality plays an important role in shaping inequality between women and men, there is much debate concerning the amount of emphasis which should be placed upon it. Radical feminists, such as MacKinnon (1982) and Rich (1984), argue that it is at the core of men's ability to control and exploit women. Social-ist feminists, such as Hartmann (1981), tend to prioritize other sources of inequality, such as the labour market, motherhood and the family. A major problem for resolving these debates is the lack of empirical evidence demonstrating the importance of interpretations of sexuality in shaping gender-differentiated opportunities. Feminists have shown ways that women's employ-ment circumstances are constrained by sexual harassment/

violence and ideas about the presentation of appropriate femi-
ninity/sexuality, but much more work is needed to illuminate
the full implications of sexuality in shaping gender inequality.
The current trend towards post-modern analyses of sexuality
(for example, Butler, 1993) which emphasize the discursive at
the expense of structural constraints, although exciting, offers
little help in establishing links between sexuality and the material world (Jackson, 1995).

This study seeks to build bridges across the different perspectives which inform feminist thinking by showing ways that
interpretations of sexuality deeply shape the conditions of
women's work, both in the home and in the workplace. Until
now, research has considered factors shaping women's work
from a heterosexual perspective and this limits our ability to
recognize the *impact of heterosexuality itself* on the conditions of
women's lives. This volume seeks to extend our understandings
by focusing on the home lives and employment experience of
women who have moved beyond heterosexuality. Drawing on
life history data from 60 non-heterosexual women, it will highlight the material dimension of sexuality. We will see ways that
moving beyond heterosexuality is experienced as empowering.
A relationship will be shown between interpretations of sexuality and women's experience of employment opportunity: the
pursuit of a lesbian lifestyle both necessitates and facilitates
financial independence. Further, we will see that, because of
the range of commonalities women share on the basis of their
gender, lesbian relationships provide greater opportunities for
the operation of ideals relating to co-operation and egalitarianism. By illustrating ways that interpretations of sexuality mediate gender to produce different outcomes, it is hoped that this
volume will encourage other researchers to extend their analysis beyond gender so as to reveal the implications of institutionalized heterosexuality for structuring the conditions of
women's work.

The remainder of this chapter will provide the theoretical
and methodological background to this study. The first section draws on empirical and theoretical material to outline my
argument as to why feminists have common interests in undermining the way that institutionalized heterosexuality is taken
for granted. It will first present data which illuminate the socially constructed nature of sexual outcomes, and will then discuss
ways that institutionalized heterosexuality is deeply implicated

in shaping gender inequality. After outlining the research questions which shape the analysis of the life history data, the second section will provide details of the way in which the study was carried out.

SEXUALITIES AS SOCIALLY CONSTRUCTED

Diversity across time and space

The diversity of sexual meanings that exists across time and space flies in the face of commonsense understandings which link heterosexuality with the expression of some essential sexual nature. The variety of different primary relationships formed by people at other times and in other places problematizes the apparent 'naturalness' of heterosexual partnerships as the medium through which we must live our adulthood. Instead, we have to recognize that the ways that we give voice to and act upon our sexual and emotional feelings are powerfully shaped by our social and economic environments. Importantly, these insights allow us to examine critically the processes that shape and construct sexual identities just as we have been doing so successfully for gender. This offers scope for change in ways that simple essentialism does not. Let me very briefly outline some anthropological and historical evidence.

There is a small but growing body of cross-cultural material which documents a wide range of social meanings attached to sexual expression in both its heterosexual and homosexual form. Of particular interest are edited volumes by Caplan (1987), Blackwood (1986) and Ortner and Whitehead (1981), the classic theoretical analysis of links between sexuality and culture by Rubin (1975), an important ethnography on male homosexuality by Herdt (1993) and an extensive review in Greenberg (1988:25–88). The study of other cultures indicates the prevalence of homosexual activity, the different meanings and significance attached to it, and ways that people can shift unproblematically between heterosexual and homosexual behaviour. In many small-scale societies we find that homosexual behaviour is ritualized and even institutionalized. These findings confound contemporary western beliefs about the integrity of sexual identities. While there is much more evidence available on male homosexuality, female homosexuality tends to remain far more hidden, particularly from the gaze and

judgement of western observers. Shepherd's (1987) illuminating ethnography of homosexuality amongst the Swahili in
Mombasa suggests that it is common to find both Swahili men
and women shifting between homosexual and heterosexual
relationships over the course of their lives. People can be open
about their sexuality without risk of censure and what Shepherd calls 'lesbianism' is common. For women, adult status comes
through marriage, but once this has been achieved it is socially acceptable for women to set up independent lesbian
households. Wealthy lesbians may even arrange marriages of
convenience to facilitate their partnerships with women.

Greenberg (1988:25–88) reviews a wide range of fascinating
ethnographies on homosexual relations in kinship-structured
societies to show the prevalence and importance of homosexuality for male rites of passage. Good examples come from
Melanesia, where homosexuality has been most studied. Here
semen is symbolically associated with male substance and is
linked with the acquisition of masculine power and special
knowledge. Initiation rites involve the sexual transmission of
semen from older men to boys. Another example comes from
the Coerunas Indians of Brazil. Here, becoming a healer involves the sexual transmission of special healing powers from
the male healer to young male apprentice. In the past, amongst
the mountain dwellers of northern Morocco, a common view
was that a boy could not adequately learn the Koran without
first having intercourse with a saintly master. At the beginning
of the century in Morocco a widely held belief was that a range
of highly valued masculine qualities could be transferred from
man to man through penetration with the penis. Rather than
implicating men's gender identities, homosexual acts are often essential to its acquisition.

Greenberg provides examples of societies where male homosexuality has been institutionalized (see also Whitehead, 1981).
For example, in some Melanesian societies custom dictates that
a boy leaves his mother's hut to form sexual relationships with
his mothers' brother or his sister's husband, and boys remain
in these relationships until they marry. Amongst the Sambia of
New Guinea, heterosexual intercourse is associated with the
depletion of men's vital forces. As there are extensive taboos
on sexual activity with women and none on homosexual ones,
homosexual activity dominates the sexual lives of adult men.
Thus institutionalized male homosexuality can co-exist along-

side marriage. Another example comes from Swat Pukhtun of northern Pakistan. Men usually have their first sexual encounters with each other and often retain male lovers after marriage. Evidence points to the existence of a slightly different form of institutionalized homosexuality in some past native North American cultures (Greenberg, 1989:42; Whitehead, 1981:84). Here we find that anatomical sex did not necessarily correspond with gender or sexual behaviour. There was space in the middle for a status known as 'berdache'. Whitehead observes that gender identity was gauged mostly by the labour someone did, rather than by sexual behaviour or *bodily characteristics*. Thus, if a child had a particular interest in the activities associated with the opposite gender, there developed a suspicion that they may be a berdache. Greenberg suggests that sometimes there were very practical reasons for deciding to bring up a girl as a berdache. If a family comprised only female children it made sense to encourage a daughter to enter the male world. They could hunt and bring back meat when parents become frail. Alternatively, at some time before puberty rites, a young person might have been visited in a dream by a spirit who ordered him on her to take on the personage of the opposite sex. A berdache adopted the social roles of their chosen gender. Thus a 'female' berdache joined the men in their hunting and fighting and could marry a woman. A 'male' berdache entered the community of women and found a male partner. According to Greenberg, a main factor underpinning a person's willingness to cross gender boundaries was that this movement did not imply loss of status: gender was shaped around notions of complementarity, and this translated into a less hierarchal gendered ordering of power than in most other societies. However, Whitehead points out that, in berdache cultures, both berdaches and non-berdaches could engage in homosexual behaviour. She concludes that in these cultures there really was no link between sexual activity and gender identity.

There is contemporary cross-cultural evidence (and, as we will see later, historical evidence) to suggest that women's same-sex friendships can be passionate and represent a central source of practical and emotional support throughout life. Gay's (1986) investigation of female friendships in Lesotho, Southern Africa, finds that romantic relationships between women have become institutionalized and often run in parallel to heterosexual relationships. Adolescent girls form 'mummy–baby' relationships with young women. These are passionate and sensual relationships which often involve 'falling in love' and perhaps sexual expression. These mummy–baby relationships, together with the more equal friendships formed between older women, are seen as central sources of emotional and practical support in the context of a nation disrupted by high levels of labour migration. Another interesting feature of female sexuality in Lesotho is the involvement of other women in young women's sexual awakenings. According to Gay, a common practice involves lengthening the inner lips of the vagina. This provides opportunities for auto-eroticism and mutual masturbation between women.

The anthropology of this issue indicates a wide range of possibilities in linking anatomical sex, gendered behaviour and sexual activity. Further, it shows that in many cultures, particularly kinship-based ones, sexual behaviour has very little to do with the expression of self, but much more to do with expressions of social or cultural status. Ritualized homosexuality in Melanesia is really about group membership and maintaining the strength of that group. It involves the suppression of the self rather than the expression of self (Herdt, 1993). Rubin (1975) attempts to make sense of the fact that some cultures (for example the Euro-American one) have the categories heterosexual, bisexual and homosexual and others (for example Melanesian) have cross-cousin sexuality. She suggests that this results from cultural rules which define sexuality in either *proscriptive* or *prescriptive* terms. In western societies, sexuality is defined proscriptively: that is, you learn who you should *not* have sexual relations with (which includes immediate members of your family as well as members of the same gender). This leaves it to the individual to choose from anyone else who does not belong to those groups. In many kinship-based cultures, sexuality is defined prescriptively. Here all people are excluded as potential partners except for one category: the category from which a marriage partner is to be selected, for example their cousins. Homosexuality and heterosexuality therefore do not come into it at all. Such categories only exist when cultural ideas about these things make it *appear* that individuals have a personal choice of sexual partner. It is therefore only when sexuality is defined proscriptively that there can be a possibility of making sexuality appear as if it is something which 'belongs to' and defines the individual and therefore make it appear to be a part of one's identity. Where it is defined prescriptively, it 'belongs to' the social group of which you are a member, and it does nothing to define the individual.

The variety of sexual meanings across the globe alerts us to the breadth of the human capacity to express sexual and emotional aspects of self. The diversity in the dominant forms that this expression takes brings issues of control into sharp relief. This is particularly evident when we consider sexuality in contemporary western societies. The influential French philosopher Michel Foucault (1979) characterizes the history of western sexuality as one that has been socially constructed through *definition* and *regulation*. From the nineteenth century onwards the moral authority of the church gave way to new regulatory bodies: for example, the medical profession, psychiatry, the law, the state. By the conflation of sexual acts with identity and personhood the sexual categories *heterosexual* and *homosexual* were created. Thus previously ambiguous or fluid behaviour became rigidly categorized and imbued with social meaning. In this way the boundaries around appropriate heterosexual behaviour could be more vigorously 'policed'. Transgressions from the 'norm' could mobilize the full weight of scientific knowledge, drawing on powerful ideas about sickness, abnormality and perversity. Interestingly, these judgements seem to affect us more deeply than moral ones based upon notions of good and bad – it is easier to live with the idea of being a rogue than that of being a sick pervert!

The silence surrounding women's sexuality in Foucault's analysis has begun to be filled by the work of feminist historians. In the quest to develop a lesbian history, historians have been particularly interested in making visible the homoemotional worlds constructed by women in the past.[1]

A major problem in linking women's homoemotional worlds with a lesbian history relates to definition: can we transpose contemporary western definitions of lesbianism (and, I would add, heterosexuality) into different historical and cultural contexts (Jeffreys, 1989; Ferguson, 1981)? How do we define sexual? Is it simply about genital sex? How are we ever to know the extent to which women's relationships involved sexual expression or the interpretations they gave to sensual pleasure? In relation to other times and places, do relationships have to be sexual to be defined as lesbian? These problems are hard to resolve if we constrain ourselves with contemporary sexual definitions. Instead, I think that our historical and cross-cultural focus should be on exposing the myth that heterosexuality is the only normal adult expression of sexuality, and that heterosexual partnerships are the only ones that count. Given the magnitude of social, economic and sexual constraints on women in the past, do we call women who wished to make their homoerotic relations central, but could not, heterosexual?

The search for a 'lesbian' history has yielded fascinating insights into the homoemotional lives of middle- and upper-class North American and British women. Faderman (1985) and Smith-Rosenberg (1975) show that the separate spheres which developed in wealthy households during the late eighteenth and nineteenth centuries supported an environment which gave rise to a rich homosocial world for women. Smith-Rosenberg tells us that there is 'an abundance of manuscript evidence [which] suggests that [during this period] women routinely formed emotional ties with other women. Such deeply felt, same-sex friendships were casually accepted in American society' (p.1). Faderman points out that these intense 'romantic friendships' were much encouraged in Britain and America. The emphasis on chastity for women in Victorian society, the belief in women's asexuality and the formality which existed between the sexes ensured that women's emotional energy was 'safely' directed towards other women. This encouragement was reflected in many novels of the period. Faderman suggests that, had some of these been written 50 years later, they might well have been at the centre of an obscenity trial. Indeed, Faderman gives examples of nineteenth-century classic literature being suppressed in the more sexually 'sophisticated' twentieth century: for example, Henry James's *The Bostonians*. In this book James has two of his female principal characters living together in a 'Boston Marriage'.

As women were generally robbed of any possibility of economic independence, these passionate friendships could be advocated as charming 'preludes' to the 'real thing': the ability of women to act on these primary emotions being practically unthinkable. This did not, however, stop women from wishful thinking. Quite unself-consciously, women wrote of their desire to run away with each other and set up home together. In a letter to her great friend Ellen Nussey in 1836, Charlotte Brontë complains bitterly of the economic constraints that prevent them living together:

Ellen, I wish I could live with you always. I begin to cling to you more fondly than I ever did. If we had a cottage and a competency of our own I do think we might love until death without being dependent on any third party for happiness . . . Why are we so divided? Ellen, it must be because we are in danger of loving each other too well. (Weeks, 1977:89).

They did in fact attempt to elope together, but this was thwarted by parental intervention (Miller, 1989).

The letters between Jane Welsh Carlyle, wife of Thomas Carlyle, and the unmarried writer Geraldine Jewsbury serve as another typical example (Faderman, 1985). Jane, an intellectual who was mistreated by her husband, found her passionate friendship of 25 years with Geraldine a source of immense support and encouragement. In 1841, Jane wrote of her feelings towards her friend: 'I love you my darling, more than I am conscious of myself, and yet I can do nothing for you' (p.164). Geraldine craved that they should live together, but was all too aware of the legal (Jane was married) and economic constraints preventing this. While Geraldine had relationships with men, which made Jane very jealous, Geraldine wrote that 'you are of infinitely more worth and importance in my eyes . . . You come nearer to me' (p.165). Faderman provides countless other examples of women wishing to develop their friendships further. Given the social and economic constraints on women, these deeply felt relationships could not challenge the institution of marriage and motherhood.

As the nineteenth century drew to a close the idea of marriage as the only career for middle-class women was being challenged. The economy had given way to absorb 'surplus' unmarried women into 'respectable' middle-class work. The growing networks of special friendships increasingly became important sources of emotional support and encouragement as women negotiated entry to the hostile public sphere (Vicinus, 1982). A privileged section of the female population had the possibility to prioritize their relationships with women (Faderman, 1991). This they did, and substantial numbers began to forgo marriage. According to Vicinus (1982) these women saw their relationships as differing from those formed by women in the past. Rather than 'preludes' to marriage or 'wise substitution,' a second best option for those who could not find a husband, women viewed them as positive and enabling. According to

Faderman, the term 'Boston Marriage' was used to describe the long-term monogamous relationships between unmarried women in late nineteenth-century New England (p.190). These women were usually feminists, or 'New Women', who were pioneers in the newly opened professions.

Single women played a major role in campaigns aimed at social reform and economic and political emancipation for women. As society became more concerned at the growing power of women, spinsters and their friendships came under increasing attack (Vicinus, 1982). They were 'openly accused of sex-hatred, and pilloried for preferring their own sex to men' (pp.622–3). Vicinus notes that 'women's homoerotic friendships became especially suspect because they symbolized the single woman's sexual autonomy and economic freedom' (p.605).

Just when some women were beginning to experience the financial independence needed to sustain alternative ways of living, these alternatives became subject to widespread attack. Freudian analysis and the work of early sexologists, such as Havelock Ellis and Richard von Krafft-Ebing, provided anti-feminists with a powerful new vocabulary to describe women's hitherto socially approved passionate friendships (Faderman, 1985, Jeffreys, 1985; Vicinus, 1982). According to Faderman (1985:241) twentieth-century stereotypes of lesbianism were influenced primarily by the late nineteenth century writings of Krafft-Ebing and Ellis. These sexologists 'cast love between women in a morbid light and associated it with behaviour which had nothing to do with same-sex love but did have a great deal to do with the insanity of some of the patients they examined' (p.241). The category 'sexual invert' was invented, and seen as the result of cerebral anomalies, a condition of the central nervous system. Normal women were those whose instincts were aroused through relationships with men (p.241). Thus spinsterhood itself became suspect, and women's same-sex friendships were increasingly linked with morbidity and perversion. Women who loved women became 'inverts', their relationships 'lesbian' and therefore perverted and morbid.

The employment gains experienced by many women during the First World War fuelled the emerging climate of growing female self-confidence and raised expectations. By the 1920s an attempt was made to address middle-class women's reluctance to marry. This involved a general reappraisal of the relationship between husband and wife: the old authoritarian marriage was to be transformed into a new 'companionate marriage' (Simmons 1979). The joys of heterosexual love became highly propagandized through the influential writings of sexual reformers such as Stella Browne, Iwan Block and Edward Carpenter (Jackson, 1987; Jeffreys, 1985). These writers viewed female celibacy and 'inverts' as the cause of antagonism between the sexes. Long-term chastity, in their opinion, was a source of physical abuse, a stimulus behind 'man hatred' or possibly thinly disguised homosexuality. According to Browne, 'after [age] twenty-five, the woman who has neither husband or [male] lover and is not under-vitalized and sexually deficient, is suffering mentally and bodily. [She is] nervous, irritated, anaemic, always tired . . . or else she has other consolations, which make her so-called "chastity" a pernicious sham' (quoted in Jeffreys 1989:66).

It seems that it was no accident that this new emphasis on sexuality occurred just at the time when women began to experience greater independence and their friendships offered positive alternatives to traditional forms of male control through marriage. Until the twentieth century there was no need to encourage women to *desire* heterosexual relationships. There was little choice in the matter: the social and economic world was structured around the institution of marriage. Clearly the prioritising of the sexual and the mobilization of beliefs and processes geared to heterosexualize women's desire are deeply implicated in bolstering men's power in the wake of women's challenge. Thus, in illuminating this historical dimension to sexual politics, lesbian historians expose more than a lesbian history, they present *women's* history.

As will be shown later, material constraints on women's ability to live outside heterosexual relationships remain powerful. However, these constraints are compounded by a wide range of ideological processes and social practices which ensure that most women perceive heterosexuality to be the *only* available option.

Heterosexuality as social institution

Our greater awareness of the existence of social and cultural processes shaping sexual outcomes allows us to ask questions about whose interests are served by current arrangements. In her trail-blazing article, 'On Compulsory Heterosexuality and the Lesbian Existence', Adrienne Rich (1984) challenges the

the taken-for-grantedness of heterosexuality. From this critical perspective, psychological evidence can be reinterpreted, allowing Rich to conclude that men and women's primary emotional attachments are towards women and that *social* mechanisms exist to redirect women's desire towards men. One does not have to agree with psychological understandings to recognize the persuasiveness of Rich's argument as she builds a strong case to support the view that powerful social processes shape women's sexual preferences. The range and variety of processes (economic and ideological through to the threat and mobilization of physical violence) that exist to ensure a heterosexual outcome suggest that this is far from natural. Rich argues that, under these conditions, heterosexuality is not simply a freely chosen sexual practice but a social *institution* which shapes sexual outcomes in such a way as to maintain gender inequality.

These important insights have yet to be fully developed in feminist thinking, partly because, as Jackson (1995) rightly points out, there has been too much focus on heterosexuality as practice and not enough on heterosexuality as institution. Further, there is a prevailing assumption that because something is socially produced rather than natural it cannot be experienced as *real*. These misunderstandings have led to unfortunate and unnecessary disputes within feminism, as accusations are made and defensive postures are adopted (see Wilkinson and Kitzinger, 1993; Segal, 1994). To invalidate heterosexual feminists' sexual choices or to fail to recognize the significance of constraints on choice perpetuates divisions within feminism. While we turn our energies inwards, an institution which does not serve women's interests stays unchallenged and Rich's insights remain underdeveloped in feminist analyses more generally.

It is far more helpful to conceptualize heterosexuality as a social institution. The term 'social institution' is used to describe basic regulatory patterns which order and reflect everyday social activities: for example, the nuclear family and the education system. The power of institutions lies in their appearance as objective realities which are universal and legitimate. We experience them as 'givens' and they shape our everyday habits and routines. They exist as part of the fabric of society and are essential elements for supporting social stability and the reproduction of the status quo. Institutions are flexible and subject to change because people are involved in negotiating the meanings attached to social practice (Giddens,

1979:5). At the same time, however, change is constrained because action is informed by knowledge which supports the legitimacy of institutionalized practice. This implies the illegitimacy of alternative arrangements and transgression mobilizes sanctions – moral or coercive. Institutions appear as 'givens' and are supported by belief systems which comprise a range of mutually reinforcing ideologies. Our knowledge of social 'reality' can only be partial and ideologies represent taken-for-granted ways of making sense of the world – instruction manuals for life. Because we cannot simply write our own manuals, we rely heavily on those who are in a position to produce knowledge. The historical and contemporary monopoly of the 'legitimate' knowledge production process (science, medicine, media, the academy, the Church) by elite white males means that dominant accounts of social reality, that is ideologies, reflect the interests of dominant groups[2]. This monopoly privileges ideologies through the mobilization of truth claims, thus limiting the formulation, availability and credibility of alternative accounts which may more fully reflect the interests of subordinate groups.

MacKinnon (1982:515) argues that 'sexuality is to feminism what work is to Marxism', and this is a crucial insight. Sexuality and emotions can take many forms, but ideological and material processes limit their expression, and provide justification for drawing women into relations of inequality with men. Institutionalized heterosexuality as a 'given' is constituted through and embedded in processes of legitimation, reification and prohibition. These processes involve a range of ideologies (often gender-specific) bound by and binding each to another to form a belief system. Examples of ideologies forming this web are those which tell the 'truth' about appropriate forms of sexual and emotional expression, about reproduction, about parenthood and, of course, about masculinities and femininities. This, by implication, leads to the silencing, denying and denaturalizing of contradictory sexual and emotional practices and the alternative forms of social relations they comprise. Significantly, most women are denied access to positive images of non-heterosexual alternatives and it is these alternatives which may provide possibilities for resolving many of the contradictions and constraints they face in the home and the workplace. The privileging of hetero*sexuality* limits creativity in forming relationships. Adult primary relationships (partnerships and

parenting) must be heterosexual and the base should be *sexual.*
Thus, usually, women are not only denied the opportunity to
experience sexual relationships with other women, they are also
denied the opportunity to form primary (partnerships or parenting) relationships with women and men which are *not sexual.*
When we start to problematize the *naturalness* of heterosexuality exciting new questions beg exploration: for example, what
factors are involved in creating desire as heterosexual? Much
more work is needed to illuminate the different sources of
constraint on how we may experience our sexual and emotional capacities. Clearly, the media are central to the production of heterosexual desire and eroticism. Research on girls'
magazines shows that the promotion of heterosexual desire
begins well before puberty and reaches a climax during adolescence (Walkerdine, 1990; Christian-Smith, 1988; McRobbie,
1981, 1990a). Heterosexual romance and imagery dominates
the visual arts, popular music and literature. In contrast, images of lesbianism are rare, positive images even rarer, and
any that might indicate why women should wish to desire women
in the first place, almost taboo.[3]
   One interesting line of enquiry might be the exploration of
links between music, visual image and the production of heterosexual emotional responses. Psychologists are beginning to
become interested in the links between music and the emotions. Empirical research by Sloboda (1991, 1992) indicates that
music is capable of penetrating our consciousness and arous-
ing very deep and powerful emotional responses in people.
Different kinds of musical structures are linked with different
emotional responses – fear, sadness, joy – and may also produce
physical responses such as racing heart beat, stomach sensations,
shivers and tears. Film makers are well aware of the importance of music for reinforcing visual and spoken meaning.
Advertizers employ music to help create desire for their prod-
ucts. We all seem to know what sort of music to play to further our romantic goals. Surely it is possible that the constant
use of particular forms of musical structures (melodic, harmonic
tensions) to emphasize heterosexual romantic imagery and
meaning plays some role in unconsciously shaping desire.
   Again, research on youth sub-cultures provides some indica-
tion of the role of compulsion in generating heterosexual outcomes. Studies such as Lees (1989), Griffin (1985), McRobbie
(1978) and Wilson (1978) provide insights into the range of

social mechanisms which draw young women out of their homoemotional worlds into romantic heterosexuality. Lees's (1989) work in particular highlights processes which police the boundaries of appropriate female sexuality. She shows that actions such as social ostracism and labels such as 'slag' and 'slut', 'tight-ass' and 'lesbian' are commonly employed by peers, and serve to direct young women into steady heterosexual relationships and curtail more independent expressions (or non-expressions) of sexuality. Lees also suggests that the sexual double standard often leads young women to misidentify feelings of lust as romantic love (1989).

Institutional heterosexuality/gender inequality

The social production of a heterosexual outcome is central to shaping gender inequality in a number of important ways. It shapes the very meanings that we attach to being women and men. It is deeply implicated in the construction of dichotomous and hierarchical gender categories and practices. As Butler (1990:17) observes, 'The heterosexualization of desire requires and institutes the production of discrete and asymmetrical oppositions between "feminine" and "masculine".' Likewise, Rubin (1975) argues that union between women and men is assured through the suppression of similarities between them, so that a 'reciprocal state of dependency' will exist between the sexes (p.178). In Rubin's view, 'gender is a socially imposed division of the sexes. It is a product of the social relations of sexuality . . . [whereby] male and female [are transformed] into "men" and "women", each an incomplete half which can only find wholeness when united with the other' (p.179). As these reciprocal differences become *eroticized*, heterosexuality becomes the attraction of opposites (Connell, 1987:246).

Clearly, without the polarized eroticism which produces gender, interpersonal relationships would be negotiated on the basis of individual qualities. In these circumstances the dominance of heterosexuality might be hard to sustain. Since much of what makes women and men socially different relates to the structures of power that feminists are challenging, women have common interests in undermining the institutional dimension of heterosexuality.

Another reason why we need to problematize institutional heterosexuality is that it informs the social conditions under which women and men may relate to each other within and across 'gender boundaries'. It provides the logic underpinning the legitimacy of marriage – or at least heterosexual cohabitation – as a commonsense 'normal' adult goal. Thus institutionalized heterosexuality, in its diverse forms, is central to taken for granted patterns of living. Its apparent naturalness conceals the arbitrary and exploitative nature of gender-specific experiences and conditions that arise. As such, it is a central, but not the sole, medium whereby men's domination over women and each other is structured and reproduced.[4]

Furthermore, institutionalized heterosexuality shapes and is shaped by relations of production.[5] On the one hand, the low wages generally offered women serve to bind women into dependent relationships with men, and may practically limit women's ability to move beyond heterosexuality. On the other hand, heterosexuality provides a framework of often gender-differentiated meanings for perceptions of paid work. For example: 'my job is worthwhile because it enables me to be the breadwinner for my family', or 'my employment is dull, but bearable, because I gain my esteem from the home', or 'the acquisition of qualifications is unnecessary, given my future role as wife and mother'. The role of sexual image has been shown to have some bearing on maintaining the appeal of sex-typed occupations and deterring entry into non-traditional jobs (Williams, 1992; Cockburn, 1987; Griffin, 1982; Willis, 1977). Black feminists, however, have warned against the tendency of universalizing the experience of White women, pointing out the diversity of Black women's interpretations of gender/sexual identities, together with differences in employment expectations and constraints (Dugger, 1991; Dill, 1987; King, 1988).

As we see, institutionalized heterosexuality does not stand in isolation from other institutions, such as the family and the labour market. Instead, it affects and is affected by them. Thus a plethora of overlapping ideologies are mobilized which construct the conditions of its practice, confirm its taken for grantedness, and generate its internal logic.

Heterosexuality as a site of struggle

The sexual practices and social relations which comprise heterosexuality are various and have been subject to change over time. Often these changes have been derived from the wider social context: economic and demographic factors, access to alternative beliefs about sexuality and, particularly, the popularization of feminism over the past hundred years. The meanings and practices within heterosexuality have been and are constantly contested and redefined. Individual women and men do subject heterosexuality to critical evaluation and many have made individual deviations. However, these struggles are more often confined to the level of the social relations, meanings, and practices *within* heterosexuality, rather than at the 'givenness' of the institution itself. The supporting ideologies, in a sense, set the agenda for the way conflict may be expressed; opposing views become framed within them, leaving their 'givenness' unchallenged.

Institutionalized heterosexuality has been remarkable in both its versatility and its persistence. The 'sexual revolution', for example, provided a space for discussion of sexual possibilities, and greater tolerance of a wide range of sexual conduct. However, as Walby (1990:123) points out, it may well have also acted to lock women more securely into active heterosexuality. In many ways, the ability of heterosexuality to remain legitimate and to appear natural has been precisely the result of this flexibility, as evidenced by, for example, the move towards companionate marriage discussed earlier. Thus broad-scale discontent becomes incorporated, and change remains limited, localized and reformist.

The rise of the Gay Liberation Movement in the early 1970s, and most importantly 'Second Wave' feminism, have generated more positive images of alternative sexual practices. Consequently, it is becoming increasingly possible to question the appropriateness of heterosexuality. However, some versions of social reality have more power and authority than others, and dominant ones may suppress those of marginalized groups. The process of legitimation integral to institutionalized heterosexuality has been effective in suppressing contradictory sexual practices and, thus, its evaluation through comparison. As mentioned earlier, there are few positive images of homosexuality in the media. The UK government has been active in preventing young people from gaining access to knowledge about alternative lifestyles. For example, in 1988 the UK government's response to more inclusive discussions of sex education in some schools was the introduction of legislation. Section 28 of the Local Government Act has served to limit discussion of homosexuality as a positive alternative to heterosexuality. Discriminatory treatment deters visible transgression of heterosexuality, which serves to support heterosexuality's 'given' appearance. If individuals believe that no one they know, like or admire is lesbian or gay, then their commonsense knowledge is unlikely to contradict stereotyped dominant understandings of what being lesbian or gay means. This is a major factor inhibiting individual comparisons and thus an identification with homosexuality.

Questioning dominant accounts of social reality

Let us briefly consider here the many British studies which explore adolescent girls' attitudes towards marriage and motherhood. Although almost all the girls in these studies expected to marry and become mothers, this was often tempered with feelings of resignation and ambiguity (Cockburn, 1987:41; Lees, 1986:95). On the one hand, marriage and motherhood represented the end of freedom and fun, possibly offering a life of isolation and domestic drudgery (Prendergast and Prout, 1980:520; Griffin, 1985:55; Sharpe, 1976:217). On the other hand, few could envisage a future outside marriage. Marriage and motherhood symbolized social status for many. To remain unmarried and/or childless was seen as personal failure (Lees, 1986; Leonard, 1980; McRobbie, 1990a). Consequently, for many young women, marriage represents the taken for granted social, sexual and economic 'solution' for adult living.

All of these studies suggest that experiential insights often become subordinated to ideas supporting romantic heterosexuality, which act as important sources of reconciliation for the contradictions that girls experience. The problems inherent in marriage and heterosexuality become reformulated: 'My marriage will be different because I will fall in love with the right man.' Thus marriage remained a goal, despite the mismatch between the romantic ideal and their often negative experience of relationships with boys, and their observations of the marriages of kin, neighbours and friends.

These studies suggest that the fact of marriage and motherhood being taken for granted was particularly evident for White working-class girls who had not expected to achieve access to social mobility through education. In the light of the structural limitations on their entry into meaningful and adequately paid work, they may well have every reason to adhere to the belief that adult female status is achieved via a taken for granted heterosexual journey to marriage and motherhood.

In order to understand better how an institution which reproduces inequality retains its pervasiveness, and under what circumstances individual resistance may occur, it is useful to consider factors which shape individual perspectives on social 'reality'. Blackburn (1988), Prandy (1981) and Stewart and Blackburn's (1975) research into ways that social inequality is reproduced in the workplace may be helpful here. Their concern is with the 'apparent acceptance by the least privileged, or the most deprived, of the social order within which their deprivation occurs' (Prandy, 1981:442). Through empirical research, they demonstrate that this acceptance is not simply the result of 'false consciousness'. Instead, they call for greater emphasis to be laid upon the cognitive aspects of ideologies. They suggest that through cognitive understandings (practical personal experience which contradicts an account provided by an ideology) an ideology may be evaluated and conventional accounts of social reality may be recognized as incomplete or inaccurate (Blackburn, 1988:226–7). However, although we may, at an abstract level, wish that things did not have to be as they are, the capacity to bring about change usually requires practical personal experience whereby alternative social arrangements are believed both to exist and to be *attainable* (Blackburn, 1988:227; Stewart and Blackburn, 1975:503).

Social location and constraints on experience limit the ability to become aware that 'things could be different' (Blackburn, 1988:227; Prandy, 1981). The ability to question the status quo is usually linked to an individual's or a group's sense of competence in generating change or exercising control. This may offer another way of thinking about how heterosexuality persists, which links interpretations of sexuality with economic constraints.

Access to educational opportunities, for example, may provide an individual with a sense of personal and economic control over aspects of her or his life. Through the expansion of options, which educational success can mobilize, individuals may have every reason to expect their futures to be very different from those of their peers. Thus educational success can offer the possibility of holding a belief that 'things could be different'. On the one hand, if an individual is critical of taken for granted ways of living it may provide access to the economic means to sustain an alternative lifestyle. On the other hand, it is not difficult to imagine that academic success, together with the possibility of economic independence, might facilitate women's evaluation of taken for granted patterns of living. The ability to achieve economic independence, together with experiential knowledge, and perhaps access to feminism, may lead to the development of a critique of hierarchical gender relations, marriage and, in certain circumstances, institutionalized heterosexuality itself. This would link with our understanding of the emergence of First and Second Wave feminism. Conversely, limited access to this power may engender the view that 'things simply are the way they are'.

Clearly, the issues are complex and sources of empowerment are various. Changes in the British economy – the decline of traditional sources of working-class male employment and the expansion of the female-dominated service sector – may be having some impact on young people's anticipated futures. This is suggested in recent research by Prendergast and Forrest (1996) on the role of schools in constructing masculinity. In many of the households of the young people in their study, mothers were the sole breadwinners. Prendergast (1995) suggests that, in contrast to her earlier research (Prendergast and Prout, 1980), teenage girls appeared to be far more optimistic about their futures. The trend was that girls expected to have jobs and relished the idea of being independent. They also held low expectations with regard to the value of their male peer group and were reassessing the significance of marriage and motherhood in their futures. The more 'girl-friendly' schooling process, changing economic relations in the home and popular feminism mean that girls have access to more positive images of womanhood. These images may provide a sense that a different sort of life is attainable. Prendergast, however, is careful to point out that girls' expectations may have to be reassessed in the light of the poor quality of jobs available to them. In contrast, the futures of the boys in her study appeared much bleaker. The decline of traditional male manual employment, together with the dominance of unreformed masculine identities, may mean that a generation of underprivileged young men will have little to offer their more choosy female peers.

The lives of lesbian women: some research questions

This discussion highlights the two broad themes which have shaped both our general approach to, and the analytical framework underlying, this study of the lives of lesbian women. These themes can be summarized in the following way. The first theme – which although not quite so central in the shaping of this study as the second is nonetheless an important issue – relates to the implications of sexuality being socially constructed. It suggests that, just as conditions exist which *facilitate* heterosexual outcomes, other conditions may also exist which lead to its being *evaluated, questioned and challenged*. The second, more predominant, theme draws upon the idea that institutionalized heterosexuality is central to men's ability to control and exploit women. This would imply that for women non-heterosexuality may be linked to the experience of empowerment.

The issues and questions that arise out of these two themes and the ways in which they are woven through the different chapters of this book are described below. Those arising in relation to the *first* theme are considered mainly in (Chapters 2, 3 and 4), while those related to the *second* theme are broadly covered in Chapters 3–6. The concluding chapter summarizes and discusses both themes as they relate throughout.

Theme 1: issues and questions, Chapters 2–4

Theme 1 broadly explores the ways in which, given the overwhelming prevalence of a heterosexual outcome, we might begin to identify those conditions which may lead to the reverse: conditions which facilitate the evaluation, challenging and questioning of the inevitability of this particular outcome. The intent is not to *explain* lesbianism per se, or to outline *predictive* categories of social construction. Rather, it is to explore some of the meaningful experiences, and social and economic influences and processes, whereby a questioning perspective on conventional accounts of social reality, and in particular gender relations, may come about. While a critical perspective may be shared by many (lesbian and non-lesbian) women, it is interesting that the decision to move beyond heterosexual relations is only taken by some.

Chapter 2 looks at respondents' memories of childhood. It asks whether and how this time may have provided experiences which contradicted dominant accounts of adolescent femininity and romantic heterosexuality. It looks at respondents' recollections of gendered play and active, practical knowledge, as well as parental influences, and asks how these may have enhanced their ability to resist dominant taken for granted scripts of female existence. Chapter 3 asks how it is, once young women have identified their differences with normative paths into conventional heterosexuality, they find or make alternative scripts. What possible 'avenues of escape' from incorporation into romantic heterosexuality were available to respondents during their adolescence? The first section of Chapter 4 looks at this question another way round. Instead of asking how a critical perspective on heterosexual relations is sustained, it asks whether access to employment opportunity itself makes women more critical. Does it offer possibilities for re-evaluating the desirability of marriage and heterosexuality itself?

Theme 2: issues and questions. Chapters 3–6

Theme 2 concerns the ways in which institutionalized heterosexuality is central to men's ability to control and exploit women. This implies that moving beyond the constraints of heterosexuality is an empowering experience for women. Several questions are considered which explore a complex interrelationship between economic independence and lesbianism.

Chapter 3 explores respondents' reported experiences of secondary schooling and asks whether the recognition of the need to achieve economic self-reliance informed perceptions of paid work, approaches to employment and skill development of those who questioned traditional gender paths or had an early recognition of sexual preference. Chapter 4 looks at the impact a later recognition of sexual identity might have on approaches to employment. Often respondents made an identification with lesbianism in their twenties, thirties or later. Many were initially guided in their approaches to employment by the assumption that they would marry, and some did in fact marry. Thus Chapter 4 focuses on respondents' employment histories. By drawing on case-history material, respondents' approaches to and experiences of paid work are compared and contrasted in the context of changing boundaries of sexual image. Chapters 4 and 5 asks if non-heterosexual women see themselves as having to be economically self-reliant in the long-term. If so, does this influence their employment 'choices', their approaches to skill development, their decisions about the kind of employment they wish to be in and their views of career advancement? Chapter 5 tests this by comparing respondents' occupational locations and pay levels with national data. Finally, Chapter 6 asks what is the relationship between employment circumstances and home life, and vice versa. What happens when women move outside the parameters of intimate heterosexual couple relationships? This chapter looks at the way women balance their home life and employment commitments in lesbian relationships. Of particular interest are ways that *similarities*, based upon their shared structural positioning within gender hierarchies, and *diversity*, derived from other sources of inequality, are manifested and managed between women.

We now move on to discuss how the research was carried out.

RESEARCH STRATEGY

Given the exploratory nature of the research and the complexity of its aims, a qualitative approach was employed. A life-history approach was used to illuminate processes of change and continuity over the life-cycle and how this related to perceptions of choice. This approach provides a sense of how an individual's life has evolved and changed over time. As Bogdan points out, it allows us 'to understand better the choices, contingencies and options open to the individual' (quoted in Faraday and Plummer, 1979:777). Because of the need to explore commonalities and differences through comparison and to provide extrapolations based on a wide range of lesbian experience, a 'multiple biographies approach' was chosen. The analysis of a relatively large number of biographies facilitates the identification of dominant themes based upon commonalities in experience and enables the possibility of generalization (Graham, 1984:109).

Sixty non-heterosexual women of different social backgrounds or circumstances at different stages of the life-cycle were interviewed. The sample comprised younger women at the beginning of their working lives looking forward in their careers, women in their thirties looking forward and backwards, and older women who were well established in their employment. Table 1.1 presents the age range of the sample.

The youngest woman was 17 and the oldest was 59; the median age was 30.

Table 1.1   *Age of respondents*

Age	Number	%
Under 20	3	5
20–29	24	40
30–39	16	27
40–49	14	23
50–59	3	5
Total	60	100

Field work

The fieldwork was carried out within a personally familiar lesbian community in a city called 'Whiteabbey' in the South East of England.[6] This was done for two important reasons. First, personal 'insider' knowledge provided a sense of the social shape of this community, knowing where the formal and informal gathering places were, and sensitivity to the diversity of social circumstances of the women who frequented them. Recent history and politics of the community were appreciated. Second, many members of this community knew me. This was important for several reasons. Like Finch (1984:79), I shared fundamental commonalities with the women I sought to interview, which made it easier to establish the high levels of trust necessary for conducting sensitive research. Furthermore, this commonality helped to ease the hierarchical relationship between interviewer and interviewee. My motives for conducting the research were more self-evident than they would have been had I been a stranger. As a consequence, my research was greeted with enthusiasm and women were keen to publicize and participate in the project. As was the case for Kitzinger (1987:74), I believe that many of my respondents would not have agreed to be interviewed had I not been a lesbian.

The lesbian community

The lesbian community comprises a diverse range of women, of different ages, social circumstances and political interests. This tends to shape the community along social and political lines. Separate social gatherings organized by those who attended a large college of higher education, serve to create a gulf between these college women and local lesbians, whose social life usually centres upon town events. Historically, tensions existed between the organizational aims of lesbian feminists, who emphasized 'consciousness raising' and women's movement politics, and less political lesbians, whose concerns related more to the availability of more light-hearted social get-togethers. At the time of research, the boundaries between these social and political groupings had become blurred. The political extremes of the 1970s and early 1980s were less apparent, and efforts were being made to better integrate both college women and local women, by organising joint social activities.

The community is a social medium forming an umbrella over a network of interlocking sub-groups of women: discussion groups, organized by the 'Lesbian Line' (a telephone help line); an older lesbian group; a young lesbian group; various feminist organizations; and friendship networks. Social gatherings, such as 'women only' or lesbian and gay discos; a lesbian and gay pub which serves as a temporary lesbian 'hang-out', act to bring together the various participants in these networks. All of these gatherings importantly provide a safe space, where women can meet and form friendships, find lovers and discuss problems. It draws together lesbians on the geographical fringes. Its significance to lesbians often relates to their relationship circumstances, becoming less important when women are in long-term relationships, and more important when they break up. Consequently, the community is always in a state of flux, new women enter the community, women move away, others return. New women often bring organizational energy into the community, while a core of long-term participants ensures a basic continuity of social activities.

Selecting the sample

Defining 'lesbian' has been a highly problematic enterprise in lesbian scholarship. The plurality of meanings which shape 'lesbian identities' have provided a diversity of definitions, which have initiated high levels of debate amongst lesbian scholars.[7] Developing a working definition of lesbianism has been important for those seeking 'lesbians in history' and 'lesbians in other cultures'. However, each definition appears either to exclude women who may see or have seen themselves as lesbian (for example, Ferguson 1981), or to include women who do not (for example, Rich, 1984). The problem of definition, which I do not think can be resolved, may be directed equally towards the category 'heterosexual', thus attesting to the multiplicity of sexual and emotional meanings through time and space. I asked each respondent to define her sexuality and there were almost as many variations in definition as there were respondents. Definitions ranged from 'me', 'a woman-identified woman', 'bisexual with heavy lesbian tendencies' 'ninety-nine per cent lesbian' and 'transsexual'. Often women had experienced important heterosexual relationships in the past, which they did not see as the product of 'false-consciousness'. Many of the women were aware of the changing nature of sexuality in their lives and did not rule out the unlikely possibility that they might form relationships with men. However, what was important to my study was that all of these women were organizing and approaching their lives on the assumption that they would form primary, loving relationships with women. They were living a 'lesbian lifestyle' which involved being independent of a man for economic and emotional support. It was these two aspects of their lives, rather than simply how they defined their sexuality, that was of central interest to me. These women therefore form only part of the continuum of 'lesbian' experience. Respondents' commentaries suggest the existence of large numbers of women who have lesbian lovers but remain married, not wishing or unable to follow a lesbian lifestyle.

Locating respondents

My first criterion was to establish the feasibility of my study. Several colleagues had expressed concern that I would be unable to find 60 willing participants for my project. The easiest way to find respondents would have been to network amongst women in the college of higher education. I ruled out this approach for two reasons. First, I was more interested in the local resident lesbian population, as they appeared to be more representative of a wider spectrum of lesbian experience and contained a greater diversity of women of different class and ethnic backgrounds. Second, I did not wish to confine the study to young college-educated women at the beginning of their careers. As it turned out, I only interviewed two women who were known to me solely by their participation in the college lesbian sub-culture. The fact that so many of the 'local' women interviewed had experienced higher education came as a great surprise to me.

The marginality and relative secrecy shaping the lesbian/ gay existence means that 'random' sampling is impossible (Plummer, 1981:214). Studies of lesbians often draw their samples through advertising in newsletters, radical book stores, women's centres and lesbian and gay coffee shops.[8] This method can produce a highly self-selected sample (Burgess, 1984:57–8). I decided to use a 'snowball' sampling technique to gain access to participants in the study. I was aware of the problems this could pose insofar as it can provide access to a discrete network of respondents. I therefore set out to find as diverse a range of sources as possible to initiate the snowball sampling. My hope was to provide a snapshot of a relatively small community by drawing on the diversity of its participants.

I discussed my project with organizers on the 'Lesbian Line' and facilitators in discussion groups and regularly participated in social activities, so as to meet women who could put me in contact with other women. I was aware that many lesbian women were not regular participants on the 'scene', and I wished to include them in this study. I was invited to enclose information about my proposed research in a mail-out that published lesbian events. This mail-out went to approximately 50 women. This served to further publicize my study in the community. The 'Lesbian Line' discussion group proved to be an important source of respondents. It was set up to serve two functions: first, as a forum to discuss lesbian concerns and, second, as a place for women to make friends. I was invited to discuss my research with this group of about 20 women, most of whom were in their thirties and forties, many had been married. Although the group organizer informed me that this was not a feminist group, I explained that my research had a feminist perspective aimed at providing a positive discussion of the lesbian lifestyle, which would focus particularly on the experience of employment. Like Kelly (1988:9), I believe that this face-to-face contact was important for enabling respondents to make an initial assessment of my 'trustworthiness'. Almost all of these women agreed to be interviewed.

Some of the older women in this group belonged to an 'older lesbian discussion group' and put me in contact with this group. I also met a young woman who was involved in a group called the 'young lesbian and gay discussion group'. There were only five women in this group, and these women proved to be the most difficult to interview, as most still lived with parents and were worried about explaining my interest in them. I interviewed only two women from this group.

I began interviewing in January 1990. Each respondent was asked to contact other friends who would possibly be willing to participate in the research. I explained that it was important that they should not discuss specific details about the questions and themes which we covered.

Very quickly I reached my number limit for women aged under 30. I then turned my attention exclusively to making contact with older women and Black women. During the early stages of field work, I luckily came into contact with several lesbians who had been involved in the community for 20 years or more. These women were able to contact and introduce me to a large number of lesbians who were no longer regular participants on the 'scene'. These included many of the older women in couples. Through these older women I was able to gain access to several friendship networks which existed on the periphery of the community. These women included two of the three Black women interviewed, and they and others agreed that they knew of no other Black lesbians in the area. It is unfortunate that the sample contains so few women of colour. Two African–American lesbians volunteered to be interviewed, but my desire to limit the study to British women ruled them out. The area where the field work was carried has a small ethnic minority population (5.5 per cent).

As the interviewing stage of the research progressed, many members of the community became enthusiastically involved in the project. Women would approach me with the names of friends who had agreed to be interviewed. The project was a popular topic of conversation during social gatherings, with women jokingly calling each other by their interview numbers. Although I did not disclose the names of participants in the study, it was clear from listening to their conversations that many women were surprised at the extensiveness of the sample. I began to feel reassured that I was gaining access to the diversity of experience that I sought.

This method of sampling may appear ad hoc. However, I believe that most of the women interviewed would never have considered volunteering had they not been reassured by friends that the research was worthwhile and, most importantly, that I could be trusted. Most of the women were not politically active. They generally had feminist sympathies, but did not necessarily define themselves as feminists. They usually described themselves as 'ordinary' women.

The interview

Each participant had been contacted initially by one of their friends or by me. When arranging the time of interview, I explained that we should allow approximately three hours for its duration. Respondents were often surprised that it could take that long, saying that they did not think their lives would be interesting enough to sustain a lengthy discussion. Before the interview, I explained that we would be covering a range of themes from childhood, schooling, through to a discussion of their work histories. I stressed that the interviews would be confidential and that I would transcribe the taped conversations myself. I assured them that the location of the study, their names and occupations would be disguised. Before the interviews, respondents were sent a background questionnaire which asked for details such as age, parents'/guardians' occupations, marital status, type of education experienced, qualifications, work history and salary.

Interviewing

The interview schedule initially took the form of a modified life-history semi-structured questionnaire. Questions were designed to guide the respondent through key stages of her life. They were open-ended, allowing for probing and lengthy responses. However, on relistening to the first few interviews, it became clear that by keeping closely to this interview schedule I was both cutting short respondents' discussions and imposing a direction on a life story which was not necessarily in keeping with their own sense of sequence. I therefore decided to use the themes of the questionnaire as an 'aide mémoire' (see Table 1.2) as described by Burgess (1984:108). In moving towards this more fluid 'conversation with a purpose' approach, I discovered that respondents usually covered most of the key questions I had placed on the initial interview schedule. By doing this I felt much more assured that I was not leading the respondent and that the respondent was less inclined to provide a 'right answer'.

Table 1.2 *Interview themes*

A. Growing up: Family background, geographical location,
definition of ethnicity, experience of ethnic difference,
grandparents, siblings. Parental employment and expectations for
you (marriage, education, jobs). Divisions of labour in home,
decision making. Early influences/role models. Early views on/
expectations of marriage and employment. Childhood interests,
friends.

B. Experience of schooling: Type of school, stream, ability, subject
choices, best subjects. School philosophy – expectations of pupils'
futures, encouragement, class/gender bias, careers advice. Your
interests and activities. Hopes then for future, perceptions/
expectations of marriage and employment, particular job hopes.
Comparison with male and female peers.

C. Sexual politics at school: Centrality of boyfriends for self and
others. Views then on romance. Interaction with boys/boyfriends,
ideas about appropriate behaviour in relationships with boys.
Perceptions of peer pressure. How easy to avoid? Other interests,
activities, etc. Friendship networks. Knowledge and image of
lesbianism then.

D. Coming out history: Length of process and how it was
experienced. How beliefs, understandings, expectations changed as
the result of 'coming out'. Experience of discrimination. Centrality
of sexuality for sense of self. Positive and negative aspects of
sexuality. Definition of/theories about sexuality. Why do women
marry? Do you want/plan to have children? How would this fit
with career? How far are you 'out' – friends, family, work? Social
life, importance of the lesbian community.

E. Lesbian lifestyle and employment: Economic consequences of
'coming out'. Has sexuality had positive/negative influence on
work, job choices, relations with workmates? Do you see yourself as
having to work for rest of your life? Has this influenced approach
to employment? Views on economic independence. Comparison of
employment attitudes with those of single/married women, and
men. Experience of discrimination.

F. Experience of heterosexual relationships: Partner's job, your job
while in relationship, children. Divisions of labour, decision
making, childcare. Negotiation of career development. How should
partners work these things out? Any job relocation – whose job?
Partner's attitude towards your job/career. Feelings on power in
relationship. How balanced was it?

G. Experience and expectations of lesbian relationships:
Perceptions of differences between lesbian and heterosexual

relationships. Partner's job, your job while in relationship,
children. Divisions of labour, decision making, childcare.
Negotiation of career development. How should partners work
these things out? Any job relocation – whose job? Partner's
attitude towards your job/career. Feelings on power in
relationship. How balanced was/is it?

H. Higher education/vocational training: Experience of, future
expectations. Reasons for choices.

I. Work history: approaches to career and changes over time: First
job, what appeal? Thoughts about the role of paid work at that
time. Was it seen as a long-term commitment? Views on economic
independence. Discussion of career. Reasons for job changes,
feelings about different jobs held, present job. Gender composition
of occupation, reasons for this situation and your experience of
being a woman in this job. Type of skills used at work.
Opportunities for advancement. Centrality of employment for
sense of self. Appeal of particular jobs, pay, ambitions and
expectations for future. Comparison between your approach to
employment and that of co-workers, male and female. Different job
pathways for men and women in your occupation? Experience of
gender discrimination. Why may women get a raw deal at work?
Influence of sexuality on employment experience. Ability to be
'out' at work.

J. Politics: Views on feminism. Other political interests – labour
politics, unions.

K. Life goals and leisure interests: Does sexuality influence these?
Aspects of the lesbian lifestyle straight women might usefully
emulate.

Like many researchers I was surprised at the ease with which
respondents talked to me. Interviews were more like 'intimate
conversations' (Finch, 1984, Oakley, 1981:34) with women re-
vealing private aspects of their lives which would more usually
be shared with a lover. Respondents 'welcomed the opportunity
to try to make sense of some of the contradictions in their
lives in the presence of a sympathetic listener' (Finch, 1984:75).
My impression was that, in most cases, respondents enjoyed
talking about their lives. In two cases the interview provided a
forum for a respondent to 'come out'.

I was taken by surprise by the effect of the research on me.
In the first place, I often experienced feelings of intense
emotional bonding with a respondent, while engaged in the

somewhat artificial situation of being with a virtual stranger, who was discussing very personal, often highly sensitive issues. The similarities we shared sometimes lead to 'counter-transference' where 'emotions are evoked in the field worker while listening to respondents' accounts of their own lives' (Warren, 1988:47). Like Kelly (1988:17) I found that interviewees raised issues and touched on aspects of their lives which often uncovered buried memories in my own past. I sometimes felt so drawn into both the discussion and the role of friend that I had consciously to hold myself back from interjecting my own experience of a situation. After an interview I usually felt emotionally and intellectually drained. Furthermore, as was the case for Kelly (1988:14–19), the content of the interviews, and immersion in the data thereafter, had a major impact on my own interpretations of self and past events, forcing me to reinterpret and re-evaluate my understandings of past motivations and experience. Again, this proved to be unsettling, sometimes deeply troubling and, at other times, exciting. It always led to greater reflexivity and careful re-examination of individual accounts. I believe that the emotional and experiential relationship which I had with the project did not detract from the scholarliness of the research. Instead, it forced me to work harder, to immerse myself further in the data, and to probe and question the accounts more carefully.

Life-history or life fiction?

A difficult problem for understanding experience arises when research is based on autobiographical accounts. Research by memory theorists supports the concerns raised by anthropologists, historians, psychologists and sociologists as to whether we are able to convey accurate accounts of our past. They suggest that life-history narratives cannot be read as mirroring the past, as memory does not grow merely though addition (Kohli, 1981:65,67). Instead, the memory's retrieval system involves a complementary process of forgetting and remembering, this being a reconstructive process whereby individuals make sense of their lives (Andrews, 1991:66). It is part of a self-regulatory system that allows the individual to develop a sense of continuity between the past and the present (Hankiss, 1981:204). Kohli (1981:67) sums up the view first formulated by Bartlett (1964), which is now the position of many memory theorists:

'narratives always contain a reconstructive element. The reference to past events occurs in the context of the present situation, and under the criterion of their significance to it.' Consequently, an individual's history is not simply a reflection of past experience, it contains an explanatory element, an 'ontology of self'. According to Hankiss (1981:203) what constitutes an 'ontology of self' is highly selective: memory selects, emphasizes and rearranges, endowing fundamental episodes with 'symbolic meaning', transforming them almost into myths. Furthermore, connections are made between past events using perspectives that would not have been available to the individual when they lived through those experiences (Andrews, 1991:65). Good examples of this in my own research were provided by some of the discussions of 'coming out', by those who perceived this as extending back into adolescence. From the perspective of *being* a lesbian, early discomfort with heterosexuality could be redefined as *becoming* a lesbian.

The perspectival nature of ontologies of self raises additional problems for research into non-conventional people. Ready-made theories often exist within popular culture, which offer understandings in the form of causal relationships. For example, there is a commonsense notion that a causal relationship exists between being a 'tomboy' or 'sissy' in childhood and homosexuality. This may influence the meanings attached to childhood experiences for homosexuals (Ross, 1980:524, Kitzinger, 1987:69). An example of this comes from my own research. June illustrates the symbolic meaning attached to an event where the only significance lies in a commonsense causal relationship between early gender non-conformity and lesbianism.

> I remember the mother of my two male cousins giving my mother a pair of jeans that one of them had grown out of. And I always remember this because of course they were boys' jeans, and in those days you used to get boys' and girls' jeans, and I thought this is wonderful. This was obviously triggering things off, and I was about seven then. (Age 44)

Clearly, the influence of these popular understandings has a bearing on the accounts of many of my respondents and raises implications for my own research findings. In some cases respondents may have selected and emphasized aspects of their past in order to comply with this explanatory model, while in other cases those who rejected this model may have played down aspects of their past that appeared to confirm popular understandings. This has posed difficulties for analysis. On the one hand, I have recognized this aspect of selectivity that underpins respondents' representations of their early lives, while, on the other hand, I have tended to believe that there are some factual bases to these representations. Taking their accounts seriously has led to broadening the analysis and the consideration of other factors that may have been relevant.

According to Wingfield, 'modern memory theory has come to learn that we are not studying the dream, but the dreamer' (quoted in Finnegan, 1992:115). At one level it does not matter how far life narratives reflect an accurate account of past experience. For as Thomas and Thomas (1928) have stated, if people define situations as real, they are real in their consequences. Andrews (1991:65) describes a dialectical relationship between the present and the past: we reconstruct our past and our present is constructed by our past. Memory of past experience is routinely used in everyday life, to plan, guide and justify action (Robinson, 1986:23). Thus life stories reveal how individuals construct, negotiate and interpret their experience (Kitzinger, 1987:71, Kohli, 1981:70). What people select from their past tells us a great deal about what is significant for them in their present context (Andrews, 1991:63). Consequently, if a respondent tells us that her mother was in full-time employment throughout her childhood, as many of my respondents did, this attests to its significance for that respondent, rather than its factual quality.

However, if one wants to move beyond individual understandings, to explore the social processes that have shaped experience, one needs to be confident that there is some relationship between autobiographical narrative and the events described. Kohli (1981:69) suggests that this is possible; despite the reconstructive nature of autobiographical narratives, 'we are inclined to think that usually there is at least *some* truth in what is being narrated, that there is some specifiable relation between the narrative reconstruction and the events to which it refers'.

Brewer (1986) offers a compromise between the two main theoretical schools of memory. This compromise takes the form of a 'partial reconstructive view'. Although he disagrees with 'copy theorists' who argue that memory is a 'copy' of sensory input, unmediated by intervening interpretation, he argues that memory may be a great deal more accurate than reconstructive memory theorists suggest. He suggests that recent personal memories are reasonably accurate copies of the way we originally *interpreted* a phenomenal experience, and it is with the passing of time that these memories become subject to reconstruction (1986:43). However, certain 'flash bulb' memories may be accurately recalled (Brewer, 1986:44). Circumstances that influence accurate recall are uniqueness, consequentiality, unexpectedness and emotion provoked by the memories. Trivia are poorly recalled and accuracy is diminished by successive accounts of a particular memory episode. Andrews (1991:66) concludes her excellent discussion of reconstructed memory by suggesting that, when an experiential episode event is of great interest to the individual, this may provide the basis for more accurate recall: 'It is by virtue of the internal significance associated with the events described that they have been stored for so long. . .'. She points out, however, that the listener must be sensitive to the possible motives that a speaker may have to misrepresent past events. She goes on to argue that examples of misrepresentation found by researchers interviewing individuals who have been involved in illegal activities should not be used to discredit findings in other self-report studies (Andrews, 1991:66).

Thus, although there are irresolvable problems associated with life-history narrative, the nature of my research questions made a longitudinal study inconceivable. It must be remembered that, despite these difficulties, no one knows her own history better than the individual herself (Kohli, 1981:69). As was the case for Andrews (1991:65), I cannot be certain that all the accounts were strictly accurate. However, like Gerson (1985:246), I found that many of the autobiographical narratives reflected lives that had experienced change and contradiction, with respondents reporting earlier hopes and expectations that did not correspond with later beliefs or approaches to life. This suggests a degree of accuracy, rather than misrepresentation for the sake of internal consistency. During the interviews I also felt that respondents were recalling events that they had rarely, if ever, discussed in detail previously. Often respondents suggested that in their discussions with me they had made what Robinson (1986:23) calls 'discoveries' which are 'spontaneous insights into one's history brought about when chance or circumstance evoke latent memories that reveal connections or themes in one's experience'.

I also feel that, by having access to a relatively large number of life-histories, individual anomalies or misrepresentations could be counterbalanced. As the sociologist Bertaux (1981:187) points out:

> A single life story stands alone, and it would be hazardous to generalize on the grounds of that one alone, as a second life story could immediately contradict those premature generalizations. But several life stories *taken from the same set of socio-structural relations* support each other and make up, all together, a strong body of evidence. (Bertaux's emphasis)

The analysis

My analysis was greatly assisted by the qualitative computer package, Textbase Alpha. Descriptions (codes) could be attached to segments of text and a wide range of variables (age, class, qualifications and so on) could be entered for each transcript. This organizational help facilitated the generation of theoretical insights because of the ease with which patterns and relationships could be identified. Clearly all research involves selectivity. The sheer volume of data I had collected meant that I exercised intellectual, political and ethical judgements as to what represented relevant themes to develop and highlight. I was guided by the principle that a researcher 'must not write what she knows to be untrue, but she need not write all that she knows' (Andrews, 1991:49). Analysis was shaped by the desire to reflect accurately relevant insights that were suggested by the data, in a balanced and honest manner.

The process of writing up each section of the research was carried out in conjunction with high levels of immersion in the data, rereading transcripts, relistening to interviews in some cases, exploring contradiction and rethinking concepts. Throughout this process, I tried to keep a picture in my mind of each respondent, and carefully considered how each might react to my arguments (Andrews, 1991:49).

The advantage of having access to the accounts of 60 women, whose experiences could be compared, together with knowledge informed by related literature, and personal experience allowed for the formulation of alternative understandings of respondents' lives to those offered by them in the interviews (Gerson, 1985:247). My hope, however, is to have maintained a balance, that my analysis of respondents' lives will be recognizable to them, yet offer new insights.

NOTES

1. Good examples of this work include Faderman (1985, 1992), Lesbian History Group (1989), Jeffreys (1985), Vicinus (1985), Cook (1979a, 1979b) and Smith-Rosenberg (1975).
2. The concept of ideology is highly debated in sociology and I recognize that it can be defined in other ways (see, for example, Giddens, 1979, 1991; Thompson, 1990) For all its problems, I prefer this definition of ideology to 'discourse', because it enables us to retain some sense of the relationship between ideas and hierarchies of domination.
3. See the very readable edited volume by Hamer and Budge (1994) on images of lesbianism in music, 'soaps' and popular film.
4. I agree with Walby (1990:20) that it is important to recognize the centrality of the state, labour market and cultural practices, in reproducing and maintaining structures of inequality within and between genders. However, just as each of these areas interacts with the others to reproduce inequality, so too does 'institutionalized heterosexuality', and its centrality is too often ignored.
5. Foucault (1979), Weeks (1989) and Brake (1976) argue, from their different perspectives, that the stigmatization of homosexuality is related to the bourgeois concern to promote the monogamous nuclear family. For Foucault this was part of the process of creating a bourgeois identity as separate from the upper classes. For Weeks and for Brake, this shaping of sexuality is related to a concern, within capitalism, to control workers. However, Marshall (cited in Walby, 1990:118) points out that institutionalized homophobia has stronger links with the maintenance of gender stratification than with capitalist control, because of its importance for controlling men's gender behaviour (and, I would add, women's gender behaviour).
6. The name of this city is fictionalized to protect the identities of the participants in the study. In Chapter 5, the characteristics of the local labour market are described.
7. See, for example, Rich (1984), Addelson (1981), Zita (1981), Ferguson (1981), Jeffreys (1989).
8. See, for example, Johnson (1990), Blumstein and Schwartz (1985), Peplau *et al.* (1978).

CHAPTER TWO

Negotiating femininities: childhood worlds

INTRODUCTION

The first chapter argued that sexual preferences are socially produced within the context of institutional heterosexuality. A range of ideologies and social practices exist to limit our choices so that heterosexuality is the usual outcome. Underpinning heterosexual desire is the construction of dichotomous and hierarchical gender categories. As these reciprocal differences become *eroticized*, heterosexuality becomes the attraction of opposites. As childhood represents an important period in the lifelong process of gender socialization, I was interested in respondents' memories of this period to see what sort of experiences informed their sense of the meanings associated with being born female.

In the first chapter we also discussed ways that commonsense notions of social reality can be evaluated and suggested that this possibility involves having access to contradictory practical experience and knowledge. The analysis of respondents' life-histories suggests that most held an early predisposition towards a desire for independence and a long-standing critical perspective on gender hierarchies.

This chapter will explore respondents' remembered childhood experiences to see how far this period may have provided broader conceptions of gender identity and the establishment of their questioning perspectives. I do not support the position held by psychoanalytic and many socialization theorists that childhood experience is the sole determiner of adult attitudes and outcomes. This cannot explain the ambiguities and contradictions experienced by people as they negotiate very different social contexts from those in childhood (Ferree and

Hess, 1987:15). While not wanting to overemphasize the significance of respondents' childhood experiences, like Gerson
(1985:37) I feel that the knowledge and experience gained in
childhood play an important role in shaping later perspectives
and choices, particularly during adolescence.

As discussed in Chapter 1, relying on people's accounts of
childhood poses problems for our analysis because of the
reconstructive and selective nature of memory. Further, childhood is qualitatively different from adult experience and may
be only 'half-remembered' (Coe, 1984:1–3). In the absence of
a longitudinal study, we must be careful about what conclusions we may draw.

I shall now turn to respondents' accounts of childhood, most
of which relate to home life experience. I will begin with a
brief consideration of ways in which some respondents understood their early experience of ethnic difference to inform their
perspectives. I will then move on to discuss three themes which
emerged in their accounts of divisions of labour at home: the
role of mothers in offering daughters broader conceptualizations
of womanhood; respondents' early perceptions of, and feelings about, the domestic division of labour in their homes;
and the impact of father figures in encouraging and/or reinforcing the development of non-traditional interests and attitudes. Finally, I will draw on respondents' accounts of their
childhood self-concepts to illustrate ways that they perceived
themselves to have constructed less gender-stereotyped
subjectivities. We will then see that, in their transition from
childhood to adolescence, many felt at odds with the dictates
of emphasized femininity and romantic heterosexuality.

'I THINK YOU TAKE YOUR LEAD FROM YOUR PARENTS': EARLY HOMELIFE

The social and ethnic background of the sample

Measurements and concepts of social class have been extensively
debated in sociology, and I cannot enter these debates here
(see, for example, Prandy, 1990; Marshall *et al.*, 1988). For ease
of comparison of respondents' social backgrounds with other
data sets, I have used the popular 'Goldthorpe Schema', which
can group occupations into three categories: service, intermediate and manual. Their social backgrounds are calculated on

Table 2.1 *Respondents' social class background (Goldthorpe)*

Class	Description	*n*	%
I	High grade professionals, administrators, officials	11	
II	Low grade professionals, high grade technicians, lower grade administrators and officials, managers small businesses	16	Service 45
IIIa	Routine non-manual higher grade	5	
IIIb	Routine non-manual lower grade	1	
IVa	Small proprietors – with employees: industry, business, shops	3	
IVb	Small proprietors – no employees: industry, business, shops	5	Intermediate 30
IVc	Small proprietors – agriculture	1	
V	Lower-grade technicians, gen. manual, could be supervisory	3	
VI	Skilled manual wage earners	5	
VIIa	Manual wage workers: industry	8	Manual 25
VIIb	Manual wage workers: agriculture	2	
Total		60	100

the basis of their fathers' occupational level when respondents were aged 16.[1] As we can see in Table 2.1, 27 respondents came from service class backgrounds, which roughly corresponds to professional/managerial middle class. There were 18 with intermediate class backgrounds. Examples of fathers' occupations which fell within this grouping include tenant farmer; 'fish-and-chip' shop owner and factory foreman. The remaining 15 came from manual backgrounds. When relevant, respondent's class background will be indicated either in the main text or in abbreviated form in italics at the end of an extract.

The sample includes women from England, Scotland and Wales, three of whom are Black. Consequently, there was some diversity of cultural contexts in which respondents were brought up. I will turn first to the Black women. All three of these women grew up in family contexts which offered competing cultural values, and their ages ranged from the mid-twenties to early forties. One was brought up in a series of wealthy foster homes. Each of the other two had one Black parent and one White parent. For the Black women, ethnic difference was mediated by the cultural and social context of their families, and had a profound effect on their self-concepts. This mediation is evident in the following extract from Jade, of African-Caribbean descent. She finds that the liberal political values that she holds are not always perceived as consistent with her ethnicity:

> Colour played no negative part of my life, I wasn't rebuked because I was Black, until I joined the Forces... because the Black girls didn't accept me because what come out of my mouth was not consistent with the colour of my skin.

I asked Jade how she felt about being brought up in a White family:

> I don't know. I don't think I missed anything at all. I think I learnt [about my cultural heritage] through reading and media as well... I think if you are interested about your culture you can go out and find it. I don't think you should blame your parents altogether, they should hold some blame... You take initiatives... There's a lot of Black kids being fostered by Whites because nobody will have them... I think they should teach the child about its own culture.

For Susan, the main problem she experienced, while growing up in an almost completely White rural environment, was that if she was naughty she was easily recognized:

> We lived in a small village. Because being of an ethnic minority as well [my mother] said, 'You and I have to be very careful what we do, because people will put us down.' She said, 'Whatever you do don't [be naughty], 'cos people can spot you a mile off.' She said, 'With us we have to be a bit more aloof than everyone else, because people will look for things to sort of...' She said, 'Don't let yourself down, people will expect you to let yourself down, but don't do it.' So I got a bit devious really if I was naughty, made sure no one was looking.

We discussed how her ethnic background informed her sense of self-reliance (her mother was of African-Caribbean origins).

> That's it, you find that [Black women are very independent and less reliant on men], I think that's what it probably is. Because you are Coloured, you have an attitude to life that is totally different, and you do. Although I am loath to admit it... I suppose in a way I am arrogant... People think you are looking down on people, but it's not, it's a protection.

All three of the Black respondents spoke of their mothers or
foster mothers encouraging them to be proud and self-reliant.
Their predominately White upbringing did lead to problems
in their gaining acceptance within the Black community, and
their skin colour clearly marked them off as different within
White culture. Early feelings of ethnic 'difference' were also
experienced by several White respondents who, as children,
had moved to England from Scotland or Wales. Maggy explains
how she initially experienced this:

> Very traumatic. For a start I had a very broad Glaswegian
> accent, and nobody understood what I said, and they really
> didn't understand what I said. It was horrendous going into
> school. I remember people turning around and saying, 'Don't
> bother talking to her, you can't understand a word that she
> says.' It was really weird because they didn't seem to com-
> prehend that I could understand everything they were say-
> ing about me. It was like talking as if I was speaking a different
> language, and that went on for some time. (26S)

The trauma generated from such a move was perceived by Val
as having a profound effect on her sense of social reality. She
had left behind a small tight-knit farming community and an
extended family within which she had been the centre of attention. She found herself in the East End of London, where,
at a practical level, the differences between her accent and the
accents of her peers made even simple communication difficult. She sees this experience as having provided her with a
critical perspective on the taken for granted, including marriage:

> I had [the fact that I didn't want to marry] sussed at a very
> early age. I really think it was the move, right! From Scot-
> land to England, when I was jolted out of a whole culture
> into another one, I guess. I mean, obviously that wasn't
> meaning that to me at the time, but it makes you see that
> there are no absolutes. That there are different choices and
> ways of living, and that one isn't more real than another.
> That was a big culture shock for me.

In terms of the theoretical discussion of possible ways of developing questioning perspectives, outlined in Chapter 1, these
women are similar. The ways in which they experienced their
ethnic difference provided practical personal knowledge that
alternative social arrangements existed. This knowledge may

have played some part in the construction of their questioning perspectives.

The effect of maternal employment upon daughters' attitudes

No pattern emerged regarding the family forms that respondents were reared in. However, a surprisingly high proportion of the sample (80 per cent) had mothers who had been engaged in paid work while they were growing up. Only 12 respondents had mothers who were full-time housewives throughout their childhood and adolescence: five of these were in service class households, five in intermediate class household and two were in manual class households. The main areas of employment of mothers who were in paid work included a factory owner ($n = 1$); health, welfare and teaching professions ($n = 12$); secretarial, bookkeeping and clerical work ($n = 20$); shop work ($n = 3$); factory work, usually supervisory ($n = 4$); catering, bar work, housekeeping, and cleaning ($n = 8$).

Historical period seemed to be much more relevant than class for shaping the employment patterns of respondents' mothers. For respondents aged over 30, nine mothers (30 per cent) were full-time housewives, 11 (37 per cent) were described as employed full-time, and ten (33 per cent) followed a more intermittent or part-time employment path. By contrast, in the case of respondents aged 30 and under, only three (10 per cent) mothers were full-time housewives, 11 (37 per cent) were described as employed full-time and 16 (53 per cent) followed an intermittent or part-time employment path. It appears that the mothers of the younger women had filled the increased numbers of part-time and casual jobs that have become available since the 1950s.

The level of maternal employment experienced by the sample across age groups is significantly higher than we find for women more generally. For example, I compared my findings with British Household Pannel Survey (BHPS) data (a nationally representative sample of over 5500 households collected in 1991).* An

---

* The data (and tabulations) used were made available through the ESRC Data Archive. The data were originally collected by the ESRC Research Centre on Micro-social Change at the University of Essex. Neither the original collectors of the data nor the Archive bear any responsibility for the analyses of interpretations presented here.

analysis of these data shows the same generational effect, with younger women more likely to have a mother working outside the home at age 14. Sixty-two per cent aged 45 to 59 had mothers who were full-time home-makers. This falls to 47 per cent of those aged 30 to 44, and 38 per cent of those under 30.[2]

There is evidence to suggest that maternal employment may have an impact on daughters' expectations because it facilitates the development of broader conceptions of women's capabilities. A growing body of predominantly North American literature explores the effects of maternal employment on children, particularly girls.[3] This research suggests that an image of a mother whose identity is not solely derived from home life involvements may encourage the development of more flexible conceptions of the gender identity in children (see the review in Lamb, 1982b; Hoffman, 1974). Links between maternal employment and the development of more egalitarian perspectives in their children have also been identified (Lamb, 1982b, Hoffman, 1974). There is some evidence in British sociological studies to support this view. Statham's small-scale study (1986) of parents who are practising non-sexist childrearing strategies found that the mothers of most of her female respondents had been employed and this had provided very positive early messages regarding the diverse capabilities of women (pp.174–5).

There is also evidence to suggest that maternal employment encourages a positive attitude towards employment in daughters (Agassi, 1982; Angrist and Almquist, 1975:167; Marini, 1978:741). This view is borne out in an analysis of BHPS data. The statement, 'A husband's job is to earn money; a wife's job is to look after the home and family' was significantly more likely to be rejected by daughters of employed mothers than by daughters of home-makers. This held across age groups. Daughters of employed mothers are more likely, during childhood and adolescence, to expect and want to be employed, and to see paid work as a lifelong commitment, than daughters of home-makers (Banducci, 1967). They may also be more likely wish to complete college education and make non-traditional occupational 'choices' (Marini, 1978; Angrist and Almquist, 1975; Hoffman, 1974; Banducci, 1967).

However, there appears to be an important mediating factor for daughters' employment attitudes: whether a mother experienced difficulties and conflict in pursuing her career (Colangelo

et al., 1984:693; Gerson, 1885). Consequently, Colangelo *et al.*
(1984) extend the discussion by arguing that a daughter's attitudes to employment may be shaped by her perceptions of
her mother's satisfaction with either her domestic or her employment experience. This view is supported in Gerson's (1985)
life-history study.

When considering the value of the above claims it is important to recognize that daughters are different individuals from
their mothers and must negotiate their lives in different historical contexts (Gerson, 1985:39). As we will see later, an
emphasis on the influence of mothers may rely too heavily on
the assumption that women may only learn from their mothers.
My own data suggest that a daughter's early attitudes towards
future employment were shaped in more complex ways, and
that both parents may have had important influences. Furthermore, perceptions of the quality of a mother's life are clearly
subject to reinterpretation in the light of a daughter acquiring
more knowledge of self and the social world.

I now want to consider respondents' interpretations of the
meaning of paid work in their mothers' lives. Respondents whose
mothers were in paid employment usually reported receiving a
range of positive messages about the meaning of paid work. A
mother's employment was, in 41 out of 48 cases, associated
with pleasure. It was often seen to provide a measure of economic independence and, very importantly, an alternative source
of identity to that of wife and mother.

Although many of the respondents' mothers were in paid
work because they needed the money, only seven felt that their
mothers really disliked their jobs or would have preferred to
have given up paid work. This is not to say that respondents
were unaware of the frustrations that their mothers often experienced, through lack of opportunity in the workplace and
limitations imposed by inadequate education (16 respondents
expressed this awareness). However, these mothers were often
most encouraging of their daughters to take advantage of training
and education that would enable them to find more rewarding jobs. Pat illustrates this point:

> She said, I should either go and get further education, or at
> least a job that would give me training, and not end up like
> her. She used to say, 'You don't want to end up and be like
> me, and be at my age with no qualifications, no experience

and be in a dead-end job.' She always said, 'Don't go for a dead-end job.' (2O*I*)

Generally, respondents interpreted their mothers as enjoying their jobs. Hazel, a university-educated woman from an intermediate background, describes her mother's feelings towards her job:

> There were a whole series of clear ideas from my parents. One was the fact that my mother was working, and was happy in her work, and it was work that involved effort and discipline. (42*I*)

Often a mother's positive attitudes towards her job were seen to contrast with her feelings towards her home life and/or domestic duties. Some respondents spoke of feeling that their mothers would have been much happier had they been able to devote themselves to developing a career. Polly, a successful businesswoman, describes her mother's attitude towards home life and career.

> She was living a life she didn't enjoy. She was born in the wrong age, she would have been a career person, and I could feel that. She enjoyed her work much more than she enjoyed motherhood and her wife position. (35*I*)

A similar impression comes from Grace, who has recently started a degree course:

> A very talented lady really, it was a waste, waste of a good brain . . . She definitely liked being at work, she didn't like being a housewife . . . She told me, it wasn't an impression . . . She would have liked to have started a business of some kind, but my father didn't have the courage; thought it was much too risky and so they didn't do it. (44*I*)

Many respondents' mothers were in the cohort which had experienced the transformative effects of the Second World War.[4] Evelyn, a college-educated woman from a manual class background, explains how she perceived her mother's wartime experience contributing to a change in her family and employment attitudes. Her mother spent most of her working life in factory jobs, having initially been employed in a munitions factory during the war:

> While my dad was away at the war he didn't appear much, and I think women became very independent – I am sure

that my mother did in those years. And I have this vision of her having to do everything. And when the men came back from the war, and there weren't any jobs for them, and the women had been used to coping, I think they were very different. I think it was very difficult for the women to go back to what men wanted them to be at home . . . She had had to cope . . . and the men wanted them back in the 'little wife at home', and I don't think it worked. (49)

Importantly, through having access to their own money, mothers were perceived as having a measure of independence. Tracey explains her mother's situation:

Yes, I think she enjoyed her independence and she still does. She's a very strong woman, who to an extent has gone against the grain of working when she had children, because [my parents are older]. My mother is 60, my father 70, so that was very much not a thing to do when she was growing up. So she's always struck me as quite independent, and independent with her money and enjoyed it. (26S)

Mothers often encouraged their daughters to think of their future in terms of being self-reliant. This was the case with Becky, who now works in a male-dominated profession:

My mother's strong thing was, 'You don't want a man for a meal ticket. Have men if you want them, but not to support you, you have to support yourself.' (35I)

This advice seemed to have influenced her early feeling towards economic independence and employment:

I felt that work was going to be important in my life – forever, even with a marriage work was still going to be important . . . That's got to have come from my mother.

Mothers, importantly, gave the impression that participation in paid work offered an alternative source of identity to that of wife and mother. Lucy, from a manual class background, who works in a traditionally 'male' profession, describes this:

[Work was] the most important thing [laughter] . . . She has always worked. From what I am told, there was a short period when she looked after me. Then she gave me to her mother-in-law and then carried on working – it was only a matter of weeks that she wasn't working . . . The message has

been very clear, that work is the most important thing in
your life, everything else will fall to bits, but as long as you
are doing something worthwhile in your work, then you are
validated as a person. (24)

The positive images of paid work provided by respondents'
mothers may well have been a contributing factor underlying
their desire for independence and their early positive attitudes
towards employment. Of the 48 respondents whose mothers
were in paid work, 37 reported early feelings that paid work
would be an important feature of their adult lives. The rest,
however, held highly ambivalent attitudes towards the role of
paid work for their adult lives. Despite having mothers who
were either happily or unhappily involved in their jobs, they
reported thinking that paid work would have an insignificant
role in their adult lives. This would suggest the existence of
mediating factors in the relationship between maternal employment and daughters' views on employment.

Even respondents whose mothers had limited experience of paid
work often reported picking up positive messages about the importance of having a job. The mother of Maud had been forced
to give up her job because of her husband's frequent career moves:

I think she enjoyed [her clerical job]. I think she resented
giving it up. She talked about it. I was with them last week-
end, and she was talking about it then, and this was 40 years
ago! And she still talks about it with fondness. (45S)

At least half of the 12 respondents whose mothers had been
full-time housewives reported learning from their mothers that
having a job was really important. These respondents interpreted their mothers as dissatisfied with their domestic responsibilities and felt that they would have been happier had they
been able to have jobs. This seemed to be particularly the case
for the mothers of the older women in the sample. Clearly, a
mother does not necessarily have to have a job for a daughter
to pick up messages about the importance of paid work.

Respondents' perceptions of the household division of labour

Respondents' interpretations of the organization of household
tasks in their families seemed to have an important influence

on how they, in turn, thought about 'roles' in relationships. Those who perceived the division of labour at home as fair expected to reproduce this in their own adult relationships. However, those who perceived their mothers as taking sole or primary responsibility for domestic tasks often reported having developed an early critical perspective on gender hierarchies. We will now explore this in more detail.

Domestic rebels

Almost a third of the sample ($n = 19$) interpreted the division of household labour in their homes as unconventional. Domestic arrangements ranged from those based on negotiation, where parents were perceived as sharing tasks fairly, or where fathers were perceived as 'helping out' in domestic routines, to those based on conflict, where mothers were considered domestic rebels. In the latter 'conflict'-based arrangements, mothers had been perceived as non-conformists who had refused to adhere to aspects of a 'housewife' role. Unconventional divisions of labour were more likely in manual households than in intermediate or service class households. Interestingly, many of the arrangements in which higher levels of sharing were reported predated the impact of 'Second Wave' feminism; slightly more than half of the respondents reporting these arrangements were aged 30 and over. Respondents often linked their parents' more egalitarian arrangements with their adherence to left-wing politics. Others, particularly the older respondents, felt that their parents' roles reflected regional variation in working-class domestic practices. Janet, a 42-year-old woman from an intermediate class background, describes the regional influences on the domestic situation in her extended family:

> My grandfather was a Hampshire man who was perfectly competent about the house. Like many rural working-class men he didn't have any macho sense of division of labour. So he found nothing difficult or strange about preparing the meals. My father similarly was very proto-feminist and saw no shame attached to doing housework – so much so that it was a rude shock to realize this recognition was not universal . . . My grandfather would darn socks, which was again a countryman's skill and not gendered at all.

Another example of a sharing arrangement comes from Sandy, a 33-year-old Scottish woman from a manual background. She went as far as to describe the power relations in her family as very matriarchal:[5]

> My experience as a child was that the domestic duties were shared. Father took parenting very seriously. He did ironing etcetera. They had a rota, and I then was involved ... that was done by negotiation, we would sit and talk about who would do what.

Again she sees this arrangement as reflecting regional practices:

> I think [dad] got [this attitude] from his own father [who was a miner]. He was one of five brothers. And his father brought him up not to expect his mother to do everything ... There was a sense of a very matriarchal society ... as a cultural thing. Women were the bankers of the family. It's not like English working-class experience, where the man comes home and gives the wife the housekeeping. What happened was, my father went out to work and gave my mother the pay packet, unopened, and she gave him back his pocket money.

There were several other examples of this style of financial arrangement, a working-class practice which has been noted in Pahl's (1989) study of household money management.

Max, aged 26, from a service class background, linked her parents' unconventional domestic arrangements with their class and age differences.

> They have always taken equal roles in the house. My father doesn't like cooking, so my mother cooks. My dad does all the housework, and he does the ironing and cleaning and shopping ... It's how I have always known it ... It was quite a scandalous marriage to start with, so they were starting with that. My father was working class from Lancashire, and my mother was middle class from the Midlands, and there was a ten year age gap between them ... So they have always gone against the grain ... I recognized it was unusual, I always have done. And my parents, to my friends, have always been seen as role model parents.

It is interesting to note that those respondents who perceived their parents as having negotiated a more sharing arrangement in the home by consensus were also likely to have initially held positive attitudes towards marriage.

In some cases an unconventional division of labour arose out of conflict. These respondents described their mothers as having rebelled against their domestic role. This was the case for Ellen's mother, who was not in paid employment:

> My parents had a very up-and-down relationship. I think [when I was] seven, my father objected to my mother's cooking, at which she threw the whole dinner across the room and swore never to do any cooking again, and indeed she never has . . . I picked up that she was tremendously unconventional in not cooking. And as far as I am aware the last time she cleaned the house as you and I might, was 25 or 30 years ago! (47*S*)

Although most recognized that their parents' sharing arrangements were not the norm, they had been presented with a model which they expected to replicate in their future relationships. Clare illustrates this kind of thinking. She found that her experience of marriage contrasted strikingly with her early expectations:

> I wasn't expecting it to be [a traditional division of labour] for me. Although I knew from an early age that women cooked the dinner, and did the shopping and housework, and men went to work and sat in the arm chair when they came home – I thought it was weird. Because it didn't happen in my house . . . It wasn't strictly divided in our house, as it was in the houses of my friends. My mother would help take the car engine apart, she did painting in the house, my father did shopping on Saturdays, because my mother worked . . . So I was expecting to do domestic things, but not because it was my job, but simply because there were things that had to be done, and I assumed that we would do them together. (44*I*)

A traditional division of household labour

It was, however, much more common for respondents to report a traditional division of labour in the home ($n = 41$). Mothers were seen to carry a 'double burden' of domestic work and paid work. At least 25 respondents had the impression that their mothers resented this domestic situation. Often respondents reported feeling at an early age that this was an unjust situation. This was the case for Patty:

Mother ran the household. It infuriated me that my mother cooked, and cleaned for my brother and father, and even made my brother's bed. I'd say to her, 'You're working just as many hours, why are you doing two jobs, why can't you share?' Mother would say, 'They're tired. Yes I'm tired too, but it's hard to get out of a 20 year routine...' Mother used to get up at 6.30 in the morning to do the housework, and she didn't enjoy it. She'd go to work and then come home, get the meal ready and clean up. (22*S*)

Mothers who were employed outside the home often utilized the help of their daughters for domestic tasks. Consequently, some respondents experienced, at an early age, first-hand knowledge of the meaning of domestic work. Some spoke of becoming aware of gender injustices because their brothers and fathers did not share this burden. This often had an early radicalising effect, as was the case for Monica:

I took over [in the home] really. I looked after my sister, and cooked my brother's dinner from when I was about 11... When I look back, I got very angry about it as I got older. Why should I be here to cook [Dad's] dinner? No matter what time he came in, he had to have his dinner ready on the table. But my brother was never expected to do it. But because I was the eldest daughter it was my responsibility... my brother seemed to go out, and do whatever he wanted to do. (43*M*)

Respondents' early perceptions of the meaning of domestic work often stood in sharp contrast to the positive messages many reported receiving from their mothers about the meaning of paid work. A total of 27 respondents, that is, almost half the sample, reported holding early critical opinions on the gender division of domestic labour in their homes; they felt it was unjust and most recalled feeling that they did not want to replicate this in their own adult relationships. The desire not to grow up to be in a similar situation to their mothers was often reported. Kerry describes these feelings:

It was just basically, Christ no! please don't let me grow up the same way. Really, no! I mean she cooked all day for school meals, had to come home and cook for us, awful really. No, I was happy round the garden, actually helping out in the garden. I wasn't into housework. (34*M*)

The word 'slave' came up quite often in respondents' description of their mother's situation, as for example in Julie's account:

> I think she didn't enjoy [her domestic role]. I think she tolerated it . . . I think she didn't question it. She just did it. [*Did you get this impression when you were young?*] Yes, yes, of course I did. I thought that I didn't want to do that myself, that I never wanted to be in that slave situation, yes. From I would say nine years, already I had that opinion. (44*M*)

The critical perspective many respondents held towards their mothers' circumstances, may have informed their thoughts on the desirability of marriage. Of the 27 respondents who held this critical perspective, 20 reported an early awareness that they did not want to marry. The rest hoped that their marriage would be different.

As we will see in later chapters, almost all of the sample developed an egalitarian perspective towards their relationships. It may well be that, for many of them, childhood experience provided the basis for the establishment of this perspective, which was reinforced through later experience. However, not all of my respondents questioned the status quo in their homes. Some reported being too involved in their childhood worlds to think about it, while others reported assuming that it was inevitable that women would carry the burden of domestic work. Consequently, there were enough respondents who reported an early unquestioning attitude towards the division of labour to suggest that the formation of attitudes is highly complex, continuous and subject to change.

The contribution of male caregivers

Very little has been said in this chapter about the influence of male caregivers in developing interests and shaping expectations of respondents. Research on childhood and socialization often assumes that, as mothers are usually the primary caregiver, fathers are remote figures, who have little impact on the development of attitudes and interests in their daughters. Most studies on fathers tend to focus on the father–son relationship, the implication being that it is through the mother–daughter relationship that girls learn to become women (Droughn, 1986). Since the mid-1970s, studies have begun to take into account the influence of fathers in the formation of daughters' attitudes

and expectations. Some of these finding will now be briefly
summarized. However, as was the case with research on maternal employment, it must be emphasized that these findings
should be treated with caution, as they require more detailed
empirical support.

Despite the fact that fathers may have little involvement in
routine childrearing (Statham, 1986:13), they may still be
influential in shaping the characteristics of their daughters
(Lazoff, 1974; Lamb, 1982b:14). Not surprisingly, fathers appear
to have the greatest influence when they have close relationships
with their daughters. These close relationships, however, may
encourage very different outcomes, depending upon a father's
own sense of gender identity. Research suggests that fathers
who hold traditional gender concepts will encourage gender
stereotyping and discourage autonomy in their daughters (Lamb,
1986:147; Droughn, 1986). Conversely, those who form close
relationships, behaving towards their daughters as they might
towards a son, may be influential in their daughters developing
a desire for a more autonomous lifestyle. By interacting with
their daughters in a less gender-differentiated way, they may
pass on skills and generate interests that are more usually re-
served for sons (Droughn, 1986:210; Lamb, 1979). Supportive
father–daughter relationships appear to encourage self-
confidence (Lamb, 1986), independence and greater flexibility
in gender self-concepts (Lamb, 1986; Lazoff, 1974). It is also
suggested that these fathers have a positive influence on the
way daughters approach their careers. Research on college
women and successful businesswomen links father support with
achievement orientation and high levels of ambition (Droughn,
1986; Lamb, 1986; Hennig and Jardim, 1979). The influence
of fathers obviously requires further attention in life-history
analysis and longitudinal studies. These findings also beg the
question: do fathers create or reinforce these tendencies in
their daughters?

I would now like to explore my own data to see what influence
fathers had in encouraging their daughters to develop less gender
stereotyped skills, interests and aspirations. I would also like to
extend the discussion to include other close adult male caregivers.

Although many respondents experienced their fathers as rather
remote figures, a third ($n = 20$) of the sample reported high
levels of valuable interaction with fathers or other male relatives,
which had a very positive influence on their early attitudes and

interests.[6] These relationships were seen as special: respondents saw themselves as their father's (or caregiver's) 'favourite', and in turn often described them as friends.[7] Importantly, these male caregivers shared their knowledge and encouraged these respondents to develop practical and/or intellectual skills which may be less common in girls.[8] An illustration of these points comes from Sara who has become a scientist:

> I was very much daddy's girl, rather than mummy's girl. Dad was a much greater influence. When dad was working on the car, I was asking him questions on it, and my sister was asking mum about the flowers in the garden, and stuff like that. Quite a true divide. My dad is much more like a friend, and my mother is much more of an authority figure in my life ... At 13 I decided I wanted to build a radio, so dad took me to a company that sold more easily assembled stuff, bought a book on easy electronics... That helped me immensely when I was doing physics. (25*S*)

Similarly, Chris, who came from a manual background, suggested that the practical skills she learnt from her father helped her to tackle science subjects at school. This led her on to study electronics at university:

> Yes, I could wire a plug at seven. His view was that you should be able to do these sorts of things... I never had any fear or anxiety of taking on [science at school], it was quite normal. If the washing machine broke down and my dad was fixing it, he would call me over to have a look at how it worked. (33)

She also felt that he encouraged her to be both successful and independent:

> The stuff I got from my father was much more about: 'You are not subservient to a man, you will never be. If you want to look after yourself, you have to do it yourself. You shouldn't have any expectations of anyone doing anything else for you. You make what you want out of what you've got.'

Positive male involvement in early learning was not limited to fathers; in some cases respondents spoke of important relationships with uncles and grandfathers. In this next example, of Diane, a successful businesswoman from a manual background, we can also see how she actively sought out the company of her father and grandfather. In this way she was able to develop her interest in practical skill learning. Like many respondents she was unwilling to restrict her interests to traditionally female pastimes:

> I loved being with my grand-dad building things, 'cos he was a carpenter. I loved taking things apart and putting them back together – hated dolls and prams. I wanted to be with my father, washing the car, gardening, used to love all that . . . My sister was very much with my mum, and I with my dad. My sister finds it natural to do housework and things like that, and she's a very clean person, never got her hands dirty. I can't keep clean for two minutes. Didn't want to be clean; that was partly because my dad wanted a boy and I tried to be that boy. I wanted to be, I was quite happy to do boy's things, I used to get love from my dad in that way. I loved learning less academic things. (35)

Unfortunately, she was unable to develop these more 'masculine' interests at school, because of the very rigid gender division in subject choices offered at her secondary modern.

For Elsie, a carpenter, access to practical 'male' skills came through her uncle. She was luckier than Diane, insofar as she was able to pursue her interest in carpentry at school:

> [*How did you get involved in carpentry?*] My uncle, who was living with us, was very much into woodwork and as kids you're fascinated and just, sort of, got drawn into it, and model-making and things like that. (41*M*)

What comes across clearly in these commentaries is the interactive, rather than one-dimensional, nature of the relationship between encouragement from fathers and the development of non-traditional interests and skills in daughters. Daughters were not being passively moulded by these close male caregivers. Instead, they seemed to have wanted to expand their repertoire of interests, and these men were willing to oblige. The process of learning was mutually reinforced by the predispositions of both daughter and caregiver. As such it seems impossible to untangle the variables.

It did appear that, as children, these respondents developed more independent attitudes towards their futures. These respondents were much less likely to assume that they would marry than the remainder of the sample. During adolescence only

25 per cent expected to marry, as compared with 43 per cent of the rest of the sample. They also tended to be academically successful; all but three reported having been in the top stream. However, I think that the most obvious impact that these relationships had on respondents was that they were able to become familiar with, and cultivate, skills and interests that are more usually made available to boys. This was reflected in both their academic and occupational 'choices'. Eight out of the nine respondents in the sample with higher qualifications in science-related subjects came from this group. Moreover, at the time of interview all but three were located in occupations or positions in an occupational hierarchy which were male-dominated.

It appears then that, when fathers are available and willing to share their knowledge and skills with daughters, as they might with their sons, daughters have an opportunity to build upon and extend their repertoire of interests. Consequently, they may be in a better position to make decisions that reflected their interests and personalities, rather than simply their gender. However, there were limits as to how far some could formally develop these interests. Some, usually secondary modern-educated, found themselves confined by a gender-differentiated school curriculum that offered craft subjects to boys, and domestic subjects to girls.

AGENCY IN THE CONSTRUCTION OF FEMININITIES

Problems with theories of socialization

Theories of socialization tend to regard childhood as the period when gender characteristics are established.[9] By concentrating on childhood, this research fails to recognize the range of ideological and structural processes which shape understandings of gender throughout life, for example workplace culture (Walby, 1990:94). Another problem with psychological, and early sociological and feminist theories of socialization (see, for example, Chodorow, 1978) is that they take for granted normative notions of what it means to be a woman or a man, and ignore the social, cultural and age-related differences amongst women and amongst men. For example, Black feminists argue that the historical legacy of slavery, together with contemporary social and economic circumstances informed by

racism, offer African-Caribbean women conceptions of womanhood based on self-reliance and autonomy, as opposed to normative definitions of femininity which stress passivity and
dependency (Dugger, 1991:40; Dill, 1987:98; King, 1988:47).
Nor can these approaches account for the historical specificity
of the content of gender categories (Walby, 1990:105, Connell,
1987:63).

The Australian sociologist of gender, Connell (1987), prefers
to conceptualize gender as a *process* rather than a 'thing'. He
suggests that gender is better understood as a verb: I gender,
you gender, s/he genders (p.140). Connell views gender as a
'practice organized in terms of, or in relation to, the repro-
ductive division of people into male and female' (p.140). He
stresses the importance of individual reflexivity within the process
of gendering. Individual action, together with the interaction
of gender with other social identities, leads to the existence of
a wide range of femininit*ies* and masculinit*ies*. There are, however,
constraints on this flexibility. Major structures or 'gender regimes'
shape gender meanings so that hierarchies exist within and
between gender categories (p.120). Certain definitions and forms
of masculinities and femininities achieve ascendency. Connell
calls these *hegemonic* masculinity and *emphasized* femininity (p.183).
A central aspect of hegemonic masculinity is its heterosexuality and connection with the institution of marriage. It is linked
with power, authority, reason and aggression. Connell suggests
that it is more of a cultural ideal to which men aspire rather
than correspond. Because it sustains and justifies their power
to dominate women, men have an interest in consenting to
and collaborating in the maintenance of this image. In contrast,
emphasized femininity is defined around compliance with gender
subordination, is oriented towards accommodating men's desires and is linked with the home and the bedroom (pp.183–8).

Because mainstream theories of socialization usually assume
two monolithic gender categories comprising dichotomous
gender characteristics, they focus on gender 'difference' and
ignore the overlap of personality characteristics between women
and men. This focus on gender difference may influence the
findings of small-scale studies of children's activities. For example,
Henshall and McGuire (1986:139) argue that those who observe
children's play in controlled situations comment on children's
use of gender-appropriate toys, while ignoring the fact that
they actually spend most of their play time using toys that are

not gender-differentiated. When girls have access to a choice of toys, they usually spend more time playing with 'boys' toys than 'girls' toys.

It is important to remember that girls grow up with a variety of often conflicting images of how they may behave as girls and women. As Gerson (1985:34) points out, 'the values of the wider society also exert a powerful influence on children. When there is inequality in the rewards associated with masculine and feminine attributes, all children, including girls, are likely to adopt to some degree the more highly valued masculine orientations.'[10] In support of this argument, there is some North American research which suggests that being a tomboy is a very common experience for women (Green *et al.*, 1982; Hyde and Rosenberg, 1977, 1974). Plumb and Cowan (1984) carried out research into tomboy experience. Their study was based on 210 North American females: young women whose ages ranged from seven to 16, and adult women. They found that just over half of the sample reported being or having been tomboys (p.708).

Research suggests that being a tomboy has positive advantages in terms of peer popularity. Hemmer and Kleiber's (1981) study of 11- and 12-year-olds concluded that there is every reason for a girl to aspire to be a tomboy. Their findings show that tomboys are usually the most popular individuals in the class. It is also suggested that the tomboy experience may influence the development of more flexible gender characteristics. Plumb and Cowan (1984:711) argue: 'Perhaps the girls who are able to transcend gender-role behaviour in childhood are the ones who will be the most flexible and androgynous as adults.' On the bases of observations of tomboy activities, they suggest that, rather than rejecting female activities, tomboys had expanded their repertoires to 'include both gender traditional and non-traditional activities.' This contrasted with the activities of 'non-tomboys' and boys, which tended to be more gender-appropriate, particularly amongst 15–16 year olds. There is some evidence to link 'tomboyism' with a strong career orientation. Hennig and Jardim's (1979) life-history study of top female North American managers found that most reported having been tomboys as children.

The tomboy poses a problem for conventional socialization theory, insofar as she does not conform to strict lines of gender demarcation. Socialization theorists have tended to ignore the 'tomboy' phenomenon or, if it is mentioned, to link it with homosexuality.[11] I would suggest that this simplistic linkage is derived more from the need to maintain the integrity of various socialization theories, rather than from empirical evidence. If tomboyism is as common as the above research suggests, then we would expect to find lesbians making up the majority of the population of adult women. Rather than simply equating tomboyism with lesbianism, it is much more interesting to explore aspects of tomboy existence to see if we can identify conditions (such as feelings of autonomy and the questioning of gender hierarchies) that might facilitate the evaluating of heterosexuality in later life.

Respondents' perceptions of childhood self

There was a degree of diversity amongst respondents' representations of childhood self. Only two women interviewed reported childhoods which involved the pursuit of exclusively 'feminine' activities and interests. Six respondents reported very solitary childhoods, preferring their own company or that of a dog, and they were often very 'bookish'. Three were partially or totally incapacitated by ill-health. However, the overwhelming majority, 49, reported being very inquiring, active, outdoor children, who enjoying 'boyish' pastimes. These pastimes included being in gangs with boys and other active girls, playing football and cowboys and Indians and climbing trees. They played with toys generally designated as boys' toys, such as 'Meccano', train sets, and 'Action Man'. They perceived themselves to be as competent and strong as boys, if not more so. Of this group, 40 described themselves as having been tomboys. Tomboy experience was spread across the age ranges: 11 were 40 or over, 11 were aged between 30 and 39 and the remaining 18 were under 30. In 15 cases, 'tomboy' respondents were from service class backgrounds, in 14 cases they were from intermediate backgrounds, and in 11 cases they came from manual backgrounds. We now turn to an exploration of the world of the tomboy, as remembered by my respondents.

The tomboy

The preferred dress code for tomboys was usually shorts or jeans, rather than dresses, which they felt were restrictive.

Establishing this dress code sometimes involved resisting a mother's attempt to dress them in more 'feminine' clothes, as was the case with Penny:

> No [I didn't wear dresses] because I'd feel such an idiot . . . it just wouldn't do, because I'd feel so uncomfortable . . . it's so impractical, especially when you're that age, 'cos kids do throw themselves around, and they dress these girls up in the most ridiculous outfits . . . I do know that taking me shopping was the chore of my mother's life really, 'cos I'd refuse to wear anything that she liked. (25)

Tomboys often played with boys rather than girls. Ola explains her reasoning:

> I always played with the boys, I never really played with the girls. They were just too soft, and I just didn't have anything in common. I wanted to be out on my bike, climb trees. They had their skirts and dresses on, I had my jeans on. We were on a different wave length . . . All I knew was I wanted to play and run around. I didn't want to be wearing my patent shoes and my dresses, I just wanted to be me. I was never a sheep, I was definitely a leader and I have gone on through life that way. (29)

Being a tomboy was in some cases related to the gender composition of the neighbourhood, as the comments of Judith suggest:

> I was a tomboy [laughter]. I say unfortunately, but when I was a kid, the street I lived on, I was the only girl on the street and there were lots of boys my age and a couple of years younger. It just seemed all my mum's friends had boys, so I was a real tomboy, played football, and jumped up and down fences, and created havoc really. Would pull a pram round full of mud, rather than dolls. (32)

Although some of the tomboys reported playing with girls' toys, most rejected stereotypical girls' activities and toys. They reported having been very active in discouraging parents or relatives from giving them sex-typed toys. Some had brothers of similar ages and could share their toys. This was the case for Louise:

> I had 'Action Man' with my brother. [I was able to play with his toys.] I wouldn't actually play with dolls. They gave me a doll's pram once, and I gave it to them back – 'I don't want

no namby toys!' Yes, I suppose I was more into boys' games. My brother and I would play cowboys and Indians, we played farmers too, and 'Action Man'. I didn't play with dolls, I had some but I never used them, it was only little girls that played with them. (23)

Being a tomboy was not always encouraged by parents and involved conflict. Sheena experienced violence from her father because she refused to be 'lady-like':

> I was always getting into trouble with my dad. When I got home from school, because my hair was always in a mess, he'd beat me for that ... He would always tell me off for looking scruffy. And I would come in with cuts on my legs; he would beat me for that too, because I was supposed to be 'lady-like'. I think in my own little way I may have been rebelling. (29)

It appears clear, from the repeatedly similar accounts given, that tomboys were desiring access to the freedom which they perceived boys having. Sometimes this led them, as children, to wish that they had been born boys. Netty's account expresses these common feelings:

> I just sort of thought that I wanted to be either a boy, or why couldn't I just be me? ... I have always looked up to my brother. It seemed that he had everything, and everything was so easy because he was male ... And I felt really frustrated, because I wanted to do the sort of things they did. And I thought that girls were playing things like mummies and daddies, and boy-friends, and that. It just wasn't what I wanted to do, I just felt kind of really lonely. (19)

The early desire to be a boy usually resolved itself during adolescence. Sally describes coming to terms with this:

> It was a long time before I accepted that men were basically stronger than women, and that that was something I had to accept ... I suppose [as a child], I wanted to be a boy anyway [laughter]. They had a better deal. It was so much easier, they didn't have to fight about wearing these stupid clothes. Oh God, why did I fight it? I suppose I was trying to find an identity for myself. I did in the end. Now I wouldn't want to be a man for anything on earth. I don't remember when that happened; sometime in my teens. (27)

It seems that tomboys were identifying with boys because they perceived a polarity between activities defined as appropriate for boys and girls. Within this polarity, interests and pursuits, which are interpreted as adventurous and active, have been colonized and categorized as 'male'. Faced with this dichotomy, those whose sense of self reflected a more central positioning on a gender continuum are placed in a paradox. As such it is little wonder that, as children, many tomboys had a problem with identifying themselves as girls. I think Maddie's reluctance to assign the label 'tomboy' to her childhood self reflects her adult unwillingness to attach gender labels to quite gender-neutral activities:

> They would have described me as a tomboy no doubt. I am not sure I know what I think a tomboy is, that's why I held back on that. I enjoyed energetic things. (35)

As we have seen in the literature cited at the beginning of this section, there is no reason to assume that girls are any less energetic or adventurous than boys. Yet when girls act upon this they are viewed as somehow transcending, to a limited extent, their femininity. I think more than anything else the label 'tomboy' acts to shape the boundaries of appropriate femininity. The label provides the language to contain and describe perfectly natural childhood behaviour, while at the same time protecting the dichotomy of gender categories. However, there seems to be some contrast to girls' and boys' experience of challenging these boundaries. While for pre-pubescent girls being a tomboy may be viewed as a 'natural' part of growing up, being a 'sissy' is actively discouraged by parents and peers (Statham, 1986:88–9). The boundaries around appropriate masculinity appear to be strictly 'policed' much earlier than they are for femininity. Fagot's (1977) study of nursery school children in the USA found that peers were very hostile to boys who played with dolls or dressed up. Horn's North American research (1979:34) suggests greater peer acceptance of girls who are tomboys than boys who are 'sissies'. This may well be due to the higher value assigned to hegemonic masculinity, and popular understandings which link 'sissies' to adult homosexuality.

An important consequence of being a tomboy, and associating with boys in childhood, was that boys were not experienced as some mysterious 'other' to be despised or revered. Perhaps this lack of mystery has some role to play in undermining the establishment of a sense of eroticized difference through the attraction of opposites which underpins heterosexual desire. In girlhood, tomboys had been able to measure their abilities against those of boys and, as a result, felt just as competent in practical, intellectual or physical skills. Like many in the sample, Rose acquired excellent sporting skills during childhood, which she fostered throughout her adolescence:

> I was always better than [the boys] [laughter], yes. I was great at cricket. They always used to have me playing cricket and football. I was always welcomed by the lads. (29)

Feelings of empathy often extended into approaches to intellectual pursuits. This was the case for Liz. Reflected in her final joking comment is the taken for granted view which associates tomboyism with lesbianism:

> Because I felt comfortable with them, and I was the same as them, we were all just as motivated, and had the same outlook, so that you could achieve the same as them. I suppose if I had hung out with more girls, we would have stayed at home and played with dolls, and I wouldn't have turned out like I did! [laughter]! (26)

These feelings of being just as good as the boys were held by almost all the respondents, tomboys and non-tomboys alike. This sometimes led to early criticisms of institutional practices that differentiated between boys and girls. An example of this kind of thinking comes from Holly, who had developed an interest in carpentry through her close relationship with her grandfather:

> We did domestic science and they did woodwork, and I couldn't understand why I couldn't do woodwork. And that came through earlier and I couldn't understand . . . They bought me a doll and I wasn't interested. I loved puppets but not a doll and not a pram. I would have liked a carpentry set, or screwdrivers, and felt it was a bit strange, I didn't like that. And then schooling and the social thing – 'Oh well, you do domestic science.' (35)

Similarly, Kate reported that the gender-stereotyped practices she experienced at primary school had a radicalising effect on her:

I always wanted to join in with [the boys] at school – infant school and so forth. The boys would go off and do interesting things with wood and clay and stuff, and we had to go off and sew bunnies and things, and I hated that. And that's what started off the rebellious spirit from word go. I had no intention of being caught in that trap, thank you very much . . . I used to get into a lot of strife because of that . . . I always saw it from the person point of view. I was a born feminist, I just got pissed off because the boys seemed to get the better deal, and I thought 'Why? What's so fair about that?' (32)

Serving an 'apprenticeship' in emphasized femininity

As was said earlier, childhood experience does not fix a person's attitudes and approaches. However, serving an early 'apprenticeship' in emphasized femininity may support a perspective which is less in contradiction with normative forms of adult femininity. By an 'apprenticeship in emphasized femininity', I mean the experiencing, as something taken for granted, of a range of early practices that are aimed at encouraging girls to develop interests which correspond more closely to traditional forms of adult femininity, based on notions of dependency.

The experiences of the two respondents who described a more stereotyped upbringing are examples of this 'apprenticeship'. Here we have a description of the childhood of Alice. Her childhood interests, and early negative feelings towards boys, contrast strikingly with most of the rest of the sample:

We didn't have many toys, in those days we couldn't afford much. I think I had one doll. I think I had a little pram, someone gave me a second-hand doll's house, I liked that. My parents didn't dress me prettily. My friends had party dresses and lovely frilly things they went to parties in . . . I really wanted a frilly, frilly, 'fro-fro' dress, so I always felt very envious of my friends' dresses . . . I was a real wimp. I was frightened of boys, I was a total wimp, I didn't like anything rough at all . . . I just had the feeling they were a race apart. We were little girls, and we were different from the little boys. Little boys played rough games; if you saw a crowd of rough boys you avoided them! (40)

Another example comes from Angie:

I don't remember any feelings about equality with boys. I think, for lots of years, I just accepted what I was told. It wasn't until I was a lot older that I actually began to question things. [*What were you accepting?*] Well, that girls did this, and boys did that. I had a doll's pram and my brother had a bike. I still have some of my dolls, and I did play with them and they were quite important, and my sister and I used to play with them – we used to give them a rough time. And I had a sewing machine, and an ironing board, and we had a house – a cupboard under the stairs that we made a play house ... as I say, we accepted what we had been told. (42)

These women also reported adolescent attitudes which reflected more traditional beliefs. Both grew up assuming that they would marry, neither questioning the gender division of labour, with each perceiving future employment as being of secondary significance. If this kind of 'apprenticeship' is commonplace, it raises some interesting questions. At the time of interview, one of these respondents was the only person in the sample to express fairly traditional beliefs regarding appropriate female behaviour. However, the other had experienced a marked change in attitudes.

Transition from childhood into adolescence

At some point towards the end of primary school and in the early years of secondary school, there seemed to be a greater polarization between girls and boys. The early ease which tomboys, and other active girls, had felt in the boys' world began to diminish as a greater awareness of the significance of gender crept into their interactions. Personal attributes of an individual child were becoming eclipsed by more general assumptions as to what constituted appropriate behaviour for girls and boys.

   Greater gender polarization during adolescence made it much more difficult to occupy the middle ground on the gender continuum. The availability of the tomboy identity appeared to have a limited life-span as the boundaries around gender behaviour were being redrawn and more tightly 'policed'. Betty expresses the sentiment of many when she describes her experience during this period:

Up to eight, I played only with the boys in the playground, but then they come to an age were they don't associate with girls any more. I remember feeling very isolated from then on. Because I remember them thinking it was sissy for them to hang around with a girl. I was a girl, I shouldn't be with them. I shouldn't play football with them. I shouldn't muck around on the climbing frames: 'Girls are stupid, girls are silly, we're much stronger than you.' And this whole sort of warped sexuality, that you were a poof if you played with girls, whereas in three to four years' time you were a poof if you didn't. (19S)

Whether they managed to negotiate inclusion in the boys' world, or stand outside alone or with other assertive girls, the groundwork had been prepared which would bring them into contradiction with the emphasized femininity offered by teen-age culture.[12]

Many reported feeling uncomfortable during this transitory period, and throughout adolescence. Underpinning this was their feeling of being at odds with the emerging culture of romantic heterosexuality. Hazel speaks for many when she describes her discomfort during this period:

I think my life took a plummet when I was 11. I didn't really have many friends outside school. I think it's all to do with these roles. Up to when I was 11, it was fine for me to be a 'tomboy', and do stuff with animals and so on, and be in my gang, that was all fine . . . I certainly didn't find it as easy to be myself once I was about 12 . . . It felt that I couldn't do the same things any more, it was all this teenage culture to do with make-up and boyfriends and stuff, and I didn't really feel at home in it at all. (31S)

Similar feelings were expressed by Connie:

The whole thing changed, suddenly they became totally different people. I thought what is this thing that happens to everyone else and doesn't happen to me? . . . I didn't know how to behave, quite honestly. They all seemed to have this secret code that they all learned, and I didn't. They all knew how to behave at discos, and I would sit pinned to the wall terrified. Where did they learn this? I didn't have it. It was some sort of pattern of social behaviour that everyone fell into, and I didn't have it – God! . . . The big 'goo goo'

eyes came out, the painted faces, and the frocks, and all
that stuff, and the act, the peacock act, basically attracting.
At 12, they would stop being your mate that you had always
known, and suddenly they would become this minor adult,
doing something that you didn't understand. They would
suddenly be – Oh! with the boys, flirting big eyes, all that
sort of thing; it didn't seem right for me, I could never do
it. (32)

CONCLUSION

These evocative childhood memories suggest that respondents
often saw themselves as active agents in the construction of
less gender-stereotypical self-concepts. They observed and
participated in the activities of other boys and girls, and grappled
with normative definitions of femininity, and usually found them
to be wanting. As a result, they generally occupied the middle
ground on the gender continuum, where many found that the
tomboy identity better suited their personalities. Through their
practical knowledge and interactions with boys, most experienced early feelings that they were just as capable as boys. This
may well have made many aware or indeed critical of institutional practices that supported gender inequality.

Importantly, many remembered learning from the experience
of their parents. Those who perceived their parents as offering
a more egalitarian model for gender relations expected this in
their own relationships, while others, who were exposed to a more
traditional division, tended to be critical of this state of affairs,
perceiving it as unfair. These respondents were unwilling to
experience a similar domestic situation to that of their mothers
and, in many cases, problematized the desirability of marriage
itself. From their mothers, respondents usually learnt that women
could enjoy and gain independence through a commitment to
paid work. Many, through their close relationships with male
caregivers, were encouraged to develop non-traditional skills
and attitudes. From both mothers and fathers, most were encouraged to aspire to a more independent lifestyle.

As was mentioned earlier, we have to be mindful that these
are retrospective accounts, so that we must be careful as to
the conclusions drawn. However, there are a range of interesting commonalities in respondents' accounts which I, like other
researchers, believe are associated with the development of

broader gender self-concepts and an orientation towards egalitarianism and independence. Good examples include the prevalence of maternal employment – which other researchers link to feelings of independence – and the high incidence of tomboyism, which has also been found in studies of other women who have gone against the grain.

As we will see in the next chapter, this early, less gender-stereotyped, sense of self and their more independent aspirations often placed the respondents at odds with the dictates of adolescent femininity and romantic heterosexuality. It may be that their broader gender self-concepts undermined the power of gender difference to appear erotic. It will be argued that 'avenues of escape' from romantic heterosexuality exist, and these offered many respondents refuge from incorporation into active heterosexuality.

NOTES

1. For feminist critiques of measures of social class see, for example, Crompton and Mann (1986), Walby (1990:7–13), Dex (1987:18–27).
2. The influence of social class on maternal employment is evident only among older cohorts, with service class households less likely to have had working mothers than intermediate or manual. Among women under 30 years old there is no significant class effect.
3. I use the term 'employed' and 'employment' to refer to participation in waged work, rather than unpaid household work.
4. The percentage of married women (usually young and childless) in the British labour force doubled between 1931 and 1951 (Tilly and Scott, 1987:214). The experience of the more positive effects of wage earning during the war, together with changes in the economy, contributed to a major transformation in the employment patterns and family priorities of women (Tilly and Scott, 1987:215).
5. In terms of perceived power and decision making in the family, slightly over half of the sample described their mothers as strong characters, the 'boss' in their families, and in seven cases the word 'matriarchal' was used to describe mothers and grandmothers. It is of course hard to know how far their mothers' power in the decision-making process was confined to more visible and local decisions.
6. In only nine cases were close relationships reported between respondents and fathers in service class occupations. It may be that managerial/professional fathers have less time available to devote to their daughters. Certainly, many of the respondents from service class backgrounds experienced their fathers as remote characters. These remote fathers may have been influential in

less direct ways as some respondents reported trying to do well at school in order to gain their father's attention.

7. There did not appear to be any pattern regarding ordinal position, or the gender of other siblings; ten had older and/or younger brothers, ten had no brothers (three were only children, one had a sister who was an identical twin) and none had more than two siblings.

8. Hennig and Jardim (1979: ch. 6) explored the childhood of 25 top management women enrolled in the Harvard Business School MBA programme in 1963–4. Interestingly, almost all reported close relationship, with fathers who had been a major positive influence on them. The women interviewed stressed their fathers' role in encouraging them to pursue more 'masculine' activities and interests.

9. For good reviews of the problems with socialization theory, see, for example, Connell (1987, 1995) and Gerson (1985).

10. Statham's (1986) British research on non-sexist parenting found that these parents were usually the parents of daughters. She suggests that parents see many positive advantages in encouraging their daughters to challenge traditional gender stereotypes, but were less convinced of the advantages that this would bring a son (pp.90–91).

11. Beliefs linking early gender non-conformity with homosexuality, particularly in the case of boys, are well established in popular thought (see Martin, 1990). Consequently, it is hard to know how far the high incidence of early 'tomboyism' or 'sissy' behaviour reported by lesbians and gay men (see, for example, Wolff, 1973; Grellert *et al.*, 1982; Ross, 1980) is related to retrospective reconstruction (Ross, 1980:523; Kitzinger, 1987:69).

12. Hennig and Jardim's (1979) life-history study of 25 top businesswomen reports a similar experience of the tomboys in their sample. Like many of the respondents in my study, they felt a conflict, during adolescence, between their broader sense of gender identity and the more restrictive expectations for gender behaviour in adolescence. These women later went on to reject traditional social goals for women, not only by achieving in a 'man's world', but in their rejection of passivity in their relationships and their advocation of gender equality (p.113).

CHAPTER THREE

Education, heterosexual expectations and avenues of escape

INTRODUCTION

In Chapter 1 I argued that access to educational opportunities may offer individuals a sense of competency in generating change and exercising control. It can also provide women with the material resources to construct different pathways from those traditionally available to women. Conversely, limited access to this power may engender the view that 'things simply are the way they are'. These two positions may be useful in understanding the adolescent experiences and perspectives towards employment of my respondents. However, another dimension needs to be added, and that is expectations based on interpretations of sexuality. In the last chapter we saw that, as respondents entered their teens, many felt uncomfortable with the dictates of emphasized femininity and romantic heterosexuality.

In contemporary western societies, adolescence represents an extended period of transition between childhood and adulthood. It is a crucial time, as people's future life chances often depend on educational and social skills acquired then. It is also a confusing time. As their juvenile bodies change into sexual and emotionally charged adult ones, adolescents are bombarded with images of what it means to be an adult woman or man. These images, and the social practices they inform, serve to place boundaries around emotional and sexual expression in such a way as usually to produce a heterosexual outcome. While this outcome is not necessarily fixed, I would argue that interpretations of sexuality add an extra layer of meaning through which gender is experienced. The gender-polarized futures many young people anticipate are viewed through the lens of heterosexual meanings which serve to justify difference.

Respondents usually found it difficult to pinpoint when they first began actively to question their sexuality. 'Coming out' usually came as the result of a long process of evaluating the appropriateness of heterosexual relations. In retrospect, many (n = 37) felt this process had extended back into their adolescence, with 20 reporting having consciously questioned or reinterpreted their sexuality at this time. In this chapter, I want to illustrate ways that the early problematising of a conventional heterosexual future is an important source of empowerment. Those who are not fully convinced that heterosexuality is right for them are placed at odds with dominant accounts of women's social roles. Since they can no longer assume conventional pathways, they have to create different ones.

We will begin by considering the impact of the 'culture of romantic heterosexuality' on respondents and young women more generally, and outline a range of 'avenues of escape' which provide an alternative to 'success' in this culture. These alternatives may have limited their incorporation into active heterosexuality. We will then move on to explore links between educational 'success' and future expectations, taking respondents' early views on the desirability of marriage as a fairly arbitrary measure of the degree to which they problematized normative heterosexual relations. This will allow us to compare the educational experiences, perceptions of paid work and initial employment outcomes of those respondents who reported assuming they would marry, with the experience of those who did not. This comparison will illustrate ways that interpretations of sexuality can have an impact on future life chances by mediating the effects of both educational advantage and disadvantage.

ROMANTIC HETEROSEXUALITY

Research carried out in contemporary English-speaking countries indicates that adolescence is a time when great pressure is placed on young women and men to interpret their sexuality as heterosexual and to engage in a particularly narrow form of heterosexual practice (Lees, 1986; Connell, 1995). Researchers speak of the existence of a heterosexual romantic culture which absorbs and powerfully shapes contemporary teenage experience (see, for example, Lees, 1986; Griffin, 1985; Hendry, 1983; McRobbie, 1978). This culture reinforces the taken for granted nature of heterosexuality and limits sexual 'choices' by obscuring and stigmatising alternative emotional experiences and sexual practices (Pearce, 1981). Seductive representations of heterosexual love dominate popular culture and the media (Walkerdine, 1990; McRobbie, 1981). Powerful peer pressure exists to 'police' the boundaries of 'acceptable' heterosexual behaviour (Lees, 1986). This romanic heterosexual culture offers little scope for resisting unequal sexual and gender relations. Instead, it acts as a rehearsal for marriage and domesticity. Most young women interviewed prioritized the getting and keeping of boyfriends, and assumed that their future involved marriage (Lees, 1989; Griffin, 1985; Leonard, 1980; Sharpe, 1976). Furthermore, romantic heterosexual images often shape women's employment expectations. They compete with possibly conflicting experiential knowledge to obscure the full extent of married women's participation in employment and the very real possibilities of marital breakdown. Consequently, many adolescent girls have contradictory thoughts on future employment, believing at one level that paid work involvement would be minimal or secondary to a male breadwinner (Cockburn, 1987:37; McRobbie, 1978; Griffin, 1985; Connell, 1987:4; Gaskell, 1992; Machung, 1989). Furthermore, gender-stereotyped job 'choices' have been shown to relate to the maintenance of appropriate sexual image for women and men (Williams, 1992; Cockburn, 1987; Griffin, 1982; Willis, 1977). Clearly, the distortions in many young women's expectations of the future will have some impact on the way they negotiate their schooling.

Other factors may intervene to temper these contradictions. For example, British and American research on young Black women's experience highlights the importance of ethnicity in privileging experiential knowledge over dominant romantic heterosexual meanings. Dugger's (1991) research on women of African-Caribbean origins attitudes to work demonstrates that they may hold more realistic views of future employment and marriage than their White female peers (see also McRobbie, 1978). Racist employment opportunities often deny, men of African-Caribbean origin the possibility of becoming 'breadwinners', and this, together with access to broader definitions of femininity, may engender greater independence in women of African-Caribbean origins. Bryan (1987) and Fuller's (1980) research highlights ways in which this alternative vision of the future informs young Black women's approach to education, which places an emphasis on educational achievement. Major transformations in the British economy, which have involved the decline of traditional male working-class jobs and the expansion of 'women's' jobs, may now be producing a similar situation for young White working-class people. Prendergast and Forrest's (1995) recent research on working-class adolescents, discussed at the end of Chapter 1, suggests that girls' expectations of paid work and marriage are beginning to change. Girls have access to more positive images of women's capabilities and are more critical of young men's behaviour, and this seems to be inspiring a more independent outlook with regard to future employment and relationships.

Women who have grown up with broader definitions of femininity may also feel at odds with gender stereotypes emphasized in romantic heterosexuality. Many of the women in my sample reported feeling uncomfortable with the dictates of the culture of romantic heterosexuality. They felt it was dead-end, emphasising a stereotyped passive femininity, to which they were unwilling to conform. Although they often enjoyed boys' company as friends, they did not wish to adhere to the constricting gender practices they felt shaped romantic heterosexual relationships. Just over half the sample reported having had no romantic involvement with boys during their schooling. Those who had experienced romantic relationships with boys usually did not do so until their final year at school. Some dated very occasionally in an attempt to 'fit in' with their peers. While a few of those who dated reported having modified their behaviour to appear pleasing to their boyfriends, the majority reported adhering to a more egalitarian approach.

Overall, boys did not seem to feature in respondents' lives to the extent suggested in the studies cited above. On the whole they felt this lack of enthusiasm for conventional boyfriend seeking placed them at odds with the majority of their female peers, although they often found companionship amongst less boyfriend-oriented friends. Lindsey told me an amusing story about how, in response to parental pressure, she decided to pay a boy to pretend to be her boyfriend. Ironically, when her mother met this 'boyfriend' she disapproved of him!

Given the intense pressure upon girls from mid-teens onwards to conform to a heterosexual identity, an important question is: how did they avoid this apprenticeship in heterosexuality?

'Avenues of escape' from early positioning within heterosexuality

An analysis of the accounts of respondents' schooling experience suggested the existence of four main 'avenues of escape' from incorporation into romantic heterosexuality. The first avenue is historical period. Older respondents, who experienced schooling before the 'sexual revolution' of the mid-1960s, usually reported that it had been relatively easy to avoid forming active heterosexual relationships with boys. Boyfriend seeking had generally been a low priority for themselves and their peers during schooling. They characterized their relationships with boys as fairly innocent, experiencing little pressure to sexualize relationships. If boys attempted to make sexual advances, they could reject these advances without stigmatization, by utilizing dominant ideas which supported female 'sexual purity'.[1] However, this apparent lack of pressure to conform to active heterosexuality in youth must be seen in the context of other social constraints on women. Fewer employment options existed to provide an alternative to marriage. The supremacy of marriage as a social goal was supported by the gendered curriculum at school, particularly in secondary modern schools. This is painfully evident in secondary modern schools' promotion of domestic and routine clerical skills over those which might have offered girls the possibility of financial independence (see the Newsom Report of 1963, quoted in Sharpe, 1976:121).

The second avenue is the experience of single-sex schooling. Twenty-five respondents had some experience of single-sex education in the context of secondary modern, grammar or private schooling. Changes in educational fashion are evident as the experience of single-sex schooling was much more common for older women in the sample.[2] Many reported feeling that the single-sex environment acted as both a refuge from participation in boyfriend culture and, most importantly, a space where important female friendships could be developed and sustained.

The third possible avenue of escape is involvement in sport. A very high proportion of the sample, 37 per cent, reported having been very involved in competitive sports while at school.[3] Most of these respondents described themselves as talented sportswomen. Importantly, sport offered a source of positive esteem. By providing the experience of themselves as acting

competently, sport may also have provided them with a different relationship to their bodies from that offered in romantic
heterosexuality and 'emphasized femininity'. Further, sport
absorbed much of their leisure time. Some felt that, because
of this, they did not have time to think about boyfriends, while
others suggested sport provided a legitimate excuse for their
lack of participation in boy-centred activities.

The fourth avenue is the experience of educational success.
Thirty-eight respondents reported being in the top ability stream
at school. Being successful scholastically was often reported as
providing an alternative source of esteem to that of 'success'
in the culture of romantic heterosexuality. Some suggested that
they devoted much of their time to school work because they
had felt uncomfortable with boy-centred activities. Others described themselves as being so absorbed in doing well that they
had little time for other activities and interests. Often academically successful respondents reported the existence of an academically inclined sub-culture within the top stream. This
sub-culture was described as rejecting the values of romantic
heterosexuality, which were associated with the lower streams.
Clearly, this academic success was important in supporting or
generating feelings of 'acting' purposively, and in expanding
lifestyle options.

These four 'avenues of escape' were often used actively or
passively as alternative routes through adolescence. These may
have been consequential in limiting early incorporation into
romantic heterosexuality.

EDUCATIONAL SUCCESS AND RESPONDENTS' EXPECTATIONS OF MARRIAGE

Most of the sample reported high levels of parental support
and encouragement in their schooling, particularly from fathers.
This support spread across class, with parents who had experienced little in the way of educational advantage often being
the most enthusiastic in their encouragement. As noted earlier, respondents seem to have been relatively advantaged in
terms of their educational ability. Of the 60 women interviewed,
50 reported that they had been in the top half of their school
year and 39 reported that they had been in the highest ability
stream; of these, over half reported having been singled out as
academic 'high flyers'. In the top stream were 22 out of the 27

respondents from service class backgrounds, seven out of 18 from intermediate class backgrounds and ten out of the 15 from manual class backgrounds. Their ranking of ability was in the context of a range of schooling experiences, from secondary modern to private.[4] The importance of this ranking is that, regardless of whether they were singled out as a potential 'Oxbridge' candidate, placed in an 'O' level stream at a secondary modern school or emerged as the only girl amongst her peers to have gained a place at a grammar school, within their educational or social milieu they were 'different'. This difference, through educational success, may well have engendered or reinforced feelings of competency and control.

In terms of thinking about the future it is clear that, because of their educational advantages, a large majority of the sample could realistically expect their lives to take a different course from the female norm. If they felt *negatively* towards marriage or institutionalized heterosexuality, as many reported was the case, this view could be realistically sustained because they could utilize the power derived from educational achievement to provide the economic means of living outside marriage. However, it was suggested earlier that another dimension needs to be added to that of educational success, and that is interpretations of sexuality. I now want to illustrate ways that this dimension may mediate the effects of educational advantage or disadvantage.

When respondents were discussing their experience of adolescence and schooling I asked them if they had had any ideas about what their future held and whether this image had included marriage. Almost two-thirds of the sample reported that marriage had not featured in their expectations. Not surprisingly, these 38 'non-marriage-oriented' respondents were much more likely to have been educationally successful, with 27 having been in the top stream at school. The median age of this group was 30. Of the 19 respondents who assumed that they would marry, less than half of were in the top stream. The median age of this group, 35, was the highest. The remaining three respondents changed from a marriage to a non-marriage orientation at some point during schooling. A similar proportion of each group was from service class backgrounds. Interestingly, most respondents from manual class backgrounds (11 out of 15) were in the non-marriage oriented group, these included all those who had been in the top stream.

I will now draw on the accounts of non-marriage and marriage-oriented respondents and compare their reported early
perceptions of employment. I will illustrate a complex relationship between educational success or lack of success, perceptions of paid work and initial employment outcomes for
my respondents. It will be shown that the impact of educational
advantage, or disadvantage, was often mediated by other factors related to respondents' interpretations of their sexuality
and/or their views on the desirability of marriage.

RESPONDENTS WHO EXPECTED TO MARRY

Of the 19 women who reported that as adolescents they had
assumed a future involving marriage, eight were from service
class backgrounds, seven were from intermediate class backgrounds and four were from manual class backgrounds. Twelve
saw marriage as an unproblematic given and the rest remembered having a more ambiguous attitude, perceiving it to be
inevitable rather than desirable. Women in this group tended
to be older and were often less educationally advantaged than
the non-marriage-oriented group.

These respondents were more likely to have experienced relationships with boys during their schooling, than the non-marriage-oriented group. Seven reported dating boys as something
taken for granted, usually altering their behaviour so that they
were pleasing to boys. Toni's experience of dating is fairly typical
of this group:

> On the whole boys were not friends, I saw them as mates in
> the sense that you had to attract. I always thought that boys
> were not attracted by women who were articulate and intel-
> ligent and expressed their opinions. Where this idea came
> from I don't know but it's there − you needed to actually
> play down your intelligence and let them feel superior, and
> it was difficult to find an equality in a relationship. In most
> of the relationships I had, I always found it very difficult to
> say 'Well, I think that's good' or 'I don't like that', because
> I always wanted to agree with him. I never had enough con-
> fidence with myself to say what I really thought. There were
> very few occasions when I could just be as I was. (49*M*)

Four others who dated reported holding a more egalitarian
approach to their relationships. Three women in this group

reported that they may have been questioning their sexuality during schooling. However, this did not immediately bring about a change in their perspective towards marriage.

Marriage-oriented respondents' perceptions of employment

Three respondents spoke of focusing on doing well at school and another three anticipated having careers. However, the rest usually spoke of drifting through school, with no clear ideas about what jobs they might like to do later.

Their memories of early attitudes towards employment ranged from perceiving paid work as important, a source of financial independence within marriage, to assuming it would be short-lived or of secondary significance within marriage. In keeping with the research of others, the latter was the more common view.[5] Only two respondents reported assuming that their jobs would be as important as their future husbands'. These women were both under 30 years old, academic 'high flyers', who ex-pected to follow professional careers. They were from service class backgrounds and had been influenced by feminism.

Ten respondents adhered to fairly traditional beliefs regard-ing divisions of labour in marriage. Their taken for granted understanding was that upon marriage their employment would either cease or become insignificant. This posed a contradic-tion in terms of their attitudes to education: many believed that putting effort into school work was superfluous; skill de-velopment was incompatible with their anticipated future role as wife and mother. An example of the contradictory nature of this thinking comes from grammar school-educated Bertha:

[*How about the idea of marriage?*] I just assumed it was the normal thing to do . . . because everyone around me was get-ting married, and having babies. I think [my parents] would have liked me to have got myself into university, got some qualifications, and then got married. It seems a total waste. I can't see the point of it. In their view I can't see the point of it, because once I got married, having the qualifications and just giving it up [as they would have expected me to have done – get married and have children and look after them, 'cos that's what we did . . . At that particular time, I didn't think married women ever got back into a career. They just did part-time work, or just filled the shelves at

Tesco's. I didn't see them as having a serious job . . . I thought
once you got married at that particular time, then really that
was it, and after that your family came first and your job
came second. (32*I*)

Then she left school and entered low-paid women's work.

This next extract from Lynne, another grammar school-educated woman, illustrates the power of these traditional ideas.
Her initial career orientation was transformed because she was
made to feel that it was deviant:

I did [see work as lifelong] to start with, and then I went to
this girl's school and it really hit me . . . It was a different
environment, and I thought to myself, 'Hang on! girls aren't
meant to have a career. I am meant to work in a bank and
think about getting married.' Believe it or not I hadn't really
thought about work, but I always said I fancied going in the
Forces. But then when I went there I thought, 'Oh! I don't
know if I want to do that, I think I should go and work in a
bank or something like that.' Do you see what I mean? It's
because, like, you're conditioned to think that, even though
you had passed your eleven-plus, and you were going to a
grammar school, you were going to get married so what was
the point of having a career? (27*I*)

Although she was offered a place in the sixth form, Lynne left
school and applied for a job at a bank. However, she was un-
successful in getting this job, and subsequently fulfilled her
earlier desire by entering the Armed Forces.

There were several other examples of grammar school-educated respondents not taking advantage of educational opportunity. Three respondents, who had earlier been achievement-
oriented in their approach to school work, reported losing
interest in school when they became seriously involved in a
heterosexual relationship. All three were in the top stream at
grammar schools. This process is illustrated by Shirley:

[My school work] suffered quite a bit, I just wasn't concentrating on it – for that period of a year. It went down quite
a lot. I basically wasn't bothered. I couldn't see the point of
it, because I was going to leave school and get married to
Kevin and that was it. [*Did his school work suffer?*] It didn't
seem to actually, when I think about it. (32*I*)

She left school and entered low-paid clerical work.

Two respondents gave up their 'A' level studies and entered low-paid women's work in order to save for marriage. This was the case with Brigitte:

> When I met John, this is the bloke I married, I threw myself entirely into that. But no, it wasn't an equal relationship by any means and that's where it went wrong I think – far from it. [*You threw yourself into it?*] Well, it became the most important thing. I mean, I skived off school. I really mucked up my 'A' levels completely . . . It became very important, I saw him all the time, every evening. (43*I*)

There were, however, examples of the experience of educational success mediating traditional expectations. Some found that being an academic 'high flyer' sustained their achievements despite their contradictory views about the future. In Polly's case, educational success carried her on to university. She later entered a male-dominated profession:

> [I saw work as] something that I didn't have to do if I didn't want to. [*How so?*] Perhaps not just [my parents], but the whole of society was telling me – TV and everything – that I would probably marry and not have to work. So I didn't have to think about what I was going to be. [*Did you think that at the time or are you thinking in retrospect?*] No, I thought that at the time, that I wouldn't actually have to earn my own living. But I was very caught up in exams, in doing very well. Took it very seriously, quite why I did, I am not sure. (35*S*)

Alternatively, lack of educational success was consequential. Pat had a series of lesbian relationships while at school. However, she was dyslexic and left school with no qualifications. Because she did not believe that she could achieve the economic independence she felt was necessary to follow a lesbian lifestyle, she decided that she would have to marry. She did so in her teens:

> I would just class myself as thick, so I knew I wouldn't be able to actually be a business woman or have a career behind me . . . I was resigned to the fact that what I had got in me already, which wasn't a lot I felt . . . Why do we plan to marry? 'Cos it's probably the done thing. There is only a few of you that stands out and says, the career is 'the main thing', and I don't want kids. There aren't many that are

strong enough to take that on. You just flow along with the
rest of the clan, don't you? [*Were you thinking of work as long-
term?*] No. At that stage I decided I'd have to marry, to get
out of my house, to get away from the family. (29*I*)

Pat's experience really brings home the economic dimension
to the social construction of women's sexuality. While Pat did
eventually find ways of becoming financially independent and
now follows a lesbian lifestyle, her experience begs an interesting question. How many women have had positive lesbian relationships but lack the economic power to live outside heterosexuality?

Initial outcomes of marriage-oriented respondents

On leaving school, six marriage-oriented women entered higher
education or the women's professions; all but one were from
service class backgrounds. Their re-evaluation of sexuality often
occurred within the college environment. A further two entered traditionally male-dominated occupations which offered
career prospects.

However, the majority (*n* = 11) initially entered low-paid
women's work, three were from service class backgrounds. In
keeping with the research findings of others (see, for example,
Mansfield and Collard, 1988; Cockburn, 1987:52; Cavendish,
1982; Pollert, 1981) most had an understanding that it would
be a short-term commitment until marriage. This kind of understanding is illustrated by Angie, who entered clerical work
after leaving school:

> [*Did you have any ideas about what the future involved for you?*]
> No, I don't think I saw it as a long-term thing. I suppose I
> assumed I would get married twenty-ish I suppose, and there-
> fore be rescued from this dreadful thing called work. I suppose
> I feel a bit cheated, in that you are brought up as a woman to
> think that a man's going to look after you, and nobody's look-
> ing after me. And I have had this hard fight through life,
> and it's very hard being single – as you must know.[6] (40*S*)

RESPONDENTS WHO QUESTIONED THE GIVENNESS OF MARRIAGE

The accounts of the 38 non-marriage-oriented respondents suggest that they were far less likely than the rest of the sample to

have experienced romantic relationships with boys during schooling. Twenty-eight had very limited or no dating relationships
with boys. There were several reasons given for evaluating the
appropriateness heterosexual relations and the desirability of
marriage. One reason was that their understandings of the
meaning of marriage, based on observations of their mother's
experience, were negative. Another reason was that many
(n = 30) had been consciously or less consciously questioning
their own sexuality at this time. School work and/or sport, as
opposed to heterosexual romance, was generally the main interest
and source of esteem and confidence for this group.

Non-marriage-oriented respondents usually (*n* = 30) looked
forward to their future in terms of having a career. These career-oriented women were slightly more likely (*n* = 16) to have
come from service class backgrounds. Twenty-two were in the
top stream and 13 had been singled out as academic 'high-
flyers'. As many as 25 career-oriented respondents reported
having questioned their sexuality during schooling. It was common for career-oriented respondents to report an early desire
to enter occupations that are male-dominated (*n* = 18), often
because they saw traditional women's work as offering little scope
for economic independence. Their rejection of this type of
employment was often reinforced by feelings that it emphasized stereotypical femininity, and/or their dislike of routine
work that involved being inside. This is interesting in the light
of Griffin (1982, 1985:82) and Cockburn's (1987:39,41) research
on women's transitions from school to the labour market. In
their interviews they found that masculine areas of work were
perceived by young women as being unfeminine and entry to
these jobs as undermining female sexual attractiveness.

Career orientation appeared to take two distinctive forms,
which seemed to be related to a combination of interrelated
factors including social class, educational opportunity and definitions of sexuality. The first form (*n* = 23) was focused on
achieving at school and going on to higher education and then
a career. These women were generally educationally successful
(all of the 'high-flyers' were in this group) and a high proportion were from service class backgrounds (*n* = 15). In its second
form, career orientation meant finding relatively enjoyable
employment which offered prospects. All of these seven women
were educated initially at secondary modern schools. This
employment perspective was reinforced by the fact that all but

one had 'come out' while at school. I will now illustrate these
two forms of career orientation.

A career orientation directed towards higher education

This first form of career orientation was guided by a range of
complex experiences. Few had any clear ideas about what kind
of career they would want. This lack of concrete knowledge
about careers was sometimes related to class experience. This
was the case with Mandy. The following extract also illustrates
the importance of access to educational opportunity, in sus-
taining a different life from that of family and peers:

> [*Had you any idea where university would lead?*] Hadn't a clue.
> [*What about ideas about employment?*] No I didn't. All I was
> aware of was being hell-bent on not being in a factory like
> him or a shop like her. Other than that, I didn't really have
> access to a lot of the options to have a look at . . . There
> wasn't any first-hand experience of that . . . It wasn't a ques-
> tion of knowing what I wanted to do, it was more a question
> of knowing what I didn't want to do. All it was about was
> that there must be more to what they've had, and they're
> staying. Knew there was more. (33*M*)

For educational 'high flyers', a career was often seen as part of a
taken for granted process of doing well and going on to university. An example of this kind of thinking comes from Lindsey:

> I always felt, I don't know whether it was because of mes-
> sages I was given at school, but I always felt that I was going
> to university and I'd have a career [laughter]. And I never
> actually even thought about it until I had nearly finished my
> degree. It was just something I had always had in my head,
> because I knew I didn't want to stay at home and have a
> family or whatever. (25*S*)

The linkage between wanting a career and not wanting to marry
was common in their accounts. Another example of this comes
from Paula:

> I never considered the fact that I would not be working. I
> would be working for pleasure, for stimulation and also be-
> cause I'd need to support myself. It never occurred to me
> that I would be living with someone who could pay me. (25*S*)

There were, however, several educationally advantaged respondents whose progress to higher education was not encouraged
at home. Their choice to pursue their education involved determination and often went against the wishes of their parents. Cordilia describes her experience:

> My education was a real battle. I had to fight to go on to
> college. You see, my parents didn't understand the grant sys-
> tem, or the degree system. They found it difficult to deal
> with the idea that you could go on to higher education without
> knowing what you'd do later. (22*S*)

The decision to go to college for Helen was also against parental wishes, but was reinforced by her questioning her sexuality:

> I suppose as I knew that I wasn't getting married, I felt that
> [work] would be something that I would be doing all my
> life . . . not a case of a job before you got married. [*Do you
> think that influenced you in the area of work you went into?*] Yes.
> I suppose if I thought I was going to get married, I wouldn't
> have pursued, wouldn't even have thought of going to col-
> lege, or agricultural college. So, yes, the fact that I knew
> that I would be working for most of my life then, did affect
> me – as to what I thought, what I pursued. (33*M*)

Her mother had wanted her to be 'conventional' and follow
her female peers into traditional women's work and then marry.
  An important motivation for many of these respondents' decisions to go on to higher education was the feeling that they
needed to broaden their options beyond traditional women's
work. In the case of two academically borderline respondents,
the experience of summer employment in routine women's jobs
catapulted them back into schooling, having initially decided
to leave. Both then went on to higher education.

A 'job for life'

In the second form of career orientation, respondents viewed
employment as a job for life. These respondents tended to be
older, their median age being 44. All initially went to a secondary modern school. Although they did not necessarily have
clear ideas of what job they would like to do, they did know
that they wanted jobs which could offer economic independence. Guiding this view was the rejection of heterosexuality

at some point during schooling. An example of this thinking comes from Faye. After leaving secondary modern school, she continued her education at a technical school. She has since reached a senior management position and has achieved the highest salary in the sample:

> [*Did you expect to marry?*] No, I knew I was a lesbian. One of the things that I never felt was expected, was that I would grow up and get married. [*Did you have any idea what you wanted to do when you grew up?*] I wanted to be financially independent, but that was without thinking about what I might like to do, want to do. (52*S*)

Respondents hoped to find jobs which offered security and scope for career advancement, rather than what they characterized as jobs until marriage. Maxine, who has spent all her working life in male-dominated occupations, illustrates this point:

> [*Did you get the impression that work would be central in your future?*] Oh yes, for a long time, whatever I did I would have to enjoy, because I'd be doing it for an awful long time. [*Did that influence you?*] I think it did, in as much as wanting [a career in the Forces], to know that it was a job for life. (43*I*)

Justine stayed on after school-leaving age to take 'O' levels and one 'A' level. She has reached a management position in a male-dominated occupation:

> [*When you were at school, how did you see the role of work in your future?*] I think I knew that really I was going to work for a good few years, and it was going to be a big part of my life . . . I wanted a job that I couldn't let go of . . . I knew that I had to get something that I was really quite happy in doing, 'cos I would be doing it for a long time . . . (25*I*)

These women reported having made very different career 'choices' from those of their female peers. Given the options these respondents felt were available to them as young women, access to a career usually meant entry into 'male' craft occupations. Five of these women favoured male-dominated occupations, viewing traditional female occupations as dead-end. Martina applied for a crafts apprenticeship when she left school:

> I realized that I was probably going to have to work to support myself, obviously for the rest of my working days, rather

than opting out and getting married and letting someone else support me, that was out . . . [*What appealed to you about apprenticeships?*] I wanted to be good at the job, I wanted a career rather than just a job, I wanted to be a qualified sign writer. I didn't want to be just working in the local Co-Op, I wanted to actually have a career rather than just a job. (38*I*)

In the case of five of these women, their desire to avoid dead-end female occupations and enter jobs with prospects informed decisions to stay on at school after most of their peers had left. Two organized entry into technical schools so they could develop vocational skills, while the other three remained at school to retake CSEs or take some 'O' levels. These decisions were often made in the context of financial pressure on them to leave school early.

Respondents who drifted through schooling

Not all of the non-marriage-oriented respondents had such focused ideas about their futures. Eight respondents were 'drifters' at school, with no clear ideas about the future. Several had serious adolescent problems and one had a major illness. Although these respondents were aware of the need to support themselves later, they usually gave future employment little thought while at school. Two considered becoming nuns, and two others thought about a career in the music industry. Two later went on to higher education as mature students, and two others returned to retake 'O' levels within two years of leaving school.

Initial outcomes of non-marriage-oriented respondents

In 21 cases non-marriage-oriented respondents went straight into higher education: 13 were from service class backgrounds, four were from intermediate and four were from manual class backgrounds. Within this context, many were able to make a positive identification with lesbianism. A further 11 entered jobs that offered career prospects, such as the Armed Forces, or male-dominated manual work where they could develop craft skills. Several of these women studied at evening classes or returned to higher education to improve their employment situations. The rest (*n* = 7) went into traditional women's work.

This type of employment was often entered as a stop-gap. Four later returned to education to broaden their employment options. Three non-marriage-oriented women did in fact marry, however, only one married in the conventional sense. One was a marriage of convenience to enable a lesbian relationship to be conducted without suspicion, the other was to a gay man and was non-sexual.

CONCLUDING DISCUSSION

Very contrasting patterns have been illustrated regarding the educational and employment perspectives, and initial employment outcomes, of marriage-oriented and non-marriage-oriented respondents. In my sample, non-marriage-oriented respondents, as a group, appeared to be more aligned towards educational achievement, usually seeing their futures in terms of further or higher education and a career. Clearly, the differences between the groups defy simple explanation. Social class appeared to be a good indicator of access to educational opportunity. However, women from service class backgrounds were spread evenly across the groups and the majority of respondents from manual class backgrounds were in the non-marriage-oriented group. Although women from intermediate and manual backgrounds were less likely to have been educationally advantaged, they did appear to fare much better in the non-marriage-oriented group, while educationally advantaged service class respondents in the marriage-oriented group did not always maintain this advantage. Perhaps some of the differences can be explained by the time period. As a group, marriage-oriented women tended to be older than non-marriage-oriented women. They may have faced fewer educational and employment options, and the traditional attitudes towards the division of labour in marriage held by many may also reflect the ideas of the past. Certainly, those marriage-oriented women, who questioned this state of affairs, tended to be younger women who had been influenced by feminism. However, traditional attitudes had been held by some women in their twenties. Conversely, there were many examples of older non-marriage-oriented women from intermediate or manual backgrounds expanding their employment opportunities through further education or entry into male occupations with prospects. The differences between these contrasting groups cannot be explained simply in terms of class, educational advantage or age. Instead, we must also consider the mediating impact of interpretations of sexuality.

If we consider women from both groups who had access to educational opportunity, we can see several tendencies. First, non-marriage-oriented respondents tended to take advantage of educational opportunity regardless of social class. They were usually more single-minded in their desire to have careers. For many this desire was reinforced by their interpretation of sexuality. By contrast, we have seen examples of educationally advantaged marriage-oriented respondents prioritising valued heterosexual relationships at the expense of their education. Second, amongst non-marriage-oriented respondents from intermediate or manual backgrounds, we have seen examples of those who were academically borderline or educationally disadvantaged taking advantage of educational opportunity. Motivating this was the knowledge that the employment they sought would be of long-term duration. Consequently, they wished to avoid low-paid women's work. They sought to broaden their employment opportunities, so as to gain access to jobs which they could enjoy, which also offered career prospects. By contrast, many marriage-oriented respondents, regardless of class background, reported feeling that putting effort into developing skills at school did not make sense, given their understanding of the sexual division of labour in marriage. Thus many marriage-oriented women, including some who had been educationally advantaged, entered low-paid women's work in the belief that it would be short-term.

Clearly, in many cases, interpretations of sexuality mediated the effects of both lack of educational opportunity and educational success. For those who questioned the givenness of heterosexuality during their schooling, the experience of being 'different' was consequential. It supported the mobilization of strategies which could facilitate the construction of a different life. For these women, their questioning of conventional accounts of social reality liberated them from some of the constraints which that version of social reality imposes on women. However, we have also seen one example where lack of educational opportunity mediated the early effects of problematizing heterosexuality. Pat's lack of economic and social power forced her temporarily to adhere to taken for granted female pathways. She retained a marriage orientation because she felt she needed to find a breadwinning husband. It is interesting to note also that two-thirds of respondents from the most disadvantaged social background, the manual, were educationally advantaged in terms of being in the top stream at school. Conversely, access to educational opportunity sometimes mediated the effects of a conventional interpretation of sexuality. For some who assumed they would marry, it provided the possibility of living a life that diverged from the options they had initially anticipated. Academic 'high flyers' had access to a value system which emphasized intellectual achievement, and this carried some on to university. This provided an alternative to the value systems offered within 'romantic heterosexuality', which might instead, have, carried them on to marriage.

This analysis of respondents' adolescent experiences suggests that there is an interrelationship between educational opportunity and interpretations of sexuality. Because respondents' accounts are retrospective, conclusions have to be tentative. However, the evidence strongly suggests that, if we are to understand women's economic position, we must take into account the role of institutionalized heterosexuality in shaping young women's educational and employment 'choices' *before* they enter the labour market. It also suggests that, to understand more fully the prevalence of heterosexual outcomes, we must consider the impact of structural constraints which often deny women economic independence, as well as the ideas and practices which support heterosexuality and stigmatize alternative sexual and emotional practices.

NOTES

1. Lees's research (1986) suggests that contemporary women lack this opt-out. Failure to engage in active heterosexuality can mobilize accusations of being a 'tight ass' or 'lesbian' from peers.
2. Of the 24 women aged 35 or older, 16 experienced some single-sex education.
3. According to Rosemary Deem (1986:73), most girls reject physical activity in their early teens.
4. Their schooling often involved a mixture of types of state-provided education: for example, a secondary modern school merged with a grammar school, to become a comprehensive, or a few years of grammar school education followed by some private education. The types of schools which they spent most time in were comprehensive ($n = 19$), secondary modern ($n = 14$), grammar ($n = 13$), private ($n = 12$) and other ($n = 2$).
5. See, for example, Machung's (1989) discussion of the ways that

women at the University of Berkeley, California, were expecting
to fit their careers around family commitments. Taylorson's (1980)
British survey of university women draws similar conclusions.
6. Interestingly, this was one of the two respondents who reported
stereotypically feminine upbringings.

CHAPTER FOUR

Gender, sexuality and employment opportunity

It's just having the guts to have a go; the want and the need, the need is very heavy. You get some people saying, 'Who's the male behind this?' 'What does your husband do for a living?' or 'When did daddy buy you this?' Or they say 'Haven't you done well!' If I was a 35-year old male, quite honestly to have a three bedroom house and an XR2 [sports car], that wouldn't be considered clever. I am clever for avoiding marriage.

INTRODUCTION

It was mentioned earlier that for most of our sample the questioning and subsequent rejection of commonsense beliefs that people are heterosexual was far from straightforward. Such is the power of ideologies and social practices which obscure and stigmatize alternative sexual and emotional expression that many of my interviewees negotiated their early adult lives on the taken for granted assumption that they were heterosexual. This chapter will explore their transitions from heterosexuality to lesbianism to focus on the shift in attitudes and approaches to paid employment entailed by this experience. It will illustrate ways that sexual identity mediates the effects of gender to support different outcomes in relation to the negotiation of employment opportunities. This will highlight the importance of recognizing the role of institutionalized heterosexuality in constraining women's choices.

There are very real economic consequences associated with the choice of following a lesbian lifestyle. Respondents were aware that this choice necessitated long-term economic self-reliance. Given the structural constraints shaping women's access to wages which enable economic independence, we cannot deny the socioeconomic dimension of moving beyond heterosexuality. Consequently, the possibility of following a lesbian lifestyle needs to be understood as an economic 'achievement'.

It will be argued that the relationship between following a lesbian lifestyle and the ability to be economically independent is by no means one-dimensional. On the one hand, the reinterpretation of sexuality led many respondents to develop strategies that would improve their employment circumstances. On the other hand, the experience of employment opportunity broadened respondents' options in such a way as to facilitate a critical perspective on heterosexual relations and sustain an alternative lifestyle. The first section of this chapter will use case history material to illustrate these two dimensions. First we consider those respondents who entered low-paid women's work on the assumption that it would be short-term until marriage and demonstrate ways that changing interpretations of sexuality shaped new approaches to career development. The second dimension will be illustrated by considering those who experienced employment opportunity and, subsequently, the opportunity to reinterpret their sexuality.

The experience of married respondents will be the focus of the second section. Here we will see a converse process to that outlined above, whereby correspondents' relationships with men constrained their employment circumstances. It will be argued that mechanisms exist within heterosexual relationships which may act to pre-empt the possibility of women either experiencing or expanding employment opportunity. Again, we will see that changing understandings of sexuality engendered a different approach to paid employment.

The third section draws on the whole sample to illustrate ways that respondents understood their choice of following a lesbian lifestyle to necessitate and/or facilitate economic independence. We will see that this had implications for their approaches to employment and skill development.

WORKING IN THE SHADOW OF MARRIAGE

'A job until marriage'

In the last chapter we saw that 11 respondents followed a traditional pathway into low-paid women's work on the assumption that employment would either be a stop-gap until marriage, or would take on a secondary significance within marriage. These women understood marriage to be the inevitable outcome of their assumed heterosexuality. They expected that marriage would involve the rearrangement of priorities, whereby home life and domestic commitments would eclipse employment involvement. For them, marriage represented long-term economic security through access to a higher 'breadwinning' wage. Five of these women married, while the rest had to reconsider their position on long-term economic self-sufficiency. As we shall see, changing understandings of sexuality served to erode conventional accounts of social reality, which led to the formation of different employment perspectives.

As new understandings of their sexuality took shape, different frameworks gradually developed for conceptualising the role of paid work in these women's lives. This new framework emphasized long-term self-reliance, and was more self-directed and judgemental regarding employment. I shall now illustrate these points using two case histories.

Nickie's story

Nickie, a grammar school-educated woman from a manual background, left school with five 'O' levels and entered low-paid clerical work. She is aged 32. Here, she recalls her early feelings about paid work:

> I thought of [paid work] as being: I am going to do this for a few years, but I am going to meet someone and get married – yes, and I shall not be working for the rest of my life. At that particular stage, I thought: I don't want to be working for the rest of my life, I am going to meet somebody. I didn't think it would be a woman, but I assumed it would be a man . . . I didn't look at it as a career, it was just something to do at that particular time.

She was in the clerical job for two years. During this period she became involved with a man, who wanted to marry her.

Although she was fond of him, the thought of marriage made her uneasy, and she began to wonder if marriage was really right for her. One important reason for this uncertainty was that she had also developed what she calls a 'crush' on a woman at work. Nickie and this woman had an 'experimental' relationship:

> I had this relationship with the boss's son on and off, but I also had, in between time, a relationship with a girl that worked there. It was just an experimental thing, I guess, for her, but it then started me thinking – I quite like this. She decided it was just something that happened for a couple of weeks, and she didn't really want that, and she was going to be 'normal'. And I suddenly thought, I don't know if I want to be 'normal'. I sort of liked the experience, and that sort of unsettled me.

Nickie was beginning to find her work limiting. She had been sent on day-release to study typing. However, being a typist did not appeal to her, and she could not see a challenging future in the firm she was working for. In this next extract we can see how a new framework was developing with regard to her career:

> I then realized that work was quite a serious matter, and started to think that I didn't want to get married for some time now, if I get married at all, by that stage. That I am going to have to do something that I'd like doing. Because I could be doing it for some time, it could be five years, ten years . . .

Although she was offered a more senior secretarial job and a higher salary, she decided to leave. Jobs were plentiful, and she found one in the civil service which required two years' training. This job offered prospects for advancement and provided a good salary. She describes her reasons for this job change in this next extract:

> [My old job] was a pretty rotten job. I enjoyed it for a while, but realized it was a dead-end sort of job. I then started to realize that perhaps marriage wasn't the be all and end all of everything, and perhaps I wanted to do something more with my life – there didn't seem to be a point to it. So I went into the civil service of all places [laughter]. But it seemed

to be a steady job, with a future; you could get promotion, you could become quite high up, and have quite a lot of responsibility. So I did that for four years.

She is now a manager in a traditional male-dominated occupation.

Janette's story

A similar pattern can be found in the experience of Janette, aged 38, from an intermediate background. She had been educated in a secondary modern school which became comprehensive. She left school with two 'O' levels and entered office work. This job lasted for two years. She found the work dull, repetitive and confining. Initially, she had assumed she would marry and have children:

> Because I come from where I do, all the girls that I knew, all the people that I knew, they just went and worked in a shop or factory, and then got married and had kids. That's all I ever thought there was to life [laughter], that's how I saw my life. My education . . . I never pushed myself or anything because I thought, what's the point – I just go and work for a couple of years until I get married and have kids and that's it. 'Cos I didn't know I was going to be gay or anything like that. So if I could turn the clock back on life, I would have done things differently . . .

Although at school Janette had experienced what she calls an 'experimental' relationship with a female friend, she had not questioned her heterosexuality. She dated 'normally', as she put it, throughout schooling and late adolescence.

Janette's framework for conceptualising the significance of paid work was reformulated in the light of two important events. First, she became seriously involved with a married man and, second, when that relationship ended, she fell in love with a woman. This next extract illustrates her changing perspective towards economic independence:

> I suddenly realized that I wasn't married at 18, and that I had to fend for myself. I wasn't going to get married, and stay at home and have kids. I was going to have to work for my living, my attitude changed towards a lot of things.

As with the previous respondent, the emotional intensity she felt towards her female lover was not immediately understood as 'lesbian'. However, she did recognize the experience as 'going against the norm', thinking of herself as 'a one off', the 'only one in the world'. Her feelings towards this woman seriously undermined her assumption that marriage provided the framework for adult living:

> Life was over because I hadn't found a spouse. And I think that I was probably beginning to realize then, that I wasn't going to get married, because it wasn't for me, that's not how I wanted things to be, and I was going to have to change. My whole attitude was going to have to change, because that's not how it's going to be. These inner feelings were not the norm towards Susan – things weren't going as I thought they would.

This extract clearly illuminates the impact this experience had in undermining the conventional accounts of social reality which had initially guided her. In terms of employment, she could no longer assume that marriage would provide an escape route from her dull job:

> [*What didn't you like about the job?*] The hours, being trapped inside. Didn't like the work basically, it wasn't me . . . It was pretty menial stuff . . . [*Did the other women that you worked with feel the same way?*] Yes, I think so. They were all waiting to get married, and get out of it, yes. [*And you weren't going to get married to get out of it?*] Oh no!

Janette gave up this job and found a delivery job in the motor trade. Her changing perspectives about the future, shaped by her new understanding of sexuality, were not simply confined to career considerations. Self-reliance also meant expanding her sense of competence to include practical skills which she had previously considered 'male':

> Basically I felt I had made the first step by living on my own, being independent, doing things for myself. Learning to do jobs that men do, like doing the woodwork around the house, all the decorating, putting up fences . . . Just being totally independent and not having to involve men to do what men do for women. And because my mother said lifting and all that sort of thing is a man's job, that was my first little step. You might think that's a little step, but back

in those days it was probably a big step. As for my career, I
was not happy in my job. Saw the job advertized, saw it in
terms of offering freedom and being outside.

Her new job was in a male dominated environment. She felt
that learning to be more self-reliant helped her gain respect
from her male colleagues:

> [*What do you feel they respected you for?*] I don't know ... not
> being silly and sexual, and just, I suppose, because I related
> to them better. I always used to amaze them with what I
> knew: 'Oh, how do you know that? You're a woman?'

The delivery job was considered by her employers as appropriate
work for a woman. Moving into areas which offered more responsibility and better pay proved more difficult. However, within a year
Janette entered the 'male' preserve of sales in the motor trade:

> [*What motivated you to go for this job?*] Better money and pros-
> pects, and the fact that I couldn't see any reason why I
> shouldn't. Because I knew as much as the men did, and I
> saw no reason why I shouldn't do it.

She has spent most of her career in this male preserve.

In these two case studies, we have seen that changing perspectives on the desirability of marriage and the evaluation of heterosexuality aided the reformulation of ideas about the significance
of paid work in the respondents' lives. This involved the reor-
dering of goals. Their job was no longer something to be en-
dured until the right man came into their lives. Instead,
employment would have to provide their standard of living. As
a result, their energies were directed into pursuing strategies
that would improve the quality of their work experience. Both
managed to negotiate successfully entry into what they perceive
as interesting and rewarding employment.

Only one never-married respondent in this group has remained
in low-paid women's work. The rest moved on to better-paid
occupations, offering career structures, three now being in management positions.

Discussion

These respondents' initial attitudes towards employment were
guided by taken for granted conventional accounts of social

reality, where adult womanhood was heterosexual, experienced within the context of marriage, and involved being dependent on a male wage. Within this framework of understanding, the anticipated avenue of escape from dull routine jobs was through attachment to a male breadwinner. Because of powerfully contradictory experience these respondents could no longer anticipate the arrival of a knight in shining armour. Their new understanding of what being an adult woman meant motivated a more self-reliant approach to paid work. Most were able to take steps to improve their employment circumstances and did achieve rewarding employment. Their changing attitudes and approaches towards employment were very much related to their move beyond heterosexuality. Their new understanding of their sexuality foreclosed many of the options offered within heterosexuality and allowed them to find new solutions.

The idea of being rescued from a dull job by some knight in shining amour (I am reminded here of Richard Gere's romantic rescue of a young factory worker in the film *An Officer and a Gentleman*) appears to be a very powerful one. Various ethnographies of British women in the workplace (Cavendish, 1982; Pollert, 1981) suggest that romance, and marriage and motherhood, tend to dominate the hearts and minds of young single women in dull, poorly paid employment jobs. These images prevailed even though many of these women found their relationships with men unsatisfactory.

In contrast to these women's occupational experience and identity it makes sense that the achievement of a social identity derived from marriage and motherhood should be anticipated positively. However, this gendered solution appears to act as a powerful disincentive for developing strategies that might improve their employment circumstances. Few planned to experience further training. Similarly, Crompton *et al.*'s study (1982:49) of clerical workers in local government suggests that the anticipation of a domestic future acts as a disincentive for women taking the post-entry qualifications necessary for promotion. As this domestic solution is generally unavailable to men, their avenue of escape from dull poorly paid jobs can usually only be through the development of new skills. In contrast, these women's perceptions of choice were shaped by the myth that their working lives would be short-lived (Pollert, 1981:94–106). In reality, most married British women do have paid employment: 73 per cent in 1993 (General Household

Survey, 1993). Often households could not manage financially on husbands' wages alone (Martin and Roberts, 1984:61). Yet the myth of the male sole provider persists.

As was mentioned in Chapter 1, transformations in the British employment structure (for example, the decline in traditional working-class male jobs and the expansion of employment for working-class women) may well be having an impact on young women's expectations about their futures (Prendergast, 1995). Changes in economic relations in the homes of young work-ing-class women, where their mothers may be sole providers, together with declining opportunities for young working-class men, may powerfully erode the idea that marriage represents the rescue from dull jobs. Perhaps lesbians represent a van-guard in a movement towards challenging the range and con-tent of women's work.

However, change appears to be slow. In a more recent long-itudinal study of young British newly-weds carried out by Mansfield and Collard (1988), we find similar attitudes amongst women. Their findings suggest that young women may well put up with dull jobs as a way of marking time until marriage and motherhood (pp.140–2). Indeed, Mansfield and Collard sug-gest that many young women take for granted that they will marry and 'would consider any strong commitment to work as unnecessary or even incompatible with their desire to marry' (p.147). Their research outlines ways that young women's an-ticipation of marriage, together with the understanding that their jobs will take second place to their husbands' jobs, may provide a disincentive for taking steps to improve their work-ing conditions. Few of the young wives interviewed expressed satisfaction with their jobs, which contrasted with the enthusi-asm expressed by their husbands towards their jobs (p.146). Not surprisingly, most of the wives were taking on a greater share of the domestic burdens in the home and lowering their commitment to their jobs.

Within marriage women are encouraged to gain their iden-tity from their home lives, and when women's employment cir-cumstances are unsatisfactory their energies may be directed into the home rather than towards improving their employ-ment situation. Gerson's North American life-history study (1985) of women's work and family decisions describes the interrela-tionship between the workplace and domestic life as one of 'pushes and pulls'. She found that, for women who were in stable marriages, the experience of an unsatisfactory workplace tended to 'push' them towards the home by reinforcing or encouraging a traditional orientation towards domestic life (p.193–4). Agassi (1982) found a similar tendency in her comparative study of the employment experiences of North American, German and Israeli women. She suggests that women who find themselves in poor-quality situations and have access to a 'legitimate domestic role alternative' may lower 'their interest in advancement, their self-confidence, their self-image as basic breadwinner, and their overall satisfaction with work' (p.227). Thus they become caught in a vicious circle with regard to improving their working situation. Dex (1988) takes up Agassi's point, and argues that the poor quality of jobs available to women in Britain, especially part-time jobs, may offer little in the way of intrinsic reward. As a result, women with unsatisfactory jobs might retreat into their domestic worlds rather than 'change all those work attitudes which might otherwise have propelled them to make efforts at improving their work situation' (p.154).

The expectation and experience of alternative social identities offered within heterosexual relations may act to render dull, insecure and poorly paid jobs tolerable for women. However, Gerson (1985) provides examples of previously traditional women who, through the experience of disillusionment with conventional heterosexual relationships, made major improvements in their employment circumstances. She found that the experience of an unpleasant break-up of a long-term heterosexual relationship can be so disorienting that women find themselves reassessing the significance of paid work in their lives. She suggests that 'the realization that a man would not always be there to care for them led respondents to conclude that self-reliance was the only reasonable alternative. When faced with the necessity of remaining or becoming independent for an indefinite period of time, work took on greater importance' (pp.70–73).

My respondents' experience illuminates the need to extend our analysis of women's disadvantaged employment circumstances beyond gender to include the significance of interpretations of sexuality.[1] To fail to do this is to perpetuate the belief that woman equals heterosexual and to ignore the material and ideological processes which construct heterosexual outcomes. Instead, we need to recognize the extent to which gendered attitudes and experiences are shaped and expressed through beliefs, values and practices supporting institutional heterosexuality. A vicious circle is set in motion, whereby 'heterosexual' women facing class and gender inequalities in the workplace find their ability to bring about change in and control over their employment circumstances further constrained by the very institution they seek refuge within.

We have seen above that respondents' acceptance and subsequent rejection of dominant heterosexual versions of social reality influenced their approaches to waged work. Initially, they were probably like many of the women interviewed in the above studies. However, they became much more like the men interviewed by Mansfield and Collard (1988), insofar as most achieved employment which they enjoyed.

Employment opportunity and sexual choice

Often the expansion of options associated with access to more rewarding and challenging employment provided respondents with the possibility of reconsidering the desirability of marriage, and ultimately heterosexuality itself. Eight respondents, who had assumed they would marry, found themselves in this position. Two of these women married and the rest re-evaluated the desirability of marriage and heterosexuality. We will now illustrate this second dimension of the process of change with two case histories.

Sheena's story

For 35-year-old Sheena, from a mixed-race manual background, the enjoyment and challenge she experienced in her job was an important factor in her thinking 'things could be different' with regard to marriage. She was educated in a variety of different schools, one of which was 'alternative'. Because of financial constraints, she left school at 17 before completing her 'A' levels, with six 'O' levels. She entered a career in sport. While at school, she had reluctantly expected to marry:

> At the end of the day I just assumed that I would get married because that's what everyone else was doing, even though that wasn't what I really wanted to do. I just felt that I would get swept along, at that time, because I was too young to really realize my own self.

Throughout adolescence, Sheena reported thinking that paid work would be important in her adult life. Underlying this was her great love of sport, within which she planned to make a career. She set herself a career goal which she wanted to achieve before getting married. However, as her career progressed, she felt less inclined to marry:

How can I explain this? [Marriage] obviously wasn't right, because I am not married now. I wasn't looking to get married. I thought, if it happens it happens. I felt that I would have been happy, if the pressures of society had been such that I crumbled under it and did get married, as long as I had [achieved my particular career goal]. Once [I got into my job], I felt so much open up for me that I forgot all about that . . . I felt, no, I am enjoying myself. I am enjoying what I am doing, travelling all over the show with my sport, having a great time, and I thought I am not giving this up to get married.

This view was reinforced when Sheena entered a long-term relationship with a woman. She had always felt strong emotional attraction towards women, and had had an 'experimental' relationship with a female friend at school, but had not identified this as 'lesbian'. During the early part of her employment career, she had loving relationships with both women and men. She had, however, experienced pressure from her male lover to conform to his expectations of appropriate 'feminine' behaviour, and found this constraining. Through comparison between these two types of relationships, she was able to evaluate heterosexuality, and found that she preferred relationships with women:

My mind was already made up in a funny sort of way, but yes [the relationship with Pete] told me that really the politics of male/female just were not for me. It was just too much hassle. I wasn't missing out at all, I wasn't missing anything. It's just hassle, and hassle I didn't want to have.

Sheena's experience of employment opportunity offered financial independence, a positive occupational social identity and the space to reflect upon the advantages of marriage. Her experience of lesbian relationships allowed her to move a step further by providing practical knowledge of alternatives to heterosexuality. Thus, through evaluation, she chose to move beyond heterosexuality.

Peggy's story

Another example of this process of change comes from Peggy, a 27-year-old grammar school-educated woman from an intermediate social class background. She left school with one 'A' level and originally intended entering banking, which she understood to be an appropriate job for a woman. However, she failed to get the job and decided to apply to the Forces, which had been an earlier career desire:

> [*What appealed about the Forces?*] I wanted to get out of [my home town], but I didn't have the guts to do it my own; get a job and find somewhere to live. I didn't know what to do career wise, but I'd always had an interest in [mechanical engineering], so I thought I'd go in the Forces. It would give me time to think, away from the home environment . . . stand on my own two feet and think. Did I want a career, or did I just want to be like everyone else and find myself a husband and just have children?

For most of her time in the Forces she held a very ambiguous attitude towards career development. On the one hand, she thought it inappropriate for women to be career-oriented. On the other hand, she enjoyed the challenge of her job, and felt unwilling to give it up for marriage. She had a series of relationships with men, but was aware that many of her friends were lesbians. She admits to having initially felt very uncomfortable with lesbianism, and discouraged her lesbian friends from discussing the topic in her presence. However, at the age of 24 a series of events (including falling in love with a woman) occurred which led Peggy to re-evaluate her own sexuality. She describes 'coming-out':

> I thought, this is what I have been hiding from all this time, I have been hiding from this . . . That's when I actually started being true to myself, and decided that I wanted a career. I was true about my sexuality . . . And I thought to myself, I don't want that – I am not a feminist, and I am not anti-blokes or anything like that – I don't intend getting married, and I do want a career and I enjoy what I'm doing. So that was a turning point for me, then. [*How had you seen your career before?*] It was just something I was doing until I met somebody, the right person.

Her identification as lesbian resolved the conflict she had felt between desiring a career and her understanding of what marriage meant for women. Her lesbian friends' attitudes towards their careers were seen to contrast with those of her heterosexual women friends, who expected to give up their careers or had done so on marrying. Her lesbian friends appeared to be unashamedly ambitious. She decided that after leaving the Forces she would go to college and develop more formally her technical skills:

> It was when I actually started to make a few decisions about things, and decided I was going to go to college when I came out. I was going to get the paper work, and go on a bit further with what I'd been doing; get the qualifications ... I wanted a career. And my personal life happened to get sorted out as well, like. [*How did your personal life affect career decisions?*] I was mixing with people that were the sort of people I wanted to be with, and they happened to be gay ... And everybody was open about what they wanted to do; like if they wanted a career. And nobody was ashamed of the fact that they wanted a career ... When I was younger it was, like, women didn't really have a career ... and it got to I wasn't ashamed any more of admitting to people that I wanted a career.

For both these respondents, their access to rewarding and challenging employment provided them with an alternative way of thinking about their future. In each case, their jobs provided a positive social identity and economic independence. The women recognized the likelihood that marriage would place heavy constraints on their ability to pursue their careers. Through employment opportunity, together with an awareness of different sexual lifestyles, they were offered alternative versions of social reality. Once they experienced relationships with women, they were in a position to evaluate heterosexuality by comparing the possibilities offered by both types of relationships. From this position of choice they were no longer willing to make the compromises which they understood to be a requirement in relationships with men.

Discussion

Clearly the expansion of employment opportunity for women has offered alternatives to marriage and in some cases heterosexuality. Since the 1970s, there have been major changes in the composition of British households. There has been a rise in numbers of couples cohabiting, with three times more women aged between 18 and 49 cohabiting with men in 1993 (22 per cent) compared with 1979 (7 per cent) (General Household Survey, 1993). Women are also delaying marriage. The median age of first marriage for women in England and Wales rose from 22 in 1971 to 25 in 1993 (General Household Survey, 1993). Moreover, the United Kingdom has the highest divorce rate in the European Community (General Household Survey, 1993). Walby (1990) argues that these changes are largely due to the expansion of paid employment opportunities. She suggests that, as women gain access to jobs that offer financial independence, they are in a position to exercise greater choice over the conditions of their interpersonal relationships. Single women may decide to delay marriage and/or cohabit. As more married women enter full-time employment, they have the material power to leave an unsatisfactory marriage (p.84).

Gerson's (1985) life-history study of women and their family and employment choices supports this view. She links access to more rewarding and well-paid employment with the ability to exercise greater control over the conditions of personal relationships. As women's self-esteem grew through their work they became increasingly less tolerant of oppressive relationships in their home lives (p.86).

However, ways in which women may utilize the power derived from access to economic resources must be seen in the context of the dominance of ideologies which support the givenness of heterosexuality and obscure and stigmatize alternative avenues for sexual and emotional expression. It is apparent that the way women may 'choose' to renegotiate their struggle with the constraints of heterosexual relations is contingent on the range of possibilities open to them. For my respondents there was nothing inevitable about them arriving at a point of identification with lesbianism. Their awakening to a lesbian possibility often came as a result of a chance meeting or event. Many had found themselves unable to ignore the intense feelings they held for a female friend; others found themselves in environments (often Women's Movement environments) where they learnt about alternative sexual and emotional lifestyles. Their journey towards positive identification ('coming out') was far from straightforward. They had to deal with the mismatch between their feelings towards a particular woman and dominant representations of lesbianism – such as the 'mannish' woman. As a result, many initially interpreted their experience as unique: they were the 'the only one in the world' who felt emotionally drawn to other women. A more positive identification with lesbianism generally involved coming into contact with self-defined lesbians and curiosity led many to approach the lesbian community.

Increased employment opportunities may offer women greater choice over the conditions and nature of their interpersonal relationships. However, the silencing and perverting of alternative types of relationships ensures that most women 'choose' from a limited repertoire of possible solutions. In Britain, marriage has not lost widespread appeal. The analysis of marriage rates by birth cohort rather than numbers per year (which are shaped by demographic factors) indicates that women and men are delaying rather than rejecting marriage (Haskey, 1995). While increases in heterosexual cohabitation are striking, these are often the result of people deciding to live together before marriage rather than a radical departure from marriage as a goal (Haskey, 1995:5). Furthermore, heterosexual cohabitation does not necessarily imply that women have found egalitarian divisions of labour.

As we have seen above, the relationship between following a lesbian lifestyle and employment opportunity is complex. Two themes have emerged. First, for those in low-paid employment, the re-evaluation of the appropriateness of heterosexuality was a motivating factor behind occupational change; following a lesbian lifestyle was seen as *necessitating* long-term economic self-sufficiency. Second, access to rewarding and challenging jobs provided the economic possibility of living outside dependent relations with men. It also offered a positive alternative social identity to that of wife and mother. For these respondents a lesbian lifestyle was seen to *facilitate* the pursuit of their careers.

We now look at the experience of those respondents who married, to explore further the implied interrelationships between institutionalized heterosexuality and constraints on employment possibilities for women.

HETEROSEXUAL RELATIONSHIPS AND WOMEN'S EMPLOYMENT 'OPPORTUNITY'

Feminists have argued that you cannot understand women's often disadvantaged employment situation (and men's advantaged employment circumstances) without reference to their home life situation. While there seems to be a remarkable lack of curiosity about the home and employment lives of lesbians and gay men, there has been some excellent work on the home–employment interface, usually of married couples. I now want to spend a little more time outlining some relevant findings and to extend the discussion to include research on cohabiting heterosexual couples, so that we can focus on heterosexual relationships rather than simply relationships which are shaped within the context of marriage. I will then draw on my own data to show ways that respondents experienced similar constraints on their ability to experience employment opportunities in their heterosexual relationships to those identified in the research more generally. Again, we will see that these respondents' reinterpretation of their sexuality necessitated and/ or facilitated economic self-reliance.

British and North American evidence

There is a large body of literature, both British and North American, which identifies a range of constraints experienced by women in heterosexual partnerships, with or without children, married or cohabiting, which place limitations on their employment possibilities. Finch's (1983) British research suggests that a wife's career holds a low priority right from the beginning of the marriage (p.138). This rests on the assumption that having a job is something she may *choose* to do and, as such, must be fitted around all her other duties (p.138). Finch argues that a hierarchy of priorities is constructed in marriage. The needs of a wife take third place, coming after the needs of her husband's career and her family responsibilities.

Central to an understanding of men and women's employment circumstances in heterosexual relationships are dominant ideas about the nature of masculinity and femininity. Hegemonic masculinity is associated with the workplace, and femininity with home life and the bearing and rearing of children. These ideas remain powerful in shaping the employment approaches of heterosexual couples well before the arrival of children. This appears to be the case for young people entering marriage as recently as the late 1980s. Mansfield and Collard (1988) found that, despite both partners working full-time, newly-weds anticipated a male provider career model (p.135). Within three months of marriage, a fairly traditional division of labour had developed, which was justified by the view that the wife's work role was temporary (pp.128–37). Young wives' changing approaches to employment often involved making adjustments to the working week to accommodate the demands of caring for the home and husband. They found many examples of women relocating for their husband's jobs, with some having exchanged jobs with good promotion prospects for unemployment or much lower status jobs (p.144). Mansfield and Collard echo Finch when they observe that 'the unspoken rule in most couples is that the work of the wife outside the home should not dominate her life to such an extent that the spouse or the house "suffer"' (pp.144–5).

This hierarchy of priorities may serve as a partial explanation for the downward occupational mobility experienced by a large proportion of married women *before* they enter their childrearing phase (see Dex, 1987:76). It may also provide insights into the reason for childless married women, as a group, not experiencing significantly greater occupational mobility than women with children (Dex, 1987:75).

Safilios-Rothschild (1976) argues that, for those wives who have jobs which hold the potential for advancement, processes exist to ensure that her career will rarely achieve parity of status with her husband's. Again, these processes are underpinned by taken for granted understandings of what it means to be a woman and a man in a partnership. According to Safilios-Rothschild, a 'good' wife should not put in extra hours at work, bring work home or travel excessively. Thus her career development can be only partial and is destined not to overtake her husband's career.

Ideologies which support dichotomous gender identities are crucial in explaining why change in men and women's home lives is limited even when economic roles between couples are reversed or shared. Morris (1990), for example, suggests that gender ideologies are an important factor underpinning the tendency for unemployed men to resist assuming responsibility for domestic tasks. The affirmation of femininity is suggested to be at the heart of the motivations of women who earn higher wages than their male partners and then compensate for their success by taking on a major share of the domestic and childcare work (McRae, 1986:127; Hochschild, 1989). In addition, a desire not to undermine normative understandings of masculine and feminine is thought to be a factor in these women maintaining the illusion that their partner is really the breadwinner. The 'doing of gender' (Berk, 1985) and the enactment of 'gender strategies' (Hochschild, 1989) are cited as the main reason for men failing to take on their share of the burdens of domestic and childcare responsibilities. This situation is further complicated by the fact that, given the lack of alternative sources of positive esteem, women may be reluctant for their male partners to assume too much involvement in their traditional domain (Lamb *et al.*, 1987, Lewis and O'Brien, 1987).

The persistence of gendered approaches to home life and employment has been noted even amongst more egalitarian couples. Doucet's (1995) in-depth study of British heterosexual couples who are actively engaged in constructing more sharing relationships found that 'the majority of women are still primary care-givers while men retain their identities and responsibilities as the household's chief breadwinner' (p.181). Blumstein and Schwartz's (1985) large-scale North American study of different couple forms included cohabiting couples. They found that female cohabiters tended to value the ability to be economically self-sufficient, while male cohabiters tended to reject a primary breadwinning role. However, the notion that a man's job should be of higher status than that of his female partner still prevailed. Although male cohabiters supported their partner's right to work, few were happy if their partners became too self-reliant. Women's employment success was often construed as competition (p.162). Blumstein and Schwartz conclude that inequalities in relationships between women and men are not simply derived from the institution of marriage; instead they identify the source as the construction of dichotomous gender identities (pp.153–4). This conclusion is supported by other large studies of American cohabiting couples (see, for example, Macklin, 1983).

It seems that the social emphasis of dichotomous gender identities becomes magnified when women and men enter heterosexual relationships, marriage in particular. Men and women become caught up in a plethora of expectations and practices which inform and shape their understandings of what it means to be a good wife, husband, partner. This limits the extent to which these individuals can challenge their differential employment situations. As we will see in Chapter 6, very different outcomes can be achieved when relationships are negotiated without the constraints imposed by gender difference.

Respondents' experience of marriage

Of the eight respondents who had experienced marriage in the conventional sense, all desired a measure of economic independence within their marriages and felt that paid employment was important. However, only one assumed that her job was as important as her husband's. The rest viewed their husband as the main breadwinner. All were employed throughout their marriages; even those with young children found ways of engaging in paid work. Three had professional jobs and the rest were in low paid 'female' occupations. Five had children, yet all experienced home life constraints on their ability to experience employment opportunity.

I now want to draw on my own data to illustrate two important interrelationships. The first is the relationship between heterosexual partnerships and employment constraints. The second is a relationship between lesbianism and expanding employment opportunity. I shall focus on the case histories of three previously married respondents who were best placed to experience employment opportunity. These women remained childless precisely because they felt their careers were important to them. Each one was in different employment circumstances: Trudy was apprenticeship-trained in a female-dominated occupation, Maureen was in a female-dominated profession and the third, Laura, was in a male-dominated profession.

Trudy's story

Trudy, aged 35, is from an intermediate background and was educated in a secondary modern school. She remembers holding a reluctant expectation of marriage, feeling that she would 'have to conform'. She always viewed employment as a continuing feature of her adult life, linking it with her desire for financial independence. On leaving school early at 14 with no qualifications, she entered an apprenticeship in a traditional female occupation. She was engaged when she was 16 and married at 18. She retained her desire for economic independence, and for this and other reasons sought to postpone motherhood:

> We discussed children, and it was decided we'd wait four years, so that gave me till 22. After a year went past, I felt a quarter of my freedom's gone – that's how I thought about it. He was very much a 'You have children, you stay at home,

you are not working ever again, certainly until all the kids are at school, 'cos you'll be a mother. You will not have anyone to look after our kids. I will still be able to go to the pub!'

She associated the arrival of children with the end of 'freedom', when she would have to give up employment and take on primary responsibility for childcare. However, she experienced constraints on being able to follow her career well before those she had anticipated coming with motherhood. Despite needing two incomes, her husband took steps to ensure that her employment status would not undermine his perception of himself as 'provider':

> [*You had finished your apprenticeship?*] Yes, but then he objected to the unsociable hours I worked, 'cos it was much more unsociable then. I would be tired . . . money did matter . . . he wanted me to go out and earn money. [*What sort of a job did he have in mind?*] Anything that earned money and that wasn't important. Well, a female is supposed to be at home . . . a job for the money, but not to interfere with putting the dinner on the table, and conjugal rights . . . On his darts night, which was most nights, I used to work in a restaurant, which I loved because it was with people again, and I used to go baby sitting, and I just used to love work really.

Trudy eventually found the conditions of her marriage intolerable and finally, aged 22, divorced him. She entered a series of low-paid jobs: driving, wages clerk, accounts. She then met Jude, the woman who would become her lover and companion for the next 12 years with one interruption. The break-up of another relationship with a man, and the commencement of this lesbian relationship, corresponded with her desire to establish her career:

> [*You were saying that work was taking on a new meaning, why was that?*] I had decided that I was never going to rely on anybody for material things, and I wanted something satisfying career wise, and [Jude] had got a promotion, and I needed to feel equally important in the relationship.

In contrast to Trudy's experience in marriage, when her desire to follow a career appeared to threaten her husband's status and authority, she found that Jude was central in rebuilding her confidence and supporting the establishment of her career:

I said, I didn't think I could go back to [the job I was trained for]. And [Jude] said, 'If you are going to be unhappy . . . the only way to do it is to buy your own business.' I said, 'I can't' and she said, 'Why not?' She talked to my father, and everyone had faith in me and so I became [the owner of a small business] . . . It all happened very quickly: met [Jude], changed my career, in five months had my own business.

Trudy now owns her own home and has a successful business which employs 12 women. According to her, she is the only woman in the region to own this type of business. She identified her movement out of what she called 'heterosexual role play' into a less gender-scripted relationship as central to her success. This 'role play', she suggested, was guided by links between male identity and notions of providing.

However, after living with Jude for several years Trudy decided to return to a 'conventional' life and enter a relationship with a man. She had wanted to make sure she was not rejecting men on the basis of her marriage. She explains:

I was 27 when I told [Jude] that I wanted the freedom to possibly choose whether I wanted to have children . . . I didn't want marriage, I wanted the freedom to have children; didn't want to become a bitter old lady who wished she'd had kids. In actual fact, I know I don't want children now, but I had to go through that break-up of the relationship and go back into the heterosexual world.

She describes ways which she experienced 'heterosexual role play' in her relationship with this man:

We never lived together, but I was willing to go back into the male/female . . . [*You felt it was going back into a role?*] Yes . . . I found I would then go back into role playing. [*Do you feel that you quite naturally slip into roles with men?*] Yes, yes, I feel that would be only for a while, and then I would have bucked. And I know that now, and he knew that then, that's why he finished with me . . . I can't be 'me' with a man, or I can't be the same me with a male as I can do with a female . . . With a female I am equal, with a male I still don't feel equal, do I? Because of social upbringing.

Like most of the women interviewed, she identified the problem with heterosexuality as this role play, rather than individual men. Again Trudy found that her employment success threatened this heterosexual relationship. In order to save the partnership she sold the business:

> That's part of the reason why I sold the business, because he didn't have the income . . . I thought, what am I doing this for? Because he's not going to take the benefits anyway, the benefits of my ability. [*How do you mean?*] I was doing well there, earning very good money. I would never have been able to enjoy it or share it with him because he wouldn't live off my money . . . [*You thought that your success was getting in the way of your relationship with him?*] Oh yes, yes.

She subsequently returned to Jude, and together they re-established her business.

Maureen's story

In the case of Maureen, aged 45, from a service class background, the development of her professional career was limited by domestic constraints and the inability to be geographically mobile. On leaving her comprehensive school, Maureen trained in a female-dominated profession. She expected to marry and, although she saw her career as important, she assumed it would be secondary to her husband's career. She was engaged to be married at 21. However, she fell in love with a woman, and broke off this engagement. She did not make an identification as a lesbian, and treated this relationship as a 'one off'. When that relationship ended 18 months later, Maureen thought that she would 'never be able to find anybody that I could love like I loved her' and decided to 'conform', so, at 27, she married. She entered marriage with the view that her career would be important and with a desire not to have children:

> I had from the very outset said that I didn't want children and therefore career was going to be important. [*How did he feel about that?*] He seemed to go along with the idea of my career quite happily. As far as not having children, he seemed to go along with that as well.

However, as her career developed and made greater demands on her time, she began to experience tension at home:

> I was head of [the department] and involved in quite a lot of travelling and lecturing around the country and he didn't

like that too much. In the beginning he thought, yes, that would be fine, that would be a good idea, but the reality of it he didn't like at all. And I think that's probably where the rot finally set in . . . One, he didn't like me being away, and two, I actually found that I could do a lot of things that I never dreamt I could do . . . [*What couldn't he handle?*] I think partly me being away and partly me growing, because I think he wanted the wife at home really, and I had stopped being that – no, that's not true, I hadn't stopped that, it had stopped being so important.

Throughout the ten years of her marriage she experienced a traditional division of labour in the home. Maureen describes her relationship to her husband as being overshadowed by 'heterosexual role play':

I felt I was acting, I was acting the way I had seen other people act. [*What about roles in the home?*] Very stereotyped, I did all the things that a good little wife does.

After a series of difficulties in her marriage, which were often related to her employment successes, she fell in love with a woman. After 'a great deal of heart searching and sleepless nights', Maureen left her husband and went to live with Barbara. The economic demands of these new circumstances forced her to make an important change in her career. Within six months of leaving her husband, she applied for, and got, a position three levels above the position she occupied while married:

[*Why do you think you applied for such a big promotion?*] I looked around for a job that was in an area that I vaguely knew, that was at a level of funding that I thought I could survive on, and that I thought I could do actually . . . [*Do you think that, had you been married, you could have gone for that job?*] Oh no! It took too much time. [*What about relocation: could you have relocated?*] Not for my job. We might have relocated for [my husband's] job.

Although her earlier job had been important for developing her confidence, and the belief that she could take on more responsibility, it was poorly paid and would not provide economic self-sufficiency. By moving beyond heterosexuality, economic necessity, together with what she described as the freedom from 'heterosexual role play', were central in both motivating and facilitating her rise to this higher-level post. She and Barbara had carried out a joint job search and neither career was privileged over the other. On relocation they set up home half-way between their places of work. They have been living together for the past eight years. Maureen has now reached a top management position in a female profession.

Heterosexual gender scripts

There are commonalities in these two stories. Both Trudy and Maureen found that their ability to experience employment opportunity and economic independence were preempted by taken for granted understandings that men should be providers and a wife's career should be secondary. Furthermore, the necessity for economic independence integral to the lesbian lifestyle had consequences for their career development. This was also an empowering experience, insofar as they found that their moves into demanding employment were facilitated within the context of their relationships with women.

Like all previously married respondents, each identified 'heterosexual role play' or the 'role scripting' discussed by Blumstein and Schwartz (1985) and Macklin (1983), rather than individual men, as the source of the inequalities they experienced in marriage. These taken for granted 'scripts' provided a framework of meaning, guiding how they felt they should act out their womanhood. This was evident in the words of Maureen, when she described 'conforming' in marriage as 'I felt I was acting . . . the way I had seen other people act.' However, this was a relational state of affairs, insofar as these particular 'scripts' framed the experience of being a woman in male–female relationship. Trudy's descriptions are particularly interesting because, when she says 'I can't be "me" with a man, or I can't be the same "me" with a male as I can do with a female', she has identified this relational quality of gender categories. For Trudy and Maureen, the ability to recognize these different versions of 'me' is to do with having moved outside heterosexuality, and experiencing being a woman in a relationship with another woman. If we accept Connell's (1987:140) conception of gender as a 'process' and think of the word 'gender' as a verb, then we must also recognize that the experience of 'being gendered' in an interaction will have an additional gender dynamic. In other words, how we experience our gender as women will be qualitatively different if we are being gendered by a woman as opposed to a man. I think that underpinning most women's choices to form loving relationships with women is a preference for experiencing the process of 'gendering' via other women.

Laura's story

Some respondents were already forewarned about the power and pervasiveness of roles in marriage. Laura, aged 33, from a manual background, had access to feminist ideas which informed her approach to her marriage. She was a university graduate who had initially assumed she would not marry. She entered a male-dominated profession and expected that, when she did marry, her career would be just as important as her husband's. However, although she perceived her relationship as having flexibility in terms of 'heterosexual role play', she was aware of the latent power of taken for granted expectations for contextualizing this flexibility:

> Although the actual operation of the marriage was quite equal, what comes with being married was a whole load of stuff that I didn't want anything to do with. Like expectations around being the wife. Invariably you might be working quite hard at not making that a reality, but it's still there. And I thought: I do not want to be doing all this. I do not want to live with that sort of expectation . . . But it is there all the time from everything else. I started sliding into a role, and was sort of sucked into being the wife . . . because the pressure on you to live the role is really acute and intense.

Another factor which impeded Laura's desire for a balance of power at home was unequal access to economic resources, which she experienced as economic dependency:

> When I was married, there was a sort of power imbalance, that came about through the money, which used to grate my nerves. The fact that he actually made so much more money than I had. Although you try not to let it be an issue, it's difficult, therefore, not to be in a position where you feel as though you are supported, even though you have your own money. You still find yourself in a situation where you are living up to his standard rather than living at yours.

The achievement of career parity was also undermined by what she felt was her husband's competitive attitude towards her career. In this next extract she contrasts this with her experience of relationships with women:

> In terms of getting on and achieving things and doing things, I feel as though I have done a lot more as a lesbian than I did as a heterosexual wife. [*How so?*] In terms of having more freedom to determine how much time is spent doing the job; the positive side of having a lot more autonomy... I felt as though it is more acceptable to do more than I could have done as a man's partner. I felt the element of competition. [*Competition, between you and him?*] Yes. [*In what sort of way?*] Because we were in the same sort of line of work... The rewards that I got were nay going to be acknowledged or recognized by him. [*You were aware that you could be successful but only so far?*] That's right. [*What about encouragement in your relationship with him?*] It was half-hearted. [*And with women?*] Yes, I have felt it has been more genuine.

The competition experienced within this 'dual-career' marriage appears to be similar to that found amongst cohabiting couples cited earlier. This attests to the still powerful role of employment status in signifying hegemonic masculinity. For Laura, moving beyond heterosexuality was interpreted as facilitating her ability to develop her career.

Married respondents' employment outcomes

The employment constraints experienced by my eight previously married respondents seem to be fairly typical, they echo those identified in the studies discussed earlier. Leaving their marriages and moving beyond heterosexuality was usually associated with expanding employment opportunities. Two who had previously been in poorly paid women's work returned to higher education in order to broaden their employment options. A further three described having made major improvements in their employment situation after 'coming out'.

However, previously married women were more likely than other respondents to have remained in low-paid jobs. At the time of interview, four were in low-paid jobs. Two of these women were in their forties and held higher qualifications. They thought that ageism was the major source of their employment disadvantages. However, a commonality experienced by these four women in low paid jobs was that they had all been mothers. Although their current employment situation was not simply the result of their having had children or of their class background (one was from a service class background, two were from intermediate backgrounds and one was from a manual background) it does appear that the effects of the constraints experienced by women in heterosexual relationships are less easily reversed when they have been reinforced by having been primary caregivers.

ON BEING 'LESBIAN': ECONOMIC SELF-SUFFICIENCY

We will now draw on the whole sample and focus on ways that respondents experienced their lesbian lifestyle necessitating and/ or facilitating economic independence. We will then consider how this informed their approaches to skill development.

The lesbian lifestyle: economic independence

One of the most common characteristics reported by respondents, in 57 cases, was a strong desire to be economically independent. For many respondents, the shift into a lesbian lifestyle appeared to be an extension of an earlier desire for economic independence. Because relationships between women were understood to be relationships of *co-independence*, insofar as there was a tacit understanding that each partner had the right and the need to be employed, relationships were perceived as complementing and supporting their ability to be economically self-reliant (see Chapter 6).

For many, the transition into the lesbian lifestyle was interpreted as expanding employment possibilities, even for those women who reported never having assumed they would marry. An example of this thinking comes from Jenny, who has recently 'come out'. Although she had not expected to marry, before she 'came out' she had been drifting from job to job, with no clear idea of what she wanted to do. She is now a trainee manager:

> Sexuality, and coming out, has made me feel that I can go and do those things and go onto courses, so that I can get into the field that I want to get into. Rather than that horrible feeling that you think: well I'd like to do that but I'll never get round to it ... I probably see myself as having to

do some sort of foundation course, and another 'A' level, and whatever . . . I don't feel any kind of doors to block me now. I can just be as I want to be, and not feel that I have to stop and start, or have my status disregarded. (22S)

Respondents also recognized that following the lesbian life-style necessitated economic independence. Fiona, who is training to enter a male-dominated profession, explains her feelings:

[*How does your sexuality affect your sense of independence?*] I don't think it actually encourages it, it necessitates it – which is not encouragement really, it's just an added pressure . . . [*Do you feel that you differ from heterosexual women in this regard?*] I don't think it is necessarily different. But I think in today's society that it is an option for a heterosexual woman – for a middle-class heterosexual woman who is going to marry a middle-class heterosexual man who will be earning enough for her not to have to work – it is an option for her not to work. Now that is not an option for many women, but it is an option for some, and it is an option for the woman who I would be if I wasn't a lesbian. It's an option not to work, whereas I don't feel I have an option not to work because I won't have a husband who could support me . . . There's always a need for me to go out to work which, if I was hetero-sexual, there wouldn't necessarily be. (25)

This view of the long-term nature of their dependence on *employment* contrasted with the earlier feelings of even the most career-oriented respondents who had expected to marry. Typically, these women felt that the element of choice had gone. They could not think of their future in terms of having the wages of a higher-earning partner to fall back on. Dusty, a university-educated woman from a service class background, explains:

[*Do you see yourself now as a lifelong worker?*] Yes. That fright-ened me initially. I remember when I started discussing the pros and cons of my sexuality, I guess that was one of the things that had frightened me greatly. Because I had grown up with this myth that was very strong, this idea that I would have a partner when I was 23, and a kid when I was 28. So that was quite difficult, and I had to think about that a lot. I had to think what it meant in terms of living. [*What do you*

see it as meaning, in terms of living?] I see it as meaning I have
to, I have actual financial need for survival, to be financially
independent... I have to have a job... the actual work that
you do... (26)

Similar ideas are expressed by Sonia, who comes from a manual
background. She had earlier expected to marry, 'came out'
aged 21, then returned to education and is at present studying for a degree:

> [*Does your sexuality play a role in making you think this way about
> work?*] Certainly. [*How?*]... In many ways it's more import-
> ant to me because I know that I'm not actually going to
> have [a male breadwinner] to fall back on.... There was a
> time when I think it sort of dawned on me, that I was going
> to have to support myself and I'd better start getting my act
> together and start to do it... I was the only one to fall back
> on. So I thought: you'll have to sort yourself out and find
> some sort of income, and decide what you want to do. Which
> is what I did. (24)

The conscious awareness of the long-term necessity of having
to earn a living often crept into respondents' discussions of
their employment ambitions. Olly comes from an intermediate
background. She 'came out' while she was at school, and has
now reached a junior management position in a male-dominated occupation. She enjoys her work and expects to rise further in her organization:

> My work was the first thing and work came first. It still does,
> whereas really it shouldn't quite so much, but that's really
> how I am going. Because of the way I am [being gay], I've
> got to make it work at work, so that I can afford to do every-
> thing that I want to do. [*Do you think being gay makes a differ-
> ence?*] Yes, yes, 'cos I know that I have to do it for myself, I
> have nobody to help me. (25)

Over half of the respondents emphasized that their sexuality
directly facilitated and/or necessitated the pursuit of economic
independence. Respondents recognized that they would be employed for the rest of their working lives.[2] This held consequences for the way they thought about jobs and provided
motivation to develop skills and strategies that would provide
access to jobs that they would enjoy.[3]

Skill development

The desire to experience challenging and/or enjoyable employment was usually a central priority for respondents. This was generally achieved, with only four respondents reporting disliking their jobs. Skill development, often seen as continuous, formed part of the process of obtaining satisfying work. A total of 38 women believed that the acquisition of further vocational or educational qualifications had been, and/or was expected to be, part of their career development.

As many as 14 respondents had entered higher education as mature students, and nine of these women had done so after experiencing the constraints of low-paid women's work. This was the case with Una, a 43-year-old divorced woman with children from an intermediate class background. She has lived with Sally for the past 15 years, for much of which time Una had a series of low-paid part-time jobs. When the children were settled in school she decided to take up evening classes. She finally got the chance to study on a degree course in another part of the country. Sally, who helped with childcare, gave up a senior position to relocate, on the understanding that it was now Una's turn to develop a career. In this extract Una explains what had motivated her return to education:

> I had been thinking about it for so long, and I had made such a bugger up of my 'A' levels [as a teenager]. [*Were your ideas changing about work now that your children were beginning to grow up?*] I suppose so, yes. Early on, when I had done all sorts of jobs, scrubbed floors, worked in a shop, and what have you, I'd done it in order to get the money. Yes, I think I felt that I needed to make more of a career for myself.

June, from a manual background, explains her reasons for entering a degree course as a mature student:

> Then I decided to be a student. [*Why?*] To give me options to do other things, to get out of my awful job structure . . . I've wanted to be economically independent, which I am. I hadn't had a proper education until I got it myself . . . It hasn't seemed hard for me to have achieved that independence, it just seems to have been the natural thing for me to do. (44)

At the time of interview, five women were mature students in full-time higher education. Often respondents had eased their way into higher education by taking 'O' levels and 'A' levels at

Table 4.1 *Respondents' qualifications by age*

Qualification levels[1]	16–19	20–24	25–29	30–39	40–49	50+	All	
	n	n	n	n	n	n	n	%
Degree or equivalent/member of a professional inst.	1	6	9	8	4	1	29	48
Higher education below degree – nursing, teaching, HND, etc.	0	1	1	3	3	1	9	15
'A' level or equivalen/trade apprenticeship completed	0	1	1	2	3	0	7	12
'O' level or equivalent	2	1	3	3	2	0	11	18
CSE below grade 1/other qualification	0	0	0	0	2	0	2	3
None of these	0	0	1	0	0	1	2	3
Totals	3	9	15	16	14	3	60	99[2]

[1] Includes seven respondents working towards these qualifications.
[2] Rounding error.

evening classes. At the time of interview, two teenage women, who had left school with no qualifications, were studying for 'O' levels. Both had been in factory work, and wished to improve their employment situation. For example, Peta left school at 15 and entered factory work. She 'came out' when she was 16. She explains her motives for returning to education:

> I know I have to be independent and not to rely on a man. [*Does that influence you in your approach to work?*] Yes, I know that I've actually got to work. [*Could you tell me a bit about your thoughts on that?*] I'm at college at the moment and I'm hoping that will get me into a good job when I leave, that will keep me going. [*Could you go for any job?*] No! I'd want something that I'd know I'm going to enjoy and that. (17)

The qualification levels of the sample reflect a trend towards skill development. In Table 4.1 we can see that only two respondents held no formal qualifications. Twenty-nine held or were working towards a degree or equivalent, with a further nine holding higher education qualifications. Of the 38 women with higher qualification, 23 were from service social class backgrounds, seven were from intermediate backgrounds and eight were from manual backgrounds (this represents over half of the sample who came from manual social class backgrounds). While respondents from service social class backgrounds make up the bulk, 65 per cent, of those holding degrees or equivalent, those from manual social class backgrounds are relatively well

Table 4.2   *Comparison of qualifications held by sample with those of British women of working age (BHPS, 1991)*

Qualification levels	17–24 Sample %	All women %	25–49 Sample %	All women %	50+ Sample %	All women %
Degree or equivalent/member of professional inst.	58	4	47	10	33	3
Higher education below degree – nursing, teaching, HND, etc.	8	3	16	5	33	5
'A' level or equivalent/trade apprenticeship completed	8	26	13	12	0	5
'O' level or equivalent	25	43	18	33	0	19
CSE below grade 1, other qualification	0	14	4	7	0	1
None of these	0	10	2	34	33	67

represented at 21 per cent. An analysis (controlled by age) of women with degrees or equivalent in the British Household Pannel Survey (BHPS) found that only 14 per cent came from manual social class backgrounds.

In Table 4.2 we see that the qualification levels for each age group of my sample are much higher than those of the general population of women. While the 1991 census indicates that the district where respondents lived has a particularly well qualified population, double the national average, the influence of location is not enough to account for these significantly high levels of qualifications.

Discussion

It appears that high levels of qualifications amongst lesbians are commonly found in other research. Johnson's study (1990:34) of older lesbians, found high levels of educational qualifications: 80 per cent were college graduates. Similarly, 87 per cent of Caldwell and Peplau's (1984:590) sample were educated beyond high school diploma. Green's (1992:96) ethnography on lesbian feminists in London also found high qualification levels amongst her sample: 24 (80 per cent) of the 30 women interviewed held or were studying for higher academic or professional qualifications. Weston (1991:12) found similarly high levels of education in her sample of lesbians and gay men from a wide range of social and ethnic backgrounds living in San Francisco. When Blumstein and Schwartz (1985:596) compared the qualification levels of individuals in different couple forms, they found that lesbians were the most likely to have some college education (88 per cent).[4] The education level for lesbians was closely followed by that of gay men and married men, followed by cohabiting women and married women.[5]

I suggest that the high levels of qualifications found in my study and those above are not necessarily the result of a sampling error. Rather, they supports my argument that a lesbian lifestyle represents an economic achievement and that there is an interrelationship between the lesbian lifestyle and financial independence. First, higher education provides the social and economic power to live life differently. For example, the high proportion of respondents from the most economically disadvantaged social class backgounds (manual) who held higher qualifications emphasizes this material dimension to sexual preferences. Second, university life may offer a context within which people can make a positive identification with lesbianism. Importantly, colleges recruit students from places big and small. College life allows them to come into contact with new people and new ideas, hence broadening their horizons and offering a break from past routines and the surveillance of family. For many people, particularly those from small towns and rural areas, college may provide their first opportunity to think about their sexuality as they come into contact with feminism, feminists, lesbians and gay men. Third, the necessity for dependence on employment implicit in the lesbian lifestyle may be a strong motivating factor in encouraging the acquisition of skills. It is worth noting that nine of my respondents actually left school with no formal qualifications, and seven of these women went on to gain qualifications – in two cases, higher qualifications. Given the constraints on women's access to a living wage, it would seem self-evident that women who live independently of men will need to be better placed in relation to qualifications.[6]

CONCLUSION

This chapter has outlined ways that the pursuit of a lesbian lifestyle both necessitated and facilitated economic independence. It has argued that the relationship between employment opportunity and changing understandings of sexuality is complex and multidimensional. The first section illustrated ways that expanding employment opportunity may contribute to the development of a more critical perspective on marriage and, under certain circumstances, heterosexuality. We have also seen examples of the impact of changing interpretations of sexuality on approaches to employment. Usually respondents experienced improved employment situations, with many moving out of low-paid routine women's work into jobs with prospects. These findings suggest that we need to extend our analysis of women's employment to include the role of beliefs and practices supporting heterosexuality.

NOTES

1. Adkins's (1995) excellent analysis of the workings of the labour markets in her study of women working in the British tourist industry draws similar conclusions about the need to theorize links between women's employment circumstances and institutional heterosexuality.
2. However, some of the younger women did not rule out the possibility of taking a short period out of the labour market to have a child, or to 'coparent'.
3. Arguably, this lifelong perspective may be held by heterosexual single women. One difference may be that of foresight. For example, Hennig and Jardim's study (1979:6–16) of top managerial women in North America found that, for those who remained single, career decisions were usually made in their late twenties and early thirties because they had initially held a short-term employment perspective (p.6). It was not until the women were well into their thirties that they took a more active involvement in their career development (p.6). This contrasts with most (45) of my respondents who had re-evaluated their sexuality by the age of 25. They, therefore, could make use of the knowledge of the long-term duration of employment much earlier in their careers.
4. There is an overall bias towards middle-class respondents in Blumstein and Schwartz's sample. However, I cannot see why this should affect the findings on lesbians any more than others in the sample. Consequently, the comparison is suggestive.
5. The figure for married women with some college education was 81 per cent; for cohabiting women it was 85 per cent.
6. This view is supported by other data on never-married women. Treiman's (1975) North American study, based on a large sample of women in their thirties and forties, found that never-married women tended to have much higher levels of education than women who were or had been married. His explanations are similar to mine. First, because single women are better qualified they can experience economic independence, which allows them to remain single; and second, married women may have more domestic and family constraints on their ability to develop skills and acquire qualifications. British statistics also suggest that 'non-married' women have higher levels of qualifications than married women, and are much less likely to have no formal qualifications (see footnote to Table 2 in the *Employment Gazette*, October 1988:522).

CHAPTER FIVE

Lesbians at work: why can't a woman be more like a man?

INTRODUCTION

The focus of this chapter is respondents' experiences of paid work. It seeks to illuminate the tensions arising from their employment experiences both as women and as lesbians. As non-heterosexual women, their lifestyle places economic demands upon them to be self-supporting. As women, they must negotiate an unequal labour market that often places limits on the extent to which this may be achieved.

We begin by comparing the pay levels and occupational location of the sample with national and local statistics on female and male full-time employees. From these comparisons it will become apparent that, although respondents worked in a wide range of jobs – rarely traditional low-paid 'women's' work and often non-traditional 'male' occupations – and were usually better paid than women more generally, they did not achieve male levels of pay. In order to see if this is simply the result of gender discrimination, we will draw on respondents' own commentaries and consider their experience of, and attitudes towards, employment. The experience of those in the sample who defined their jobs as 'male' and those who defined them as 'female' will be discussed. We will then explore respondents' attitudes towards employment, together with their ambitions and approaches to career development. The insights which it is hoped may be gained from this chapter will lie in the supporting commentaries, as the small sample size both generates and magnifies statistical inaccuracy.

DIFFERENCE AT WORK

As we have seen in the Chapter 4, the anticipation and experience of marriage generally places constraints on women's employment opportunities. Ideas that men should be breadwinners and that women's working life should not dominate at the expense of the needs of their home, husband and children prevail. Once married, women tend to take on the bulk of household and caring work, which enables their partners to devote their energies more fully to the working lives. Feminists have pointed out that men's ability to expropriate women's unpaid labour means that women and men negotiate the labour market under very different circumstances (Adkins, 1995; Pateman, 1988). Given this insight, and the historical evidence on American and British single women which links remaining unmarried with educational and employment opportunity,[1] it is surprising that there has been so little contemporary research on the employment experience of older, 'never-married' women in Britain.[2] There is some contemporary evidence to suggest that this would be a fruitful line of enquiry. Roos's (1983) cross-cultural comparison of the occupational location of never-married with married women shows that the former are more likely to occupy higher status and/or non-traditional occupations. Perhaps the general lack of curiosity about single women is due to the fact that older, never-married women make up such a small percentage of the British female population.[3] A further reason may be due to problems of data collection. In Britain, published statistics often group together divorced, widowed, separated and never-married women into the category 'non-married' women. Another difficulty raised by Roos (1983) is distinguishing between single women and what she terms 'premarried women'. This she sees as important because 'premarried' women's 'occupational preferences may be affected by an anticipated assumption of the traditional responsibilities of marriage' (p.855). Finally, we cannot assume that never-married women's labour is not being appropriated by men, as many may be in cohabiting heterosexual relationships.

More attention needs to be given to the lives of older single women. Feminist concern with the experience of married women is understandable. However, if we are to gain a better understanding of both the nature and sources of constraints on women, we need to extend our analysis to include the experiences of women who are constructing lifestyles beyond the boundaries of marriage and possibly institutionalized heterosexuality itself. By doing this we may gain a clearer vision of the different mechanisms which interact to place limitations upon women's autonomy. Given the problems that have just been outlined regarding the difficulties in distinguishing among single women, the experience of lesbian women may provide the best comparative data set for analysis.[4]

Pay

Despite the existence of the Equal Pay Act 1970, and the Sex Discrimination Acts of 1975 and 1986, women's skills remain undervalued. A substantial pay gap exists between female and male wages. In 1994, the average hourly rate (excluding overtime) for women in full-time employment was 79.5 per cent of men's, and their weekly pay was 72 per cent of their male counterparts' (New Earnings Survey, 1994). Further, the Low Pay Unit defines 'low pay' as two-thirds of the median male wage (*Employment Gazette*, 1994). If we analyse and compare the wages of male and female full-time employees we find that, in 1994, 42 per cent of women and 18 per cent of men fell below the low pay threshold (New Earnings Survey, 1994). As part-time workers are likely to be even more disadvantaged in terms of weekly earnings, and most part-time workers are women, female workers represent the bulk of low-paid workers in Britain.[5] Conventional wisdom suggests that inequalities in pay reflect women's interrupted career histories due to their childrearing responsibilities. As my sample's earnings usually reflect continuous labour market participation, it is interesting to see how their pay levels compare with other male and female employees.

The mean weekly wage for the 44 fully employed respondents was £218 in March 1990. In Figure 5.1 we can see that the pay levels of respondents in both manual and non-manual occupations were higher than those of full-time manual and non-manual female employees more generally.[6] However, a very different picture emerges when we compare their pay with men's pay. The mean weekly average of both manual and non-manual respondents' average pay was considerably lower than that of their male counterparts. Neither the age distribution of the sample nor their geographical location could explain these anomalies.[7]

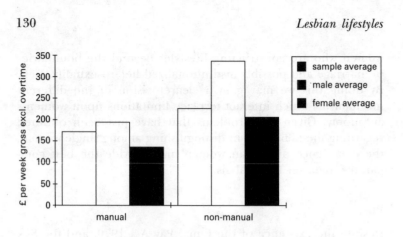

Average gross weekly pay excluding overtime, April 1990

Figure 5.1   *Sample's pay compared with British manual and non-manual workers by gender (full-time employees)*
Source: *New Earnings Survey 1990.*

Why should respondents occupy this middle ground in terms of pay? We might expect their wages to be higher than other women's, but why have they not achieved parity with men? Alternative explanations must be sought, such as gender and racial discrimination, different priorities in relation to career development, the financial undervaluing of occupations with a high social or caring component and homophobia and heterosexism. All these interrelated factors will be explored later.

'Full' and 'component' wages

To bring to life the social consequences of pay disparities, Janet Siltanen (1994) has devised a method of relating wages to cost of living by calculating the amount of money a person needs to earn in order to be self-sufficient. She makes a distinction between 'full' and 'component' wages. She defines 'component' wages as those which are *not* sufficient to supply the resources necessary for an individual to support herself in a one-person household. 'Full wages' will support a household with one or more dependants, and minimum 'full wages' will support a one-person household (p.108). Siltanen's analysis of the 1987 New Earnings Survey shows that a disappointingly high proportion, 50 per cent, of women in *full-time* employment earned 'component wages' (78 per cent for manual workers). In contrast,

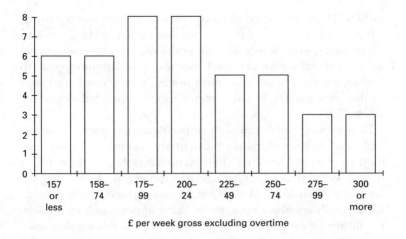

Figure 5.2   *Pay range: fully-employed respondents (March 1990)*

21 per cent of men in full time employment earned 'component wages' (dropping to 15 per cent when overtime is taken into account[8]). When overtime is included, 40 per cent of male full-time workers earn 'full wages' which will support a family, as compared with only 12 per cent of women (p.113). The social consequences of this are staggering. As full-time workers are likely to earn more than part-time workers, this means that only a small proportion of employed women are earning wages that provide the capacity to live independently. A relatively high proportion of male workers earn breadwinning wages, while the majority of women remain dependent on a male partner or the state for their standard of living.

This way of thinking about the social capacity of wages is very illuminating. It is now worth considering respondents' earnings in relation to their ability to provide financial self-sufficiency. Figure 5:2 shows that, although few respondents were earning exceptionally high wages, few were earning exceptionally low wages. This appears to reflect respondents' need to earn wages that would provide a measure of economic independence. In 1989/90, a 'full' wage for a single adult was £157 and over (Siltanen, 1991). Figure 5.2 shows that the vast majority of fully-employed respondents (86 per cent) achieved 'full' single adult wages, with only six (14 per cent) earning 'component' wages. Half of those receiving 'component' wages were within £10 of the threshold and the lowest paid worker in my sample still lived with her parents; she earned £116 a week in a temporary, manual job. Most respondents on component wages were on trainee or entry level salaries. The sample appear to fare a great deal better than most women workers and are closer to the men insofar as their wages usually provided economic self-sufficiency.

In summary, then, although respondents did not achieve the high-level salaries of male – particularly non-manual – workers, they were closer to men than women insofar as their wages usually crossed the living wage pay threshold. As we will see later, the need to be able to earn a wage which would provide a marginally adequate standard of living appears to be a motivating influence on respondents' approaches towards employment.

The occupational locations of the sample

Table 5.1 suggests a highly segregated English labour market, with women and men employed within different occupational groups. The first column of Table 5.1 shows that male workers are spread across occupational groups. By contrast, we can see in the second column that over half of the English full-time female workforce (62 per cent) is concentrated into two occupational groups: 'clerical and related' (44 per cent) and 'professional and related in education, welfare and health' (18 per cent). If we look at the right-hand column and compare my sample with employed women more generally, we can see both similarities and differences.

Respondents were well represented within the occupational groups 'professional and related in education, welfare and health' (33 per cent) and relatively well in 'clerical and related' (15 per cent). Few were in 'selling' (2 per cent) and a disproportionate number were in managerial and science occupations. Their representation in 'managerial' (15 per cent) – usually low-level management – 'professional and related supporting management and administration' (11 per cent) and 'professional and related in science' (11 per cent) was not only proportionately higher than women nationally, but higher than even the male workers.

The pattern which emerges from this comparative analysis suggests that respondents tend to be located in higher-level and/or male-dominated occupations, rather than simply 'gender-appropriate' occupations.

Table 5.1 *Comparison of sample with occupations of full-time workers in England by gender (OPCS classification)*

Occupation [1]	Employed males %	Employed females %	Sample %	n
I Professional and related supporting management and administration	10	6	11	6
II Professional and related in education, welfare and health	5	18	33	18
III Literary, artistic, sports	1	1	4	2
IV Professional and related in science, engineering, technology and similar fields	9	2	11	6
V Managerial	8	4	15	8
VI Clerical and related	10	44	15	8
VII Selling	5	6	2	1
VIII Security and protective service	3	1	0	0
IX Catering, cleaning, hairdressing and other personal service	4	8	6	3
X Farming, fishing and related	2	0	0	0
XI Processing, making, repairing and related	3	0	0	0
XII Processing, making and repairing and related (metal and electrical)	21	4	0	0
XIII Painting, repetitive assembling, product inspection, packing and related	4	5	0	0
XIV Construction and mining	3	0	0	0
XV Transport operating, materials moving and storing and related	10	1	4	2
XVI Miscellaneous, inadequately described	2	0	0	0
Total	100	100	101[2]	54

[1] Includes occupations of one part-time respondent, four training to enter specific areas, and main occupation of two respondents with two part-time jobs each and of three respondents who retired early.
[2] Rounding error.

Source: *New Earnings Survey* (1990, Part D).

Table 5.2   *Regional full-time workforce by gender, occupation and pay*

| Occupational group | Employed males | | Employed females | |
	%	Mean pay £	%	Mean pay £
I Professional and related supporting management and administration	8	392	4	n/a
II Professional and related in education, welfare and health	5	324	18	252
III Literary, artistic, sports	1	n/a	1	n/a
IV Professional and related in science, engineering, technology and similar fields	9	338	2	n/a
V Managerial	7	342	3	n/a
VI Clerical and related	10	234	44	169
VII Selling	5	241	7	139
VIII Security and protective service	2	n/a	0	n/a
IX Catering, cleaning, hairdressing and other personal service	3	193	8	128
X Farming, fishing and related	5	186	—	—
XI Materials processing, making, repairing and related	9	2	5	n/a
XII Processing, making and repairing and related (metal and, electrical)	15	268	1	n/a
XIII Painting, repetitive assembling, product inspection, packing and related	5	236	7	144
XIV Construction and mining	3	n/a	—	—
XV Transport operating, materials moving/storing and related	11	242	1	n/a
XVI Miscellaneous, inadequately described	1	n/a	—	—

Source: *New Earnings Survey* (1990, Part E: Analyses by Region) April.

The regional and local labour markets

In Table 5.2 we can see that the regional workforce distribution across occupations roughly mirrors national trends. Full-time women workers are similarly concentrated into two occupational groups, 'clerical and related' (44.2 per cent) and 'professional and related in education, welfare and health' (17.73 per cent). A slightly smaller proportion of the female workforce is employed in 'selling' and 'catering, cleaning, hairdressing and other personal service' than is the national trend.

If we look at women and men's pay in the region, we can see the impact of both horizontal and vertical segregation on pay differentials between women and men. Women's representation in three of the four highest paying occupational groups (that is, groups I, IV and V) was so low that their mean pay was not calculated in the New Earnings Survey. Furthermore, major discrepancies between the pay of women and men are evident for those in the same occupational groups (for example, groups II, VI, and VII), thus attesting to gender segregation within these groups and its impact on women's earnings.

It is worth considering respondents' occupational locations by industry in the context of the local labour market, as it differs in many ways from both national and regional patterns. For example, the sample's underrepresentation in manual occupations in manufacturing industries may be partially explained by the characteristics of the local labour market, where the manufacturing sector is in decline (see Table 5.3). The district where most respondents lived has the lowest percentage of manual occupations advertised in the country ('Whiteabbey' City Research Group, 1990).[9]

Table 5.3 shows that the sample's high representation in scientific and technological industries again reflects the characteristics of the local labour market, which is heavily biased towards 'professional and scientific services'. High technology industries employed 17 per cent of the local workforce in 1988 ('Whiteabbey' District Council, 1988). Unfortunately, there are no available local statistics which are broken down by gender. However, if we look again at Table 5.2 we can see that women in the region make up a similar proportion of the occupational group 'professional and related in science, engineering and technology' as compared with women nationally and they are not as well represented in managerial occupations. This would suggest that, although the local labour market offers a diverse range of higher level occupational opportunity, the advantage this affords has more generally been experienced by male employees. From the accounts of my respondents, it was clear that many of them were drawn to this particular district precisely because of these opportunities.

Table 5.3   *Comparison of employment by industry: sample, local labour market and Britain*

Employment by industry	Sample	Local labour market	National average
	%	%	%
Professional and scientific services	38	33	17
Primary (including agriculture)	4	2	3
Manufacturing	6	20	29
Construction	—	6	5
Other services	53	39	46

Source: 'Whiteabbey' District Council (1988).

Women's work, men's work

One of the most stable features of the British labour market is its segregated nature (Blackburn *et al.*, 1993). The persistence of the concentration of women and men into different occupations is one of the major reasons for equal pay legislation failing to equalize their pay. While gender segregation in itself does not have to imply gender inequality in earnings, the fact that women tend to dominate 'secondary sector' occupations and men 'primary sector' ones does.[10] We have already seen some interesting patterns regarding the occupational location of my respondents in relation to female and male workers more generally. We will now explore this further.

When people are asked whether their jobs are usually performed by women or men their perceptions support this view of a highly gender-segregated workforce. Among my respondents, 18 (33 per cent) said their job was usually performed by a woman, 20 (37 per cent) said it was performed by either a woman or man equally, and 16 (30 per cent) said it was usually performed by a man. These perceptions of the gender mix of their jobs appear to differ significantly from the perceptions of full-time employed women more generally. I compared these findings with women full-time workers in the British Household Panel Survey. Here 65 per cent described their jobs as mainly performed by women, 27 per cent as performed by either a woman or a man, and only 8 per cent as usually performed by men. When women in female-dominated occupations are asked to give reasons for the gender exclusivity of their jobs, they often suggest that the pay is too poor to attract a man (Witherspoon, 1988:178). Women who describe their jobs as usually performed by men are usually in 'primary sector' occupations (Burchell and Rubery, 1991:21). Measuring the gender composition of a particular occupation poses certain difficulties. Using individual workers' perceptions has both advantages and disadvantages. One problem is related to the way an individual interprets the question 'Would you say that the job that you are doing would normally be filled by a man or a woman?' The reply may be informed by the immediate employment context. For example, a sociologist in a Women's Studies department of a university may consider her occupation 'female' because in her experience it is more usually performed by women. However, if she answers the question on the basis of being a 'sociologist' she may describe her occupation as 'male'. Both assessments may be correct, with each version reflecting different dimensions of her experience in the occupation. Another example would be the case of a young female doctor. She may describe her occupation as 'either sex' because at medical school women now comprise half of the student intake (Watkins, 1987:234). She may also perceive it as a 'male' occupation because it is on the whole dominated by men, and highly segregated by race and gender (Watkins, 1987).

Another problem is that assessments of the gender composition of an occupation should also take into account the proportion of women and men in the labour force. For as long as women comprise a smaller proportion of the workforce than men it is statistically impossible for them to make up half of the workers in all occupations (Hughes, 1990:59). If, for example, a secondary school teacher describes her job as an 'either sex' occupation, she is in one sense correct because, according to the New Earnings Survey for 1991, women make up 50.62 per cent of full-time secondary schoolteachers. However, as full-time female employees make up only 35 per cent of the workforce, their 50.62 per cent representation in secondary teaching reflects an overrepresentation. Consequently, a teacher is in a 'female' occupation while her experience in the staff room, filled equally by women and men, may contradict this description. Again, both descriptions are valid, with each describing a different social reality.

Another way of seeing how far my respondents have devi-
ated from gender norms in terms of their occupational choices
is to work out the gender composition of their occupations
using Census data. From this information it is apparent that
respondents were likely to have underestimated the extent of
men's representation in their occupation. These data suggested
that the occupations of 27 respondents were male-dominated,
while only 16 had perceived this to be the case. It is perhaps
useful to think of occupations as lying on a continuum in terms
of their gender composition, with, for example; nursing (92
per cent female) lying at one extreme, clerical administrators
(49.84 per cent female) equally male or female numerically
but actually 'female',[11] entertainment managers (41 per cent
female) lying slightly on the 'female' side of the proportional
cut-off point of 39 per cent and civil engineering (1 per cent
female) lying at the other extreme. Consequently, there are
degrees of gender concentration in occupations, although it is
unusual to find occupations which have similar numbers of
women and men; most are heavily dominated one way or the
other. Of those 27 respondents in male occupations, 18 were
in very male-dominated occupations where women comprised
20 per cent or less. For the rest who were in 'female' occupations, only six were in occupations which were over 70 per
cent female. A large number, nine, lay between the cut-off points
of 39 per cent female and 50 per cent female, and these women
usually experienced their occupations as 'either sex'.

Just as indicators based on an individual's perceptions of the
gender composition of her job are problematic in terms of
'accuracy', so too are those based upon current British published occupational statistics. Although these statistics present
an important overview of an occupation, and allow us to measure
changes in gender segregation over time, they do not necessarily represent an individual's experience at the level of her
working environment. Furthermore, there is often not enough
distinction made within occupations, which may obscure the
extent to which women and men are doing different tasks – or
are defined as doing so. In other words, information on the
gender composition of occupations is not necessarily designed
to measure vertical segregation within an occupation. In the
case of my respondents, their perceptions of the gender composition of their occupations were sometimes informed by the
knowledge that they had achieved levels within their occupations

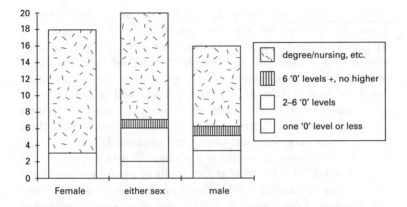

Figure 5.3 *Respondents' qualification levels by perceived gender composition of their jobs*

which were less commonly reached by women. Given that neither indicator is completely satisfactory, my data will be discussed on the basis of respondents' perceptions of the gender composition of their occupations. Where there are major contradictions between their perceptions and the statistical data, these will be pointed out.

Eighteen respondents perceived their occupations as 'female'. Slightly under half (*n* = 8) were from service class backgrounds, five of whom held higher qualifications. All but four occupations conformed statistically to the description 'female'. In the case of the male-dominated occupations which had been considered 'female', these had been reported as such on the basis of the employment *context* (for example, most of these respondents were working within 'Women's Movement' organizations). If we look at the qualification levels of women in 'female' occupations (see Figure 5.3) we can see a dichotomy: women either had higher qualifications (*n* = 15) or they had very few (*n* = 3). As we will see later, it was unusual to find respondents in traditional low-paid women's work.

Twenty respondents described their occupations as 'either sex'. On the basis of statistical information, seven of these occupations were actually male-dominated and 13 fell within the category 'female'. However, in terms of their immediate working environment, their perceptions may be fairly accurate. Nine were in occupations or at occupational levels where women comprise between 39 per cent and 50 per cent of employees. It may be important to make a distinction between 'female'-dominated occupations and the few 'female' occupations which are made up of similar numbers of women and men. High levels of men in 'female' occupations may well influence levels of reward and the status attached to a particular occupation (Crompton and Sanderson, 1990:35). Those who described their occupations as 'either sex' when they were actually male-dominated occupations were young women in junior positions who experienced a fairly equal representation of women and men at their occupational level, or within their professional training courses. These women worked alongside women and men at similar occupational levels and this employment or educational context informed their perceptions of the gender ratio of their jobs. It was interesting that three of these respondents were young women in science specialities where men comprised 80 per cent of the profession. They told me that their perceptions were based on the numbers of women and men who worked at their level in their laboratories. They all worked with female bosses.

If we look again at Figure 5.3, we can see that women in 'either sex' occupations held a broader range of qualifications than those in 'female' occupations. Thirteen (65 per cent) held higher qualifications. Most of these women were in science, teaching or management. Of those seven respondents without higher qualifications, five were in occupations where men numerically outnumbered women. It is interesting to note that two had taken exams which enabled them to rise from low-level female-dominated clerical occupations to higher level administrative positions where there were numerically more male workers.[12] A third woman had risen to a management position from an initial starting-point in female-dominated manual employment.

The statistics supported the perceptions of all 16 respondents who described their jobs as 'male'. Over half of these women ($n = 9$) were from intermediate or manual backgrounds. Fourteen (88 per cent) were in very male-dominated occupations, where women made up less than 20 per cent of the occupation. In terms of qualification levels, women in this group had the most diversity (see Figure 5.3). Nine (56 per cent) had or were working towards higher qualifications, two of these women held professional qualifications which they gained as they rose through and out of clerical occupations,[13] and another was a 'mature' student working towards a higher vocational technical qualification. However, five respondents in this group (31 per cent) held low levels of academic qualifications; all were from intermediate or manual backgrounds. Four of these women had entered male-dominated occupations on leaving school and had experienced job-related training. The fifth respondent began her working life in a 'female'-dominated occupation and was now the proprietor of several small businesses.

Factors shaping occupational 'choice'

It is not at all surprising to find this pattern of moving out of, or avoiding, traditional low-paid 'women's' work amongst the sample. It seems that, for those who had left school with low levels of educational qualifications, this had been a wise decision in terms of pay. The mean weekly earnings of the three respondents in 'female' occupations, who had left school with one 'O' level or less, were only £155; for the two in 'either-sex' occupations it was £246; and for the five in 'male' occupations it was £182.

Two important factors have already been identified as influential in shaping the non-conventional occupational 'choices' made by respondents on leaving school. First, their fathers had often been active in encouraging and supporting many of these respondents in the development of non-traditional skills and interests and, as we will see later, in helping them find jobs. Second, for respondents with lower levels of educational power, the connection between the avoidance of traditional women's work and their questioning of their sexuality has been explored earlier; however, it is worth briefly mentioning again. In Chapter 3, we have seen a tendency for women who had been questioning the desirability of marriage and heterosexuality during adolescence and were not educationally advantaged to favour occupations which offered the possibility of a career. For most of these women, male-dominated manual occupations appealed because they were seen to provide an opportunity to develop craft skills in the context of a career. They had understood that if they followed the conventional route into traditional women's work this would not provide the long-term financial independence they desired. Almost all of the unmarried re-

spondents from manual backgrounds, who had consciously
questioned their sexuality during adolescence and had not
experienced social mobility through education, chose to enter
male-dominated occupations. The importance of the evaluation of heterosexuality during adolescence, for less privileged
and educationally advantaged women, cannot be overempha-
sized. These women had a head-start in developing careers that
would offer economic independence.

Time is a crucial dimension to this study. These unusual occupational patterns that have been described have also to be
understood as the result of changes over time, which were often
related to respondents' interpretations of their sexuality. The
questioning of heterosexuality led respondents who had expected to marry to re-evaluate their more short-term occupational goals. On the basis of the knowledge that they would
have to be financially self-reliant, these women usually moved
out of low-paid women's work into 'either sex' occupations or
male-dominated occupations. Of course, not all of the respondents were able to accomplish this. It is perhaps worth mentioning that two of the three respondents with low levels of
qualifications who have remained in women's work had earlier
anticipated marriage; one did marry and is now divorced. The
third woman has remained in her particular occupation because illness had prevented her from taking up job opportunities.

Another aspect of time which shaped respondents' occupational 'choices' is historical period. It is interesting to look at
the ages of women in different professions. Of the eight respondents who qualified in the female-dominated health or
education professions, the median age was 45 and only one
woman was aged under 30. By contrast, of the 11 respondents
in statistically male-dominated professions such as medicine,
science and technology, and accountancy, only two were aged
over 30, and the median age of women in these professions
was strikingly low, at 26. This appears to reflect the recent
broadening of occupational choices available to women with
educational credentials. This finding supports Crompton and
Sanderson's (1990:127–30) view that throughout the 1980s there
had been a growing minority of well qualified women who gained
much from feminist campaigns to increase women's representation in male-dominated professions. The commentaries of the
older professional women in my sample often reveal structural
and ideological constraints on their employment choices. Many

of these women remarked on the limitations that shaped these choices, insofar as they confined their decisions to a narrow range of professions. Teaching and nursing were perceived as the taken for granted professions available to women.[14] Furthermore, older respondents' occupational choices were often constrained by curriculum limitations at school. Several respondents, who had experienced secondary modern education, complained that they had had no opportunity to study 'male' craft subjects.

We now move on to explore respondents' experiences of, and attitudes towards, employment, and begin by focusing on those who perceived their occupations as 'male' and those who perceived them as 'female'.

SUCCEEDING IN A MALE WORLD

Sixteen respondents were located in occupations, or positions in an occupational hierarchy, which they described as being usually occupied by men. On the whole, women in this group appeared to have been the most active in the sample, in terms of developing and improving their job prospects. Three respondents were located in 'male' manual occupations and a further four had moved up through 'male' manual work to low-level management positions. For another three respondents in this group, it was the achievement of senior positions in an occupational hierarchy which gave rise to the label 'male'. For half of the six respondents in, or training to enter, 'male' professions this represented a career change: one was a mature student in professional training following a career in a 'male' craft occupation, and two others had begun their working lives in female-dominated occupations.

Respondents' experience in male-dominated manual occupations

On examination of the sample's work histories, at least 15 had some experience of male-dominated manual work. These were unconventional women because they had expanded their occupational choices to include working-class jobs which their fathers and brothers, rather than their mothers and sisters, might have considered. Within these occupations, respondents' movement up the hierarchies was often slow and plagued by difficulties, but most found the experience rewarding, both intrinsically and extrinsically. The Armed Forces were viewed by some respondents as a useful entry point to traditional male occupations.

The Armed Forces

In all, five respondents, including two Black women, entered the Armed Forces, while many others spoke of having had the desire to do so. The Armed Forces provided four respondents with the opportunity to develop 'male' technical and/or craft skills, and a fifth to gain a nursing qualification. They were particularly appealing to women from less privileged social backgrounds, who did not have the opportunity to stay on at school to study 'A' levels. Given the limited job opportunities they felt were available to them, entering the Forces clearly represented a career with prospects for advancement and job security. Furthermore, it was seen to offer a chance to travel and an opportunity to keep up their sporting interests. Thelma explains her reasons for entering the Forces. She has spent most of her working life in male-dominated occupations, using the skills that she had developed while in the Forces:

> [*Were there any other aspects that appealed about going into the Forces?*] The security, the availability of travel, also the different types of sports that you could do. I would never have been able to have afforded to learn [these sports] ... The girls were doing the same sports as the boys ... I could do everything that a man could do. [*Why did you go for driving in the Forces?*] To be able to learn the mechanics of a car. I would have liked to have been a fully fledged mechanic, but they didn't actually have mechanics in the [Women's Corps]. Doing this I was affiliated to the Mechanics Corps and could go and learn from the boys, and I learnt as much as the mechanics did. I had the ability, when I came out, to maintain my own car. (43*I*)

As with women interviewed in Faderman's (1992:150) detailed history of twentieth-century lesbian life in America, the military appealed to respondents for a range of important reasons. These respondents tended to be fairly ambitious and achievement-oriented and they all wanted to learn a trade. Further, most wished to develop more technical and mechanical skills, and the Forces were perceived as being a more 'equal opportunities' environment where occupational gender boundaries were more blurred. They could perform jobs that were physically demanding, which were freer from the constraints of physical confinement that they associated with clerical and factory work. Verity expresses these sentiments:

> I don't want to be a typist, that's the last thing, that's another reason why I joined the Forces. I didn't want to go into an office, I didn't want to be a clerk, secretary etc . . . I wanted to be out and about, I wanted to do something different, I didn't want to do what the girls did. I am not saying I wanted to do what the boys wanted, or did . . . The driving suited me down to the ground: I was outside, I was learning something, I was doing something different, I wasn't doing what all the girls used to do, and I excelled in it . . . The Forces, they do try their best to make you one of the team; you have the same rank as the blokes. If you have a bloke soldier to give him orders, you have to give him orders whether you are female or male, and I take orders from males or females, and they have to accept what a woman tells them. (29*M*)

Respondents who were keen on entering the Forces had usually been questioning their sexuality. They saw the Forces as providing an environment where they might come into contact with lesbians and clarify the possibilities. All the respondents who had been in the Forces spoke of the existence of tightly knit lesbian networks. In some cases exposure to this community raised questions in the minds of respondents regarding their own sexuality; lesbianism could be seen as a feasible option. Furthermore, this community was always reported as being highly achievement-oriented and career minded. Wendy is typical of the rest in her description of her lesbian colleagues' approaches to their jobs:

> The gay girls were certainly the stronger . . . and wanted to get on more than the straights . . . Not physical strength, it's as people, they were always the harder workers. Why they were doing it or what they were doing it for I don't know, but certainly . . . the girls that had the boyfriends didn't want to work the longer hours anyway, because they wanted to meet their boyfriends at night. Whereas the gay girls – I wouldn't say they didn't want to meet their women – put their work first somehow. There was no extra money, you

got paid the same as someone that didn't want to do it. I just used to love the job, so I didn't mind how many hours I did anyway. (34*M*)

The tendency to put career first seemed to affect their approaches to relationships. As marriage was never an option for them, frequent postings meant that long-term relationships were hard to maintain. Consequently, relationships were described as being entered on the understanding that they would probably be short-lived.

Lesbians, however, appear to hold a very ambiguous position in the Forces. One respondent remarked that the Women's Corps would probably be unable to function without the competent input of the lesbians, yet the level of official homophobia was particularly high.[15] Purges were commonplace and respondents lived under the continual threat of exposure. Ali originally intended joining the Military Police. However, her experience of their behaviour towards lesbians made her reconsider:

> When I got in and saw how the military operated I thought no way [am I going to join the Military Police]. They were just a bunch of animals. I couldn't relate to that; the women were as bad as the men. They would have your bunk ripped apart, the mattresses off, looking for letters ... Because being gay is illegal in the Army and they used to have these purges ... What would happen is, the young girls coming in would get frightened of what was going on [high level of lesbian visibility] and freak, and would hand in a list of names to whoever, to the CO even, and they would have to act on it, and there would be this purge, and all the names on the list were investigated. The young girls coming in were very dangerous one way or another, which is why I kept really low key about things. (35*M*)

One respondent fell victim of a purge and was discharged. This had serious repercussions as she lost her opportunity to train in medicine. Furthermore, the knowledge that the Forces are intolerant of homosexuality deterred some respondents who would have really liked to join up. For these respondents fear of building a career and then being exposed as a lesbian influenced their decision against entry. Moreover, I was unable to interview any serving military women, as those who had been approached were worried about the possibility of being identified.

The four women who developed more 'male' mechanical and technical skills in the Forces utilized them when they re-entered civilian life. One entered higher education to develop her technical skills further, and the others entered driving or motor-trade occupations. Several remarked that they found civilian life, in terms of employment opportunities, far more gender-segregated than was their experience in the Forces. They also commented on the difficulty in reaching the relatively high levels of pay and perks which they had experienced in the Forces.

Making a career in male-dominated manual occupations

Three respondents were currently employed in traditionally 'male' manual occupations at the point of interview. A further four had moved up from male-dominated manual occupations to low-level management. All these seven women were from intermediate or manual backgrounds. Interestingly, these women tended to be older: their median age was 36, and two women were in their forties. In the case of the older women, their earlier unconventional employment choices were very much perceived as being made in the context of an extreme polarity between women's and men's work. For them, women's work offered little in the way of job security, pay or prospects; in contrast, men's work represented the possibility of developing skills and establishing a career.

Occupations which involved driving were popular with many of the 15 respondents who had had some experience of male manual occupations. They enjoyed being able to wear more comfortable clothes. Those who had experienced more traditionally female jobs often spoke of having been uncomfortable with the more feminine dress code to which they had had to adhere, and they had found this physically constricting. Some had previously been in factory and shop work, which they found highly regimented; they spoke of disliking the constant surveillance of supervisors and of having to clock in and clock out. In contrast, driving occupations represented greater freedom and the ability to exercise greater control. They enjoyed being able to organize their daily work routines, setting their own pace, and being out and about. Tamsin explains why she chose to enter a job in transport. She enjoys this work, although she

sometimes has to put up with the sexist attitudes of male co-
workers:

> It's been a very successful move for me. There are other
> women that do driving and they have a very good work
> record . . . The customers we deal with always ask for us back.
> [*How have you found the job as a woman?*] It's quite interesting;
> you get these blokes: 'here you go, we have a woman trying
> to do a man's job', that sort of attitude thrown at you. That's
> not what I am trying to do. I'm trying to earn a decent wage,
> that's all. I don't want to be a secretary, so I want to be a
> driver instead . . . They [men] do find it quite a novelty really,
> especially [with me being] in the big trucks, because they
> do find that quite hard. (29*M*)

Others found the sexist hostility from male co-workers more
enduring. Their experience highlights the important role played
by sexist male workplace culture in 'policing' the boundaries
of traditionally male occupations.[16] In the case of some respondents, their interest in particular occupations was dampened
by the sexism and homophobia that prevailed. Consequently,
they were propelled out of jobs that they found challenging
into jobs where the working environment was more pleasant.
This was the case for Christine who went to work backstage in
a theatre in the Midlands. She was involved in carpentry and
painting. Although she loved the actual job, she found having
to defend herself from the sexist attitudes of her male co-workers
too great a strain. She left the job after a year and is now self-
employed:

> I found it very hard going because of the sexism involved. It
> was very sexist, and I thought all theatres would be like that.
> It was also very homophobic. It's a total double standard, a
> lot of homosexuality in the theatre, but the sort of butch
> attitude with the people who shifted the scenery was quite
> horrible . . . I enjoyed the work, but I left there because I
> really got so spooked out by the pressure of having to always
> defend yourself while they took the piss out of women. You
> would get things you couldn't believe – it was 1983 or 1984.
> If I and another girl would lift something, he would say: 'I'll
> let you two lift that, you women's libbers, you go out and
> burn your bras', and I thought Jesus Christ what century are
> you coming from! It was a phobia about women getting into

areas that men have traditionally been able to call their own
– not that we were wielding pick axes or anything. We were
just lifting a piece of scenery. (32)

Many of the respondents in male-dominated areas of employment found that male co-workers were initially hostile to new
female co-workers. However, those respondents who have
remained in such occupations found that, once they had proved
themselves competent, they seemed to have good working
relationships with their colleagues.

Respondents who have made long-term careers in male manual
occupations usually worked themselves up to low-level management. Typically, they started their careers in driving or garage
work. However, initial entry into male occupations had been
fairly difficult for respondents as school leavers. Lenora talks
of the sexist attitudes of an employer in her first job interview
after leaving school. She had seen an advertisement for an
apprenticeship with a sign-writing company and thought it would
be a good craft to learn:

> They advertised for an apprentice. I got an interview – don't
> know why they bothered to interview me – and then got told,
> 'We're looking for a lad.' They had no intention of employing
> me. I told them I wasn't going to rush off and marry – I
> couldn't say, 'Look pal, I'm queer!' What can you say? (38)

Very unequal treatment in gaining access to training in male
craft skills was common for respondents now in their late thirties
and forties. They saw themselves as early pioneers in their chosen
occupations. Three were semi-skilled mechanics, none had
trained formally on apprenticeship schemes. They learnt their
skills on the job, picking up information from their male
colleagues. Lenora explains how she eventually learnt her trade,
after working in a garage as a petrol pump attendant:

> I got well fed up there, fed up with getting soaked. Then a
> space came up as an apprentice mechanic . . . We talked about
> it at work, and they said, 'Why don't you do that?' I said,
> 'I'd love to, nobody is ever going to give me the chance of
> doing it, however.' The guy went to see the boss to see what
> he could do, had a few words and the next thing I was in
> overalls and doing it. They knew I was mechanically minded,
> had a car and was always taking it to bits, so they knew I was
> keen. So in I went. I never went to Tech, or any apprenticeship.

I just learnt from the others. I was there for a few years and picked up most of it. (38)

For several respondents, entry into male occupations was facilitated by fathers. Carol's father helped establish her in a career in mechanical parts:

I followed in my father's footsteps [into the motor trade] – selling parts, everything to do with looking after parts, selling them, ordering them. [*Is that the sort of job that you find a lot of women in?*] Not within the garage trade. It helped that my father had been in the trade for so many years and knew a lot of people. He was able to say that I'd worked with him in the garage, which I'd done at the weekends. People were surprised to find that a girl could understand what part of the car they wanted. (43)

However, achieving equal pay proved much more difficult for her:

[The job isn't well paid] until you start getting up through the ranks. It took me about ten years to rise up and command a decent wage, but then that wasn't the same as the men were getting. [*But if you were doing the same job, how could they pay you less?*] I don't know, but they did, and what do you do? Do you lose a job that you fought and hammered and screamed for for years? [My job was advertised in the paper]. It was advertised as a certain amount [of pay] possible. I never attained that possible, and I queried it one day. He said, 'It's because you are inexperienced in the job and we were actually looking for somebody with more experience.' So I said, 'I have had ten years of experience, how experienced have you got to be!'

Promotion was also illusive for Carol. Years of experience meant little when the necessary qualifications for advancement appeared to be based on gender:

I actually changed jobs and became assistant parts manager in another garage to be able to get to being paid the same as a bloke, and then in the same garage they side-stepped me for promotion, which left me still assistant manager, working under somebody who had been my stores supervisor; he had jumped over me. I kicked up a hell of a stink about this and I had the usual things thrown at me – 'A woman doesn't do this job' – and I had been in the trade for nearly

18 years ... I had taken every single course they had thrown at me, and I had passed. Every time I went away on these courses I was the only girl there. In accountancy I got a distinction, which pissed off a lot of the men.

She left this company and finally achieved a management position elsewhere:

I was employed to do the job from I don't know how many applicants. Because I had been in the trade for so many years they thought I was the best person ... it was the first time in my life that men had actually acknowledged the fact that I knew more about the subject than they did, and deferred to me, and that was a very enjoyable and peaceful time of my life. It was still male-oriented, but that never worried me working with men ... I wasn't looking to go anywhere then. I got fed up with fighting this bloody male world, just wanted a job that would earn me x amount.

She has recently changed occupations, and is now working in a lesbian and gay organization.

Fighting against this kind of discrimination was common amongst respondents in male-dominated occupations. Jackie talks of the problem of being taken seriously by employers. She had been delivering parts for a company. She had an interest in mechanics, was ambitious and wanted to move into a better paid, more demanding job. She spent any free time at work with the parts store-man learning the trade. A chance came up to join the sales team:

[I] ended up mainly in the stores, because I knew a bit about cars and parts; ... knew more than the store-man did ... There again I came up against the male bit. We had about five reps on the road, selling the parts. If one was off sick or on holiday I got his job to go and do his round, and I was as good as he was on that ... I said to the manager, thinking on promotion lines, 'If one of the reps leaves, do I get a chance of his job if I work hard and prove I can do it?' They said, 'No, no chance! It's always men that are reps.' I thought, no, I am not going to be a toe rag just because I am female. (39)

Jackie left this company, she later achieved a management position in transport, and eventually did well enough to set up her own business.

Like Jackie, respondents usually persevered until they were taken seriously by their bosses. Jessy managed to move up from 'male' manual work to a management position in a garage:

It was very difficult to get into the actual management position. [My company] was a very old fashioned firm and there weren't any women in management positions. The manager went on holiday and I used to cover for him... No one [else] wanted to cover; no one wanted to know about [it]. It was a very difficult [area of work] to get into. It's a hell of a responsibility. They said no, so someone said 'What about [Jessy]' and they said 'She's a woman!' They said it really wouldn't hurt covering, and I covered. I got quite good at it and I did enjoy it. (34)

It was not until she became frustrated with her manual job, and decided to leave, that she was seriously considered for promotion. Her employers were unwilling to let her go, she refused to stay unless she was given a permanent management position and finally they agreed to give her the job. She has been on several management courses. However, the job pays a 'component wage'; although she has enjoyed it, she is at present considering finding a new challenge, offering better pay.

Promotion for these women came as the result of this actively putting themselves forward. They had not been considered 'natural' promotion candidates by their bosses, and attention had to be drawn to their merits. It seemed that they often had the support and encouragement of male co-workers who had perhaps a greater awareness of their individual competencies. Despite gaining respect from co-workers, these respondents were often victims of public perceptions and stereotypes of the capabilities of women. Some spoke of their feelings of frustration in dealing with the general public. Customers would assume that a woman would know nothing about mechanics and seek advice from inexperienced youths. However, this was not always the case: some found being a woman in a male-dominated occupation, such as sales 'repping' in the motor trade, a distinct advantage. In this case, respondents experienced their novelty value as beneficial. In the competition to gain access to clients, potential customers were reported as being more likely to make an appointment with a woman because of the novelty of the situation.

Respondents in male occupations tended to enjoy their work.

It provided variety and challenge. They also recognized that they had to be very good at their jobs to earn the respect of the men that they worked with. They knew that, if they made mistakes, this would be understood in gender terms by their male co-workers. Consequently, they were very aware of the need to work doubly hard to earn the respect of male colleagues. As one respondent put it, 'You have to be twice as good as the men.' Acceptance by male co-workers and becoming 'honorary men' did, however, lead to some respondents developing a more 'masculine' value system. These respondents reported being intolerant of inexperienced female co-workers when they felt these women were incompetent. As women were a small minority in their occupations, the mistakes made by female co-workers were seen as 'letting the side down'. Several respondents saw this as undermining their attempts to break down their male colleagues' gender stereotypes.

Respondents in management had to develop skills for handling male workers who were generally unaccustomed to having a female boss. Irene describes her approach to managing male workers:

> There aren't many women in charge of [transport departments]; it's usually a man's job, not that a woman can't do it . . . I get on very well with every department and I am very tolerant. I suppose I could be accused of being quite soft, but I am not very aggressive. I know I can be aggressive towards people, but the men I am in charge of, I tend to make them feel they are doing me a favour. I ask them to do things, I don't tell them to do things, and they do it. I have seen other women, especially at work, tell men to do things and they won't do it, because a woman's told them to do it. So I get on quite well from that point of view. If there is any work to be done, I just join in; if we are short-staffed I'll go out and pack boxes . . . I will move things about with them . . . I don't sit back and think, 'That's not my job, you do it.' I am accused of being soft, but the six men that work for me are not particularly bright; if they were they wouldn't be packing boxes all day long – I don't mean that disrespectfully . . . so you have to treat them different . . . I find it hard sometimes having to discipline people, especially people that have been there 25 years. (25)

She explains what appeals to her about her job and why she thinks so few women are interested in this line of work:

It's very physical, a lot of physical activity, moving things about, and I don't suppose a lot of women want to bother with carrying boxes about and shifting things about; it doesn't seem a very feminine thing to do, I suppose. I don't lift boxes all day long, but I do it. A lot of women . . . in our company think it's the worst job in the world . . . they wouldn't want to manhandle six men who are very awkward and very petty and childish sometimes, and they wouldn't want to get their hands dirty. It doesn't bother me. I am not saying I love being up to my armpits in dirt, but it doesn't bother me . . . I find it quite interesting; there are so many different things that go on and I don't want to be tied to a typewriter all day, or tied to a phone. 'Cos I've done that, been tied to a phone, I'd find it interesting for a while but that's not for me any more.

Irene, like so many of the sample, had experienced office work as constraining, repetitive and dull. In contrast, she and others experienced the world of 'male' manual work challenging, offering variety and greater physical freedom.

Sexual politics in traditionally 'male' manual occupations

I asked the respondents in male occupations how they coped with sexual innuendo and pornography that would perhaps act as constraints on their physical freedom. Interestingly, these respondents were more likely to be 'out' to co-workers than respondents in traditional female employment and the professions. However, the very fact that these were women determined to make a career in traditionally male occupations often made their sexuality suspect. Hostile attacks upon competent women in male jobs were usually directed at their sexuality. In other words, because they were doing the jobs they were doing, they could not be 'normal' women, they had to be 'queer' or 'dykes'. When they experienced hostility, it was their location in particular jobs that identified them as lesbians, rather than anything else. When the term 'queer' or 'dyke' was used it represented the 'policing' of women into appropriate gender behaviour, rather than description.[17]

Several excellent studies (Williams, 1992; Griffin, 1985; Cockburn, 1988, 1987) have shown links between men and women's occupational 'choices' and the maintenance of 'appropriate' sexual/gender identity. A person may face having their gender/

sexuality called into question if they make non-traditional occupational choices. This can play a role in deterring many women
from entering male-dominated jobs (Cockburn, 1987:
41–2). Most of my respondents in traditionally male manual
occupations, together with some in male-dominated professions,
suggested that, had they been seeking relationships with men,
their jobs would make them singularly unattractive. They felt
that in some ways they would be interpreted as undermining
the male role. By excelling in traditional male areas, they
threatened an important source of male identity. However, the
significance of these factors is often neglected in theories of
occupational segregation.

Few of the respondents who were 'out' experienced serious
difficulties from co-workers because of their sexuality. Some
spoke of having to deal with advances from male co-workers
who were intent on introducing them to the 'joys' of heterosexuality. These women felt that they represented a challenge
to some men. Moreover, respondents' accounts of their experience of the sexual overtures of male workers reveal their
awareness of the links between this kind of sexualized behaviour and male attempts to undermine women's employment
achievements. Ivy, who is in low-level management, describes
the problem she has with a male co-worker:

> There are loads of affairs going on between the women staff
> there and the blokes. There is a bloke on reception has fancied
> me for ages, and I have had a lot of hassle with him . . . it's
> very difficult for me to deal with . . . he came out with it
> quite blatantly once, and asked me if I wanted a fuck, or 'I
> will cure you' . . . He's one of these guys that can't handle
> women being an equal to him . . . Because I am good at what
> I do, he is always trying to get back at me, telling tales. (34)

The women tended to defuse the situation with banter. Sexual
jokes and banter were a usual feature of the male working
environment experienced by these respondents. Some women
reported that part of the process of becoming 'one of the lads'
involved being willing to show a good-natured approach to this
part of workplace culture, and a few even joined in. Sexual
banter and pornography were seen as coming with the territory, and these respondents did not want special treatment.
Joan, a driver, discusses her approach to pornography and the
physical attention of co-workers:

I sometimes jump into a truck, and they have their poster in
the back of a truck. Well, you know, that's what they put up.
Fair enough, it doesn't bother me, I just don't bother looking at it. Not sexual harassment as such; you always get the
chaps that will try and put their arms around you – 'Hello,
love'. Some of them are genuinely being friendly, but if I
particularly don't like them I tell them not to. If I don't
mind, I am not going to say, 'Get off.' As long as it is a
greeting hug, I don't mind. (29)

However, once women reached management levels they acquired
a degree of power which placed them in a better position to
deal with pornography. Josephine discusses how she handles
this situation:

[*Is there a lot of pornography in the workshop?*] No there's not.
At one stage they had a nude calendar in the workshop, and
I remember when we bought a new lorry and the second
day it turned up to work, the driver had this nude calendar.
I went berserk. I said, 'I am sorry, you are going to take that
out of there. I don't like it.' 'What do you mean you don't
like it? Oh, you prude.' I said, 'I am not a prude, it's company image and I do not want our company vehicle going
around with that in it. If you want it in your own home it
doesn't bother me, but I don't want it on display. I don't
want to see it and I don't want our customers to see it.' And
the same thing in the workshop; they used to have
pornographic magazines hanging around and calendars and
that all seems to have dwindled off now. (32)

Some found that being a lesbian was a distinct advantage in a
male environment. They felt that they did not have to deal
with the same amount of sexual advances and harassment as
their female colleagues in clerical and secretarial jobs. They
generally reported feeling very comfortable with their male co-
workers, and interacted with them as friends. They experienced
a sense of freedom from the more overt heterosexual innuendos
and behaviour which commonly extended into the everyday
lives of male and female workers. Some even found that their
bosses took a greater interest in their careers once they were
told about their sexuality. In these cases, the sexist attitudes of
bosses, informed by stereotypical understandings of women and
lesbians, acted in the lesbian worker's favour. Typically, they

saw their lesbian employees as 'serious' workers, unlikely to leave to get married or have children. One respondent in low-level management reported that recently she told her boss that she was a lesbian. She believes that this contributed to his decision to set her up in her own business.

Overall, many of these respondents appeared to have had to pay a heavy price for the rewards they experienced in male-dominated jobs. They had to cope with sexist attitudes of co-workers and bosses. They lived under a constant pressure of having to prove themselves competent. Many did, however, manage to succeed in a male world, earning promotion and respect.

Respondents in 'male' professions

Eight respondents, three of whom were from manual back-grounds, described their professions as 'male'. Two women had gained their professional qualifications as they moved up their occupational hierarchies. Three others had gained or were gaining professional qualifications as mature students. These 'male' professions were in fields related to technology, electronics, engineering and various male preserves in financial management and accountancy. Most of these respondents were in the early stages of their careers; their median age was only 27. However, their median weekly pay of £240 was higher than the pay of those respondents in 'either sex' and 'female' professions.

These respondents saw themselves as performing jobs that few women were doing. They saw many obstacles in their professions that might deter other women from entry. Often their jobs required high levels of geographic mobility. Those who acquired professional qualifications 'on the job' spoke of the importance of being willing to develop careers during the years that other women are often devoting to childcare. Ingrid gained professional qualifications while working her way up from an initial starting point in clerical work. She describes the crucial aspects of timing for career development:

> I think at middle management there are only maybe three women out of about one hundred people all together ... Because of the age people are likely to be at the grade I am at, if they are going to have kids they will probably have them now, because most people will be coming up to 30. There is definitely a bias in the company generally. I couldn't say

anyone specifically, it's more male-oriented; as I believe any financial industry is. It's more a thing a man would do than a woman, from their point, not from my point of view. (26S)

Like most of the respondents in male-dominated occupations more generally, she feels that having confidence in her own abilities had been very important in helping her to get ahead in her area of work, which she felt was strongly biased against women.

Experiencing male bias seemed common. Corrie is in a heavily male-dominated speciality in engineering. Although she had no difficulty finding a good job, she had experienced some very sexist attitudes in interviews:

One interview I got such a bad reaction. Why the guy even interviewed me I don't know. The guy said, 'Well, if you are going to be working on site it's long hours you know, and you have to come to work whatever time of the month.' Various questions like, 'We can't have [someone working for us who] breaks down on site and cried every time they had a problem.' Very strange attitude. By that point I didn't really want a job with them. (24M)

Often these professional women, like the respondents in male manual work, thought of themselves as female pioneers in their chosen occupation. They spoke of the importance of demon-strating competence, as some male colleagues were quick to use gender as an explanation for any mistakes made. Interest-ingly, those in charge of men in manual occupations spoke of finding greater acceptance from older men in trades than from younger labourers.

It also seemed to follow that, the more male-dominated a profession was, the more likely a respondent's sexuality would be called into question. This highlights the gendering process underpinning the meanings attached to jobs (see Cockburn, 1988) and the way that transgressions of normative gender behaviour implicate sexual identity. As with respondents in manual occupations, it was their job location, more than anything else, which suggested that they were not 'feminine' and thus had to be lesbian. The use of such labels as 'queer' or 'dyke' were used as punishment for entering male preserves, rather than description.

As with other respondents located in male-dominated

occupations, Hope believed that it was her competency in male preserves which came to be interpreted by men as a challenge to their authority, and this was seen as detracting from sexual attractiveness to the opposite sex:

> Men do find it difficult; men outside of the trade find it difficult because you are [in engineering], and stuff. They find it very strange, as if you were trying to challenge them in some way. If I was straight, I think it would be very difficult to find a man that could fit into my life (26).

An unsympathetic reader may take the view that lesbians are physically unattractive women, and that difficulties with men are the result of this. This is a stereotyped notion which raises all kinds of interesting questions relating to what actually constitutes sexual attractiveness in the first place. In Hope's case her understanding that sexual unattractiveness is related to challenging men, rather than 'looks', is supported by the fact that her identical twin sister, who works in a female-dominated area of work, has had a steady stream of boyfriends. The relationship between entering male occupational preserves and the risks this poses for women who wish to be sexually attractive to the opposite sex must surely play an important role in deterring many women. This aspect of the way sexuality affects everyday life, shaping women's and men's occupational choices, attests to the significance of interpretations of sexuality in shaping occupational 'choices'.

Despite the problems associated with following unconventional career paths, these respondents enjoyed their jobs and found their work highly challenging. Most of these women were feminists, and many wished to use their skills to promote social well-being and where possible to advance women's interests more generally. It was noticeable that those respondents who had achieved senior 'male' positions in an occupational hierarchy invested a considerable amount of energy in improving the situation for other women. Few could be accused of removing the ladder from beneath them. Silvana, who has worked her way up to a 'male' position in a female-dominated occupation, has enthusiastically encouraged other women to follow her:

> Oh yes, when they say they can't do it I tell them, 'I left school at 14. If I can do it, I am only average, so can you if you want to.' I get a kick out of seeing them succeed. Some

are married with children, and I see that as successful too. They are working with children, and it's important that they have the choice. (35)

Another respondent introduced Equal Opportunities procedures in her organization, and has been instrumental in setting up non-sexist job evaluation schemes. All of these women were strongly committed to their work. Those in the early stages of their career development were also, within certain limitations, very ambitious. We will consider some of the limitations that framed their ambitions later in the chapter when we assess respondents' various perspectives on ambition and ethics.

RESPONDENTS' EXPERIENCE IN 'FEMALE' OCCUPATIONS

At the time of interview, 18 respondents described their occupations as being usually 'female' occupations. These were in a wide range of occupations, and very few were 'dead-end' women's jobs. Six respondents were in relatively high status, professional or managerial jobs; all but one had achieved fairly good salaries, the exception being the trainee manager who was receiving a 'component' wage. They tended to be older women; four were aged over 40.

Apart from the professional and managerial women, this group was not particularly well paid. Their weekly wages ranged from between £120 and £217, and four received 'component' wages. Despite the low-paid nature of their jobs, as we see later, most enjoyed and were highly committed to their work.

Respondents in low paid dead-end women's jobs

Three respondents saw themselves as trapped in their low paid jobs. They were all aged over 40. One earned a 'full' wage, but the other two were earning 'component' wages. One was in an administrative clerical job, another was a low-level health worker who had been plagued by illness for most of her life. The third was a Black woman in a clerical/reception occupation, who had been unable to find higher-level employment. Although she does not see this as a result of discrimination, she did experience several racist interviewers when looking for jobs. Two of these women were amongst the few respondents in the sample to dislike their jobs. They described them as dull and routine, and they felt trapped because of lack of opportunity.

For Gladys, however, her poorly-paid administrative job represented a major step down from a previous job in vocational training. She was very much a victim of circumstances. She had been 'head hunted', and subsequently left a job which she had found challenging and well paid. The new job fell through, and she had to take any available job:

> So now I am [an assistant] which grates, 'cos I hate actually being told what to do, and when somebody says go and fill the kettle and write a letter, do this and do that, I find it very difficult, I must admit. But again it's a job and I need to work to survive, and I am looking for something else . . . I don't think I am looking for anything else to develop my career 'cos I have ten years left before I retire. So I think I want to do something that I will enjoy for the last ten years of my working life. (49)

When I contacted her after the interview she told me that she had managed to find a much better job which she was very enthusiastic about.

The fact that so few respondents were in low paid dead-end women's jobs at the time of interview was very much an active accomplishment, representing a process of change. Again we must remember the time dimension to this study. At least 34 of the sample had some experience in their work histories of low-paid women's work, including factory work, clerical work and shop work. As we have seen in an earlier chapter, it had been entered more usually as a stop-gap until marriage. Respondents' experience of low-paid dead-end women's work was often very negative. Certain female-dominated occupations were often perceived by respondents as requiring emphasis of a particularly narrow definition of femininity which they felt unwilling to conform to. Jill, now working freelance in an arts occupation, discusses earlier experience of 'temping':

> They got me one job as a receptionist and that's where I couldn't handle it, 'cos receptionists are supposed to have finger-nails and dress – and the 'Joan Collins look alike thing'. I could do all the necessary play acting, 'Reception, can I help you?' I thought it was a great laugh. But I just didn't

have the image when it came to 'May I get you a coffee', and all that sort of thing. I just blew it completely [laughter]. It was not my sort of thing. Having had poverty raging, I just didn't have the back-up with clothes and everything and didn't see why I should. So that didn't work and they booted me out. (32)

The links between secretarial/reception work and the requirement to conform to particular forms of heterosexual femininity have been discussed by Griffin (1982) and Pringle (1992). A recent study by Adkins (1995) powerfully illustrates the way that women's sexuality and feminine charms are central to their employment in the British tourist industry. Griffin (1982) and Pringle's (1992) work suggests that sexuality and femininity are core defining features for women employed as secretaries and receptionists, transforming them into 'office wives', 'mistresses' and 'mothers' (Pringle, 1992). In these areas of employment the strong emphasis on 'looking good', wearing fashionable clothes and make-up, and responding 'sensitively' to men's sexual advances is integral to the culture of the workplace. Griffin sees this as an exclusionary practice which discriminates against certain groups of women, such as Black women, or working-class women who do not have the 'right' accent, and older women.

There was, however, one woman in my sample who did not find the emphasis on flirtation and stereotypical femininity in reception work a problem. Amy, who has spent all of her working life in reception work, discusses her experience working as a receptionist on a building site:

I went to work ... on a site office. I enjoyed that one, great! me and about two hundred labourers, loved it ... [*How did you get on with the men?*] Fine. I don't mind men being a bit naughty and cheeky ... 'cos I can give an answer, yet some women can't or don't want to, or think it's sort of ... a lot of feminist women. Well, these guys are doing this job which isn't fun. When they see a woman pass, that's sort of a relief for them, to have a shout and a whistle. When I went into work in the morning, I used to walk down the site, they used to shout and whistle and I used to wave [laughter]. At the beginning I used to be embarrassed ... I used to wear miniskirts. (45)

The fact that so few respondents remained in these kinds of jobs is what we would expect, given that interpretation of sexuality was often an important motivating influence underlying their career moves. As we have seen, an important dimension of the process of 'coming out' is the recognition that paid employment will be lifelong, and generally the sole source of an individual woman's standard of living. This was important and empowering knowledge, insofar as these women directed their energies into finding work that would provide both a 'full' wage and a rewarding experience. Thus, out of necessity respondents actively challenged taken for granted employment norms imposed on working women. Where possible, they sought out better paid areas of work in 'either sex' or 'male' occupations. In nine cases respondents returned to education in order to broaden their career opportunities.

Working for a pittance when I could be earning thousands

Nine respondents were in fairly low-paid jobs which they defined as 'female' occupations. However, these women were highly committed to their area of work. All but one held higher qualifications. Because higher education is a source of social and material power, which can extend occupational choices, it could be said that most of these respondents had, to some extent, made an active choice to participate in worthwhile but poorly paid employment.

Low pay is not always a good predictor of the quality of a job. Many of these poorly paid women were in areas such as health care, welfare and the arts. These jobs offered challenge and reward of a different, less materialistic nature. To these women their occupational location was described as being the result of an active choice. They enjoyed their jobs and were highly committed to them. The poor financial reward was seen as reflecting the distorted priorities of society rather than any lack of complexity or value in the work that they did. Josie explains her approach to her work in the arts, despite being a graduate she earns a 'component' wage:

> I don't have any great financial expectations, and that's not because I am a woman, but because of the type of work I've chosen. I would feel guilty to be paid really well . . . because the arts doesn't make money. I mean, I'm very career-minded, but my career has already been thwarted by itself, and it doesn't particularly bother me. It's sad: it's all the wrong

way round, because they can't afford it, and yet they deserve
the right people. So unfortunately, that's my way of thinking, so I will probably sell myself short . . . That's one of the
female traits. I'll probably work for a pittance, when I could
be earning thousands. (25)

Some younger respondents were at the bottom of an occupational
hierarchy. However, they were expecting to move up the hierarchy to positions which were more usually male-dominated.
This was particularly the case for respondents in the book trade
or library occupations. At the time of interview, Katrina was in
the process of taking steps to move up in the library hierarchy.
She had recently applied for and been accepted on a post-
graduate course which would provide the necessary professional
qualification for advancement. She was very committed to her
work, believing in the importance of providing ordinary people with access to a wide range of knowledge and information.
She describes how she feels about her job, which pays a 'component' wage:

> It's not a job that I can switch off from. I come home and
> think about a problem at work and I enjoy it. It gets boring
> sometimes, but I really enjoy it and can't just switch off from
> it. It isn't a job that I do just for the money. (25)

A political dimension of occupational 'choice'

Four respondents had chosen to work in 'Women's Movement'
organizations, and many others hoped to do so. There were
two important political factors underlying this occupational
choice, or desire. One was feminist politics. Often the process
of 'coming out' developed or heightened respondents' awareness
of the inequalities women faced. Their experience of discrimination and marginality also provided most with high levels of
empathy towards other marginal groups in society. Janette
describes this:

> I suppose being a woman you grow up with an awareness,
> well I grew up with an awareness, that women are discriminated
> against . . . But being a lesbian as well, I think that's more
> so. Even if people close to you aren't doing it, you are aware
> that there are people in the wider, outside world that are
> discriminating against you . . . I sort of go on the usual anti-
> racist demos, and stuff like that . . . Until you have experienced

some kind of overt discrimination yourself it doesn't ring true. (25)

Consequently, the wish to combine more radical politics with their working lives was common in the sample. Many were highly critical of what they perceived to be 'male-stream' work structures; some hoped to bring change within the system, while others wanted to work outside it, either in self-employed situations or in Women's Organizations.

The second political factor shaping this occupational choice was the desire to work in a non-homophobic environment, where they could be 'out'. The importance of being open about sexuality cannot be underrated. In keeping with other research (Hall, 1992), many women in the sample commented on the sense of alienation they experienced in their working environment because of their fear of being open about their sexuality. By having to protect their private lives from the attention of co-workers, respondents were very sensitive to the degree to which people's private lives intersect with their workplace lives. Many of these respondents spoke of feeling 'unwhole' at work, as a result of having to guard this important feature of their personality. They felt unable to speak of loved ones, or share the personal trauma of a breakdown of a relationship. We will explore this important theme later in the chapter, when we consider respondents' approaches to career development.

Just as some respondents felt that they could better express aspects of their personality in a 'male' working environment, others felt more comfortable in politically sensitive 'women's space'. Respondents working in women's organizations tended to utilize a range of skills: counselling, administrative and managerial, and above all emotional work. Organizations were non-hierarchical collectives, where each worker shared in all the tasks. Like the previous respondent in an arts occupation, these women did not expect to earn a great deal of money in this underfunded area. Debby explains her reasons for her forthcoming job change. She was in the process of moving from a relatively well-paid job to a poorly paid one in a Woman's Organization.

Going to this job will be going to a woman-only space. It's a collective establishment so there won't be hierarchies. I'll be working in a positive way to re-empower women, and to give women the space to leave abusive situations, and to do that within a feminist analysis. I don't think you can put a price on this. (29)

Respondents in 'committed' employment shared priorities beyond that of material reward. This may offer us one clue to the disparity in earnings between the sample and men more generally. Despite holding qualifications that could lead them into relatively well paid jobs, their interests lay in areas that are not materially valued. Their poor pay consequently represents the low value assigned to dealings with people, as opposed to things.

In a society plagued by inequalities there are, of course, limitations on how far individual action may result in improved occupational location. Consequently, we have also seen examples of respondents trapped in low-paid jobs, constrained for example, by the limitations of the education system, ill health, ageism and possibly racism. Clearly, however, many respondents had strong views on the suitability of particular areas of employment. We now explore their approaches to paid work in greater detail.

GENDER, SEXUALITY AND INDEPENDENCE

A main hypothesis in this book is that there is a strong interrelationship between employment opportunity and the lesbian lifestyle. There are several dimensions of this. Briefly they are as follows. First, the experience of employment opportunity provides economic power which enables women to develop a more critical standpoint on heterosexual relationships. This economic power, under certain circumstances, allows women the possibility to consider a lifestyle outside heterosexuality, as was the case for my respondents. Second, a critical standpoint on the desirability of marriage and heterosexuality more generally encourages a desire for economic independence which may lead to putting energy into expanding employment opportunity. In the case of those respondents who had questioned their sexuality in adolescence, this early evaluation of heterosexuality was usually an empowering experience with regard to employment outcomes. For other respondents who questioned heterosexuality later on, two patterns can be identified. For some the recognition that the lesbian lifestyle necessitated economic independence provided motivation to seek employment that would offer an adequate standard of living. Consequently, for these women their understanding of their sexuality generated change in their approach to career development. For others, their experience of the lesbian lifestyle was understood to facilitate their desire to be economically independent and take on more challenging and demanding employment. These are important contexts which shape and have shaped respondents' approaches to employment.

Ambition and the importance of work

Of the 43 women who expressed an opinion about the role of paid work in their lives, 33 felt they had a strong commitment to their jobs. They viewed their careers as being important or central to their sense of identity. A further ten of my respondents, however, viewed their employment as necessarily important, but felt that if they could afford to give up work they would happily do so in order to partake in other pursuits. As with the single women in Adams' study (1976:84), freedom from family responsibilities allowed many respondents the leisure time to develop a wide range of other interests, which were often ranked higher than paid work. Respondents frequently spoke of desiring more time to become further involved in areas such as counselling, voluntary work with women, music making, hobbies and extended travel. Nonetheless, paid work was still important to them, usually enjoyed, but (rather wisely perhaps) not the only source of pleasure in their lives. Only four respondents reported disliking their jobs.[18]

As we will see later, however, there was a certain amount of ambivalence amongst the sample regarding the extent that pay acted as a motivating factor in approaches to career development. Although respondents recognized that there was a pay threshold which they did not wish to fall beneath, they often prioritized other considerations over income and promotion.

The sample held a wide range of differing approaches to career development. Many respondents were very ambitious. An example of this kind of thinking comes from Colette. She has just entered further education to train in a 'caring' occupation (she had left school at 14 when she ran away from home):

The job I want to do, once I am there I don't want to stop. I think what I'd like to do is work and work and work and get myself really established ... I know that I need a career. I need something there for security and I suppose that's what a man wants. A man wants to be successful and to prove that he is good at what he's doing. That's what I want. (17*M*)

Interesting patterns emerged, however, when respondents were asked to compare their approach to career development with that of their male colleagues. I was initially surprised to find that most of the respondents, regardless of their level of ambition, felt they differed in this respect from their male colleagues. They usually viewed men as being far more single-minded in their desire for success than they felt themselves to be. Dorothy, a scientist, explains how she perceives her ambition differing from her male colleagues':

I think science is incredibly competitive ... The men especially play a lot of games to get them where they want to get. They are not games really that a lot of women are prepared to play. A lot of them get where they get not because of how good they are, but because they've played along with the system and they've gone to the right dinners ... And I am going to get where I get because I deserve to get there, not because I've licked the bum of someone who ... is more important than me ... They will probably get further than me, but not because they are any better than me, but because they fit into the system better. Another thing about men ... they're so obsessed with getting on and becoming important, that what they do doesn't matter. They do work because it's going to get them somewhere, whereas I will only do work if I think that it ought to be done. (25*S*)

Male co-workers were often perceived as driven willingly or unwillingly by their perceived role as 'breadwinner'. They were also seen to benefit from the assistance of a wife, whose socially approved role was to provide back-up and support for her husband's career. Hillary, a professional woman, comments on how she perceives the ambition of her male colleagues. She is well aware of the advantages her male colleagues gain from the 'two person career' identified by Kanter (1977) in the USA, and Finch (1983) in Britain.

> My male colleagues are very hell bent on getting to the top
> of the greasy pole ... and for the most part are [at the top].
> Their home life continues the traditional middle-class pro-
> fessional life, where, as I say, they go home and meals are
> there, and everything else is there for them. So in effect all
> they really have to do is concentrate on their professional
> life. The women have to juggle being wives and mothers and
> professional people. (37S)

Another way that some respondents perceived differences between the career development of men and themselves was in
the shape of career goals. They felt that while men's career
strategies were directed along a straight line, theirs was or-
ganic. They described a more tree-like progression, moving in
one direction, then changing to another. Consequently, some
spoke of holding five- or ten-year career plans followed by assessment. It was not uncommon to find respondents who had
made several career changes, for example, some pursued careers in teaching and health care and then moved into other
professions.

They also perceived men as being far more interested in pay
and status than job content, whereas respondents often felt
that, once a certain pay threshold had been achieved, job content was far more important. These sentiments are expressed
by Gaye, who works in sport as a manager. She views herself as
much less instrumental in her approach to her career than
her male colleagues:

> Well to me, it's much more important for me to be happy
> within a job, because it's fairly challenging. Something I enjoy
> more than how much it actually pays, well as long as it pays ...
> enough to sort of live on. I am not particularly fussed about
> chasing another grand a year ... I don't see work as just
> money chasing ... the men that I've met are more money-
> oriented. They don't care what they do quite so much as
> long as it pays the right amount. (26M)

The differences which respondents identified between their
ambitions and that of their male colleagues may provide another
clue to the gender gap in earnings discussed at the beginning
of this chapter.

Job appeal

Regardless of respondents' levels of ambition, the desire for
financial reward, although important, was rarely reported to
be a sole motivating force in job choice. Once a living wage
was achieved, enjoyment of work and the need for a challenge
were considered as far more important than levels of pay. Ellie
has spent most of her working life as a technician. She is now
at college developing these skills to a professional level:

> [*What motivates you in your work?*] If I was purely interested
> in money I wouldn't be doing the job I'm doing. I know it's
> well paid, but there are better paid jobs that I could do. If I
> was purely interested in status there would be other things I
> could do as well, but [my profession] to me, gives me the
> challenge that I want, because there is so much happening
> in it. There's something different every day happening in it,
> so it gives me the challenge that I want. If it was just the
> challenge I wouldn't do it either, but at the same time I've
> got the status and the money. So it's all three of those
> really. (27*I*)

Many respondents were reconciled to the fact that, as women,
their standard of living would never be very high. Commonly
they spoke of not being very materialistic. This point is made
by Flis who works in a caring occupation:

> [*What appeals to you about a job?*] A bit of a challenge, not so
> much the money. As long as I have enough money to do
> what I want, to cover the mortgage, buy some clothes, enough
> to go out and have a meal once, twice a month, enough to
> feed my animals, and a bit left over. It's all I've ever been
> used to and I don't think I will ever earn a lot of money,
> and it's not one of my priorities, as long as I get job satisfac-
> tion. (38*I*)

Similarly, Frankie's career development was motivated by intrinsic reward rather than simply monetary gain. She is highly
committed to her poorly paid job in an arts occupation:

> I want to satisfy myself with my ambition. I want to achieve,
> I do want to achieve, and to feel proud of myself. I don't
> want to achieve for the sake of achieving and just to be on
> the fast track. I want to get somewhere. I want to have at-
> tainable goals that I actually reach and go out and get pleasure

from. I want to have dreams that maybe do or don't ever happen. But as I've said, I think it's all tied up with this fact that I don't feel I'm involved in a massive sort of like money grabbing cycle . . . I mean, I think my pleasure therefore does come from the work itself . . . So hopefully I would like to think, I will see my career shape through responsibility, and interesting work and actually having control over things. (24S)

Another common theme reported by respondents was the importance of a job being worthwhile socially. Glenda, who had returned to higher education as a mature student, works in the arts. She discusses the importance of a job being worthwhile rather than high-status:

Work is important to me, but I am not a career minded person, perhaps it's lack of opportunity. I tend to accept too readily things. It is important to me to work doing something that I feel is worthwhile, and that's most important to me, and to be doing something that gives me satisfaction. In terms of socially valued career that's not of great importance. (43M)

All of the respondents in science and technology professions commented on their career decisions being strongly influenced by ethical considerations. They saw their career development as shaped by a desire to avoid particular employers, such as the nuclear industry, the arms industry, or certain pharmaceutical companies which were politically 'unsound' either in their dealings with the Third World or vivisection. Consequently, some spoke of their career development taking them into charitable organizations, where they would not expect to earn as much money. An example of this kind of thinking comes from a Mary-Anne, a scientist:

I won't work for the big companies. It's a political decision, I won't be poor, but I will always be at the bottom end of the scientific scale . . . Yes [the men] are more likely to end up wealthier than I am. If I wanted to be wealthy, I could be wealthy, but I don't politically want to go and work for a multinational drug company whose ethics stink. So I will end up working for a charity or working in academia. (24S)

Typically, respondents spoke of being drawn to jobs that offered control. Control was conceptualized in different ways, and the term was used as a shorthand way of discussing power.

The most common way that respondents thought about control was in terms of control over the work routine. Twenty-six mentioned this as being important. Particularly for those in manual occupations, enjoyment of the job was very much linked with working in an environment which allowed a measure of control in the way they organized their daily routine. These women rejected the idea of working in an office job. They wanted to be more physically mobile. Often they sought work that would take them out of the confines of the workplace: jobs such as deliveries, driving, sales 'repping' or working in agriculture or horticulture.

A second way that respondents referred to seeking control was through their desire for power to influence, which was usually inspired by their feminist politics. Again this was a theme that came up in different ways. Those who were in occupations that dealt with the general public often spoke of this desire. Anne, who works in a public service occupation, explains her ambitions:

> [*What drives you in your career development?*] Power [laughter], power and influence to be honest. [*What do you want the power for?*] I would define myself as a feminist that chooses to work within the system, to change it from within. That's what drives me, rather than working outside the system and throwing bricks at it. I see myself as a mole really. That's what drives me. I would call myself a pragmatic feminist, seeing opportunities for changing things, and going for it and doing it, but within parameters that can be defined in other ways by other people. It sounds like a cop-out but it's not meant to be. Taking existing things and saying 'Look, we can maybe do this differently' and then doing it. (33*M*)

As we have noted earlier, often respondents felt that their experience as lesbians offered insights into ways in which women and other marginalized groups are exploited. Consequently, many women reported becoming increasingly more interested in feminism. We saw earlier that this led some to seek work in Women's Organizations. Others remained within the mainstream but intended to develop their careers in such a way that they might utilize their skills for the benefit of other women. For example, one graduate was seriously considering returning to higher education to retrain in law. She felt that there was a great need for feminist lawyers, and that this would be the most useful way for her to develop her skills.

Homophobia and heterosexism at work

There is no legal protection for people in Britain who have been discriminated against on the basis of sexual orientation. The workplace can be a deeply homophobic environment (Cockburn, 1991). A recent survey on the employment experiences of lesbian and gay men, commissioned by the campaigning organization Stonewall, (1995) is illuminating. It found that 68 per cent of the sample were not 'out' at work because they feared the consequences. There were clearly good reasons for this fear as 48 per cent had been harassed in the workplace because of their sexuality and 8 per cent had lost their jobs because they were homosexual.

As was noted earlier, the desire to work in a non-homophobic working environment was often reported as being very influential on respondents' job choices. Homophobia was cited as a very real problem by most respondents. At least 18 feared the consequences of their sexuality being known at work or had already suffered discrimination. Three women had lost their jobs when it was discovered that they were lesbians. Molly discusses her feelings about losing her job for this reason:

> I worked for the blood bank in 1985; I worked there for a month. Another worker found out I was a lesbian. She shopped me to one of the other girls and it went round. It got to the office and they said, 'the girls feel uncomfortable; someone says you're a lesbian. Are you?' And I said 'yes'. 'Well, the girls don't feel comfortable because you have to share rooms.' I said, 'We've been doing this for over two months', and they gave me two weeks' severance pay, and they said, 'You don't have to come back for those two weeks.' I thought that was their loss, and I walked straight into another job. They had no principles, and I stood by mine – it wasn't my hang-up. I always feel that, if I say to someone I am a lesbian and they decide to sever their relationship with me, I always feel very sorry for them. I feel genuinely saddened by how they think and feel. I am a nice person. (31*I*)

Fear of the consequences of discrimination influenced respondents' career decisions in less overt ways. Some respondents avoided certain areas of work that they might have otherwise entered because they anticipated discrimination. For example, Jody, aged 38, had wanted to enter the police force after leaving school. She worked for a while in a garage until she reached the minimum entry age. She then had to rethink this plan when she realized that homosexuality was a sackable offence in that occupation. Jody now works in low-level management after a career in a male manual occupation.

Other women made career changes because they felt that ultimately they would be unable to protect their private lives from the surveillance of co-workers and employers. Brenda decided to leave teaching for this reason. She had been seen as a natural candidate for promotion and realized that, if she took on more high-profile positions, her personal life would become increasingly subject to scrutiny. She felt frustrated because she did want advancement, but was fearful of the cost; for if her sexuality was known, she would certainly have been dismissed. Brenda is now training to enter a 'male' profession where she feels she will have more power over the conditions of her employment. She also expects that in this profession she will have a greater chance to be self-employed.

Zoe gave up medicine partly because of the sexism that ran through the teaching. She felt angered by the distorted images of homosexuality that informed medical opinion:

> It was a political decision. I suppose I could have gone through with it, but I wouldn't have been able to go through a period of indoctrination like that, and character manipulation, and still be me and still be sane . . . The whole thing was so, just so homophobic and so sexist that I couldn't stand it. I knew I couldn't be strong enough to survive that sort of thing and that's why I left, and that makes me really angry sometimes because I would really like to be a doctor, and I know I'd make a fucking good doctor, and I could do a lot of really good work. (25S)

Many respondents spoke of feeling alienated from their co-workers because they are unable to share important aspects of their lives. Hilda works in management in a sports occupation:

> I can't ever be happy one hundred per cent, because I can't be happy at work, which is a third of my life . . . Nobody asks me questions that I don't want to be asked, because when they do they get some blunt answer. Nobody pushes me on that subject. Whether it's because they don't care, which I don't think is true, I think they're just prepared to

> let it be .... I can't ever be at one with myself because I
> can't be at one with me at work, which is a third of my
> life ... Because if they knew about me I'd be sacked. (23*I*)

Some respondents found the best way to cope with homophobia
was to 'come out' in the interview. They felt that, if this blocked
their chances of getting the job, it would mean that the working environment would not be right for them. Another common solution respondents mentioned in their hopes for the
future was to become self-employed, to set up their own businesses. Some saw this as a joint venture with their lovers. Being one's own boss was seen as the ultimate in control: it offered
the possibility of setting the goals, content and terms of the
working day.

CONCLUSION

One thing that was striking about many respondents' career
discussions was a strong sense of choices having been exercised. Although some experienced difficulties in gaining access to more challenging employment, usually because of the
sexist attitudes of employers, many respondents gave an impression of having exercised relatively high levels of control
over their career development. They appeared willing to take
advantage of opportunities which they felt were right for them,
and did not hold back from making themselves available for
promotion. Juxtaposed with this feeling of control was, for some,
something that they had little control over, which was the threat
of having their sexuality exposed. A general sadness was expressed by most of those who felt that they had to remain si-
lent at work about this central feature of their lives. The shadow
of homophobia and heterosexism extended to their future work
plans. A popular solution was to become self-employed, or to
work with other women in a non-homophobic setting.

Their lesbian lifestyle necessitated lifelong economic self-reliance and this affected the way they approached their career
development. They desired employment which would both
provide a living wage and job satisfaction. However, often their
ambition seemed to be curbed by other considerations and
few appeared to desire success at all costs. Many prioritized
other values, such as caring, ethical, political and social values.
Although these values may be shared by men and women alike,

rightly or wrongly, they experienced these values as women's values. Their ability to be guided by these values in their occupational choices may, in part, be explained by their particular characteristics. As we will see in the next chapter, these women are workers, shaped neither by social expectations to be primary breadwinners, nor by the constraints associated with being secondary earners. In this way their hopes and actions, which do not follow conventional gender scripts, possibly represent a new kind of worker for sociological analysis.

NOTES

1. See, for example, Vicinus's (1985) study on the lives of the 'new women' who formed the early cohorts of college education in the USA.
2. For more general research on the experience of single women see, for example, Allen (1989) and Adams (1976).
3. In 1989 only 8.6 per cent of women aged 35 to 39 had never been married, this fell to 5.6 per cent for women in the 40 to 44 age group (Marriage and Divorce Statistics, 1991:14).
4. A similar call for the necessity of investigating the economic lives of lesbian women is made by the American economists Badgett and Williams (1992).
5. In 1994, 46 per cent of women workers in Britain were part-time (*Employment Gazette*, 1994).
6. I checked to see if this was due to the age distribution of the sample and found that their pay advantage held across the age groups.
7. It is also worth mentioning that in the county where this study was carried out, women's wages lie slightly below the national average and male wages are amongst the highest in the country. In April 1990, the average gross weekly wage (excluding the effects of overtime) for non-manual male workers in the county where respondents lived was £341, for male manual workers it was £203. However, the average gross weekly wage for full-time non-manual women workers in the county was £207, and £139 for full-time manual women workers (New Earnings Survey, 1990, Part E.).
8. Including overtime makes very little difference to the proportion of women earning 'component wages'.
9. The local female workforce has grown rapidly since 1981, with the expansion of so called low-skill service sector 'women's jobs' – mainly part-time clerical jobs. In 1989/1990 clerical and related occupations accounted for most of the non-manual jobs advertised locally ('Whiteabbey' City Research Group, 1990).
10. Women form a minority (22 per cent) of 'primary sector' occupations, that is, better paid employment offering more job secur-

ity and scope for advancement than 'secondary sector' occupations which tend to be low paid and insecure, offering limited prospects (Burchell and Rubery, 1991:26).

11. In order to calculate the degree to which an occupation is dominated by one sex or the other we have to take into account the proportion of men to women in the total labour force. In the case of the Census data, men made up 61 per cent of the labour force sample, thus a 'male' occupation is one where men comprise more than 61 per cent of an occupation. A 'female' occupation is one where women comprise more than 39 per cent of the occupation.

12. The possibility of women achieving upward mobility through clerical occupations has been discussed by Dex (1987:49–51) and Crompton *et al.* (1982). They both suggest that this is not very common.

13. Dex (1987:49) suggests that this level of upward mobility via clerical work is rare.

14. Crompton and Sanderson (1990) comment on the high levels of pressure that direct women towards 'suitable' professions. This was particularly striking for the older professional women whom they had interviewed: 'A recurring theme amongst the older women was the pressure on them, despite their position as academic "high-flyers", to take up "suitable" careers in nursing or teaching' (p. 64).

15. For a very entertaining discussion of the central role played by lesbians in the military, see Faderman (1992, chs 5 and 6) and Miller (1995). For information on brutal and underhand tactics used in catching lesbians see Faderman (1992).

16. See, for example, Adkins (1995), Cockburn (1991) and Stanko (1988) for a discussion of the implications of the sexual harassment of women by men in maintaining gender segregation.

17. Lees's (1986) study of adolescent girls clearly illustrates ways that labels such as, 'dyke', 'tight-ass', 'slut' and 'slag', used by both girls and boys, have very little to do with actual sexual behaviour. She argues that these terms are used to punish inappropriate gender behaviour, such as being perceived as too independent.

18. Johnson's (1990:108) North American study of older women in long-term lesbian relationships found a similar situation amongst her sample. They were usually highly satisfied with their employment experience; only 7 per cent of the sample of 216 were dissatisfied with their jobs.

CHAPTER SIX

Lesbians at home: why can't a man be more like a woman?

INTRODUCTION

Finally, we come to the analysis of respondents' approaches to and experiences of relationships to illustrate the significance of sexuality in shaping women's work, in both its household and market forms. The review and reassessment of the relationship between the public and the private have enabled feminists to identify ways that women and men's employment circumstances are shaped by their home life situations and vice versa. Men's ability to appropriate women's unpaid physical and emotional labour means that women and men do not exchange their labour in the labour market on the same basis (Adkins, 1995:43, Pateman, 1988). Both Finch (1983) and Kanter (1977) show that a one-way process exists to incorporate married women into the jobs of their husbands as, for example, unpaid hostesses, secretaries or accountants. By taking on the bulk of caring and household work, women in heterosexual relationships enable their partners to be more single-minded in their engagement with paid work at the expense of their own employment experience. Married women's jobs are usually geared towards accommodating their home life commitments as much as possible (Scott *et al.*, 1993:25). The constraints that women face at home leave them vulnerable to exploitation by employers in their search for a cheap and flexible workforce. Adkins (1995:30) points out that the role of sexuality as the basis for men's ability to appropriate women's labour has been neglected in feminist theorising. Given the relationship between home life arrangements and employment circumstances, it is useful to have an idea of what women can achieve when their labour is not being appropriated by a man.

Within the context of institutional heterosexuality, women and men are drawn into relationships with each other as socially, symbolically and materially different persons. Their relationships are negotiated with reference to a framework of materially shaped, pre-existing gender scripts which guide interaction. Informing these differential scripts are dominant beliefs about the complementarity of feminine and masculine identities (Pateman, 1988:140, Connell, 1987:248, Rubin, 1975:178). Practices and ideologies which reinforce gender difference, for example, the undervaluing of women's occupational skills and an employment structure which denies the time and emotional component of men's home life and parental responsibilities, place constraints on the extent to which women and men can operationalize more egalitarian ideals. The analysis of lesbian partnerships is important because it provides visions of divisions of household and market labour which are not structured by dichotomous gender scripts.

This chapter will draw on respondents' accounts of their approaches to and experience of relationships. We are interested in ways that both *similarities* based upon their shared structural positioning within gender hierarchies and *differences*, derived from other sources of inequality, are manifested and managed between women. We begin by illustrating ways in which respondents perceived their partnerships with women differing from their experience and/or understandings of heterosexual relationships. The discussion will then move on to consider some potential sources of inequality and conflict, such as money, home ownership and emotional commitment. This will be followed by an outline of divisions of labour in lesbian households. The chapter will conclude with a consideration of some employment consequences which respondents felt arose out of the context of their more egalitarian relationships which valued 'co-independence' rather than dependency.

LESBIANISM AND EGALITARIANISM

There is a small but growing body of North American research on lesbian relationships (for example, Weston, 1991, Johnson, 1990), some of which compares the experience of lesbian, gay and heterosexual couples (Blumstein and Schwartz, 1985, 1990; Caldwell and Peplau, 1984; Peplau and Cochran, 1990; Peplau *et al.*, 1978). In her review of these relatively large-scale comparative studies, Lindsey (1990:152) concludes that egalitarian arrangements are more likely to be valued and achieved in lesbian partnerships.

Peplau and Cochran's study (1990) found that lesbians, followed closely by heterosexual women, were much more likely to value egalitarianism than any of the men interviewed. In fact, 97 per cent of lesbians said that ideally partnerships should be 'exactly equal' in terms of power, and 59 per cent thought they had achieved this, which was the highest percentage of all the couple forms interviewed (p.339).[1] Lesbians also tended to be the least tolerant of inequalities in their partnerships, and this usually applied to both partners (Blumstein and Schwartz, 1985:61). When relationships were perceived as unequal they were more likely to report dissatisfaction (Caldwell and Peplau, 1984:598) and were less likely to be together for follow-up interviews (Peplau and Cochran, 1990; Blumstein and Schwartz, 1985:310).

Feelings that relationships conform to a more egalitarian model appear to be a crucial dimension to enduring lesbian relationships. This is borne out in Johnson's (1990) excellent in-depth study of 108 long-term lesbian couples whose relationships ranged from ten to 52 years in length. Johnson found that feelings of being in a partnership of equals was essential for most of her interviewees (p.120). A common belief was that their relationships allowed them to realize their egalitarian ideals in such a way as would not be possible in heterosexual relationships, which they tended to view as 'innately unequal' (p.120). Egalitarian ideals appeared to underpin couples' decision-making process, with 90 per cent reporting that they had an equal say (pp. 120–28). In terms of influence, Johnson found that 81 per cent of the sample felt that the balance of their partnerships was equally weighted (p.125).

These studies seem to indicate that lesbian women are comfortable neither with dominating nor with being dominated in their partnerships with each other. Longevity in relationships appears to be more usually contingent on partners having negotiated a satisfactory balance of power. Alternatively, sustained inequalities seem to give rise to high levels of dissatisfaction and contribute to the eventual downfall of a partnership.

An important question raised by this work is why issues of equality occupy such a central position in women's lesbian relationships. Peplau and Cochran (1990:339) take us some distance towards understanding this when they suggest that many lesbians have access to feminist analyses and may therefore be more sensitive to the operation of power. We now turn to our own data to see if we can take this understanding a step further.

'Scripting' gender inequality

When respondents were asked if they could identify ways in which their relationships with women differed from heterosexual ones, the overwhelming response, volunteered in 53 cases, was that relationships with women were 'more equal'. The degree of certainty expressed was usually related to the amount of experience they had had of relationships with men, with those who had been married appearing the most confident in their assessment. What was actually meant by this was not immediately evident. However, as we will see in their commentaries, it is clear that respondents were sensitive to circumstances which supported relations of domination – between women and men, and among women. This was manifested through their adherence to an egalitarian perspective as an ideal or a political principle, which appeared to be constructed around notions of individual autonomy. Lesbian relationships, in contrast to their understandings of heterosexual relationships, were viewed as having the potential for realising these objectives. We now briefly illustrate the main differentiating features they perceived between lesbian and heterosexual relationships, which together led them to this conclusion.

There were two main aspects of heterosexual relationships which were understood by respondents to pre-empt an egalitarian outcome. The first, and most obvious, was related to their belief that women and men do not share 'equality of conditions'. In other words, there exist structural inequalities between them. For example, men's access to greater economic power was seen to support and reinforce their ability to dominate their partners. Ursula explains:

> I just see that there is very little equality in heterosexual relationships – in like the definition of a man and a woman, the man is the one with the power. There is no definition of who takes the lead or the power in a lesbian relationship . . . It is in 99 per cent of the cases the man that will earn more money, he will make all the decisions – well, most of the decisions . . . (19)

A second important differentiating feature was related to the gendered assumptions guiding the actual operation of hetero-sexual relationships. As we saw in Chapter 4, those who had experienced relationships with men usually identified 'hetero-sexual role play' as a major medium of constraint on self-determination. This role play was perceived as a taken for granted practice whereby gender inequalities were intentionally or (most importantly) *unintentionally* translated into everyday action, expectations and outcomes.

When looking back on their relationships with men, hetero-sexual role play was understood by many respondents to have subtly controlled their behaviour. Valerie, a divorced woman who had recently 'come out', explains:

> Well [lesbian relationships] are just so much more relaxed, there's no obligation to fulfil a role, you make your own. You make your own position comfortable that fits round you, whereas, I mean in most heterosexual relationships, there's no way that people can ignore the set roles, the set expecta-tions, and it's restricting.(43)

Sheila contrasts her lesbian relationship with her previous marriage, and highlights the consequences of adhering to het-erosexual role play for decision making:

> I feel more equal, I don't feel that I could leave all the de-cisions up to [my lover] or need to. Whereas with [my hus-band] I did, and I think in many ways I was happy to leave the decisions up to him, because that was what I saw as his role... [Relationships with women are] very much more fulfilling in that I feel like a person in my own right rather than an accessory. And I think I felt very much as an access-ory when I was married. (45)

Roxanne describes some consequences of this 'role play' for women's and men's approaches to domestic tasks:

> I have never found that I am toeing the line with men... But I had been having to fight battles of role play. Like doing the dishes and just taking on those sorts of roles naturally. In my experience, if there are dishes there waiting to be done, it will occur to a woman to do it, but it won't occur to a man. So you would always be the one saying, 'Wash up.' I just couldn't cope with that side of things. Sounds a bit crazy, but it will just be too much for me. It will be the little niggly

things, which would become big, and then it gets out of hand ... And they don't arise now. (27)

Women taking the bulk of responsibility for trying to break down gender boundaries and for constructing more egalitarian conditions in their relationships with men has been commented upon in research. For example, Statham's (1986:168) study of 'non-sexist' couples, found that it was her female respondents who had to remind their husbands to do their share in the home. Gordon's (1990) study of feminist mothers in Finland echoes these problems. She makes an interesting point about the role of same-sex reference groups: her respondents' more egalitarian male partners compared themselves favourably with other men but their contributions often fell short of their partner's ideal (p. 97). My respondents often spoke of the energy and disappointment involved in their attempts to expand gender roles in their relationships with men. For these women, being in a relationship with a woman with a similar agenda and view of the world was a major reason for their enthusiasm about lesbian relationships.

A central reason for respondents' sensitivity to heterosexual role play was their experience of entering relationships which simply lacked roles based on reciprocal gender expectations. The absence of scripts based on gender difference has been mentioned in other research on lesbian couples (Blumstein and Schwartz, 1985:153, Peplau and Cochran, 1990:342). Yvonne sums up the feelings of many of my respondents:

Like I say before, it is more equal. There aren't any stereotypical images like in a man/woman relationship, it's something that is so dependent on the two different people. You just form the relationship that is between yourselves, if you know what I mean. There is nothing that [tells you] – this is what you should do, or this is what you shouldn't do and stuff. It's something that just clicks and every relationship is formed, and it is totally different from another one, 'cos it's just how the two people in the relationship make it. There is nothing there at the beginning to influence thoughts on how things should be done. (24)

Importantly, the absence of prescribed roles based on notions of gender difference was seen as emancipating, because this situation expanded choices and enabled greater creativity in the negotiation process between women. This is explained by Harriet:

> One of the things that struck me in my first lesbian relation-ship was the fact that there weren't any role models. I couldn't go and see a film on how to live. It meant that I was really free to do it the way I wanted to. I was uncluttered by im-ages of how I should be doing it. I could more easily choose what I did want, in a way, without having to go against any-thing . . . If I had got married to [my boyfriend] there would have been loads of stuff telling me how I should have been behaving. [*Why do you think this is a positive situation?*] It may be easier to fit into prescribed roles, because they are there without you having to think and you can fall into them. I think they must oppress both people actually, because it is much better if you can have the confidence to do everything in a relationship. (35)

The lack of taken for granted guidelines for conducting rela-tionships presented those involved with a 'problem to be solved'.[2] It seems that women negotiating lesbian relationships have to engage in an unusual amount of creativity, and this requires reflection upon and evaluation of what constitutes interper-sonal relationships. The flexibility offered in lesbian relation-ships was understood to provide a context within which women could more easily operate on egalitarian ideals. This is not to say that respondents were unaware of the inequalities between women and the potential this had for creating power imbal-ances in the relationship. Daniella discusses this:

> Well, I mean I don't have any sort of romantic or idealized notions about relationships with women. I think they are really hard. But I also think that there's obviously going to be power differences, and power imbalances, but I think there's a far greater chance of working them out. (25)

An important reason for the belief that power imbalances could be 'worked out' between women was that there was no clear overriding power dynamic shaping the relationship. This is discussed by Elspeth:

> I think there are lots of power factors. She sometimes had power because she was older, I sometimes because I was younger. She sometimes had power because she had money,

I because I was an academic. There were lots of power factors, none of which were overriding ... Fluctuating power
but no wild fluctuations, with a middle line of equality. (23)

In describing their relationships as 'more equal', respondents
were talking about a range of features which were often constructed as the converse of their understandings of the operation of heterosexual relationships. They believed that within
lesbian relationships they could exercise greater self-determination and experience relative freedom from domination.

The definition of power is a contested area in sociology.[3]
Rather than entering into these sociological debates, my intention
here is to consider my respondents' understandings of the different forms which they perceived power to take. The important
point to make here is that these women were often conscious
of potential power imbalances generated in interpersonal relationships. I therefore wish to place a focus on the ways that
this awareness informed their approaches to relationships.

It has been implicit in respondents' accounts throughout this
book and in the remainder of this chapter that they were usually conscious of both the positive and negative effects of power.
First, they were aware of the enabling aspects of power; ways
that, for instance, access to economic power expanded their
ability to be self-determining, to make choices over the conditions of their lives and in particular their relationships.[4] Second, they were aware of a range of negative ways in which
power operated as a constraint upon themselves and others.
They saw power expressed through structures of inequality. In
terms of interpersonal relationships (heterosexual and lesbian),
they associated, for example, excessive economic imbalances
with providing a dependency context which allowed the higher
earning partner to exercise, intentionally or unintentionally,
greater control over the conditions of that relationship.

Their recognition of the operation of power, however, extended beyond structural sources to include various 'belief systems' shaping everyday practices. One major source of this
awareness was perhaps generated by their experience of simply being lesbians and having to face the contradiction between
broader social definitions of them as sexual 'deviants' and 'un-
natural', and their own positive experience of their sexuality.
A main component of the often lengthy process of 'coming
out' is coming to terms with this contradiction. To view one's

sexuality positively requires the recognition that dominant beliefs can be fundamentally wrong, and for many respondents this insight was viewed as empowering. Gillian explains how coming to terms with her sexuality encouraged a more critical perspective:

> [My sexuality] has been very empowering and it shook me out of my middle-class marriage slot into just thinking about the ways things worked and into thinking about power structures and conditioning. It just made me think, and I don't think you can be a real person without this. Certainly society is out to stick people into little boxes and that means keeping them heterosexual ... Keeping the myths and brutalising men in such a way as to make them 'men'. It gives you a sort of understanding ... of what is going on. But you have to be on the wrong end of the power structure ... So, yes, if you are a lesbian you notice the power structure against you and you have more understanding in a experiential way. (23)

Another aspect of being positioned outside 'institutionalized heterosexuality' was that they felt they became more aware of how power worked negatively (their value judgement) through taken for granted ideas about the ways that women and men should interact with each other. Eva discusses this:

> I think there's definitely a difference ... I've had very equal relationships with women. When I see some of the relationships that straight female friends have had with men! But mostly, a lot of the time they don't see anything wrong with it, because it is what everyone around them is doing ... [They are] accepting what to me appear to be horrendous imbalances ... One friend goes home, a nine hour day at work and, the usual thing, prepares the meal and looks after the house and everything, and he just sits there and tells all his friends what a slob she is, and all this kind of thing. But how, how, how ... can we try to, to point this out to people, to other women? (25)

The inequalities that emerge though enacting heterosexual roles were often seen to be obscured from the view of participants (themselves included), because of the power of dominant ideologies which tend to naturalize and justify them. Here I am reminded of Lukes's (1974) 'three dimensional view of power'. He argues:

[I]s it not the supreme and most insidious exercise of power to prevent people, to whatever degree, from having grievances by shaping their perceptions, cognitions and preferences in such a way that they accept their role in the existing order of things, either because they can see or imagine no alternative to it, or because they see it as natural and unchangeable, or because they value it as divinely ordained and beneficial? (p.24)

There are no similar ideas that can be mobilized to naturalize and justify one woman's domination of her female partner, and so relations that involve domination will be more visible and perhaps less readily accepted. From respondents' discussions of their interpersonal relationships, it was apparent that their egalitarian position extended to include a general uneasiness about being in a situation of dominance over a partner. Déidre illustrates this:

One thing I am, I'd say, I am one for equality. I don't believe anybody should dominate anyone in a relationship. The reason I like relationships with women is because the equality is there. You help each other. You know, one doesn't tell the other more, 'cos I don't like being dominated. (27)

This situation may be reinforced by the empathy derived from a lesbian's ability to place herself in the position of her partner, which is illustrated by Catherine in this next extract:

I think there must be [a difference between lesbian and heterosexual relationships] because as a woman I would hate to be treated the way a man might treat a woman – this domineering thing. And I would never dream of doing to somebody what I would hate to have done to myself. (24)

Lesbians' sensitivity to the operation of power may provide a more conscious awareness of its abuse by self and others and, as we will see later, may lead to the development of 'damage limitation' strategies.

All these factors may inform the negotiation process between women and, because a more balanced outcome is likely to be in both their interests, their more flexible relationships make it easier to achieve.[5] Consequently, it is perfectly reasonable to assume that lesbians' home lives are more equal than the heterosexual norm, and this raises key questions. First, what impact do other sources of inequality have on their relationships? Second, what do divisions of labour look like in the absence of gender difference to shape task allocation and approaches to employment? The next two sections will explore these questions.

THE OPERATION OF AN 'EGALITARIAN IDEAL'

We now shift the discussion forward a little and explore respondents' accounts of their relationships with women to see how far their concerns about self-determination, egalitarianism as an ideal and sensitivity to power were translated into practice. We will focus on some areas of potential inequality, such as economic inequality, unilateral home ownership and emotional commitment, which may mediate the structural similarities women share with each other on the basis of gender.

Money matters

Another point raised in the studies outlined earlier is that the ability to dominate a partner in relationships between women tends to be less contingent on access to economic and educational power than is the case for heterosexual partnerships. Peplau and Cochran (1990:340) point out that economic factors may not be as relevant in lesbian relationships as access to other resources, such as status within the lesbian community. They suggest that domination in lesbian and gay relationships may be far more related to the degree of emotional commitment each partner invests in the relationship. A partner who feels greater emotional dependency will tend to have less power in a relationship. Johnson (1990:127) suggests that, for her long-term couples, domination was more likely to be the result of the personality differences, rather than age or income differentials. Blumstein and Schwartz go as far as to say that 'lesbians do not use income to establish dominance in their relationship. They use it to avoid having one woman dependent on the other' (1985:60). It is important to remember that most lesbian couples of employment age are and expect to be in 'dual-worker' relationships, and it is rare to find examples of one partner being financially dependent on another (Weston, 1991:149, Peplau and Cochran, 1990:344, Johnson, 1990:108; Blumstein and Schwartz, 1985).

It is important not to dismiss the significance of economics in the power equation. If, as the above studies suggest, there is a tendency for money to be less important in establishing power relations then this is quite an accomplishment. My research and that of others would suggest that this is an outcome of a process whereby women have actively sought to avoid being in situations where financial imbalances are too extreme. This is implied by Blumstein and Schwartz's (1985) discussion of financial arrangements in lesbian households:

> ... sharing financial responsibilities equally, neither partner becoming dependent on the other, were common goals we heard from lesbians. When a relationship was seen as out of balance – with one woman contributing less to household bills than the other – it was disturbing to both partners. Each expressed a strong dislike of such a potential for power imbalance (p.61).

Blumstein and Schwartz's observation suggests that the women interviewed were well aware of the *unintentional* consequences of economic imbalances. This is very much related to women's sensitivity to the power derived from money which may influence dealings between them. My respondents were well aware of the negative (constraining) and the positive (enabling) dimensions of economic power. They had often viewed the negative aspects of this power in their family of origins and/or experienced it in relationships with men. All recognized the positive aspects of economic power because it provided their independence. For these reasons, amongst others, respondents tended to value financial self-sufficiency and reject economic dependence. Thus, where possible, they actively avoided, or created strategies to offset the impact of, excessive economic inequality in their partnerships. We now briefly illustrate this argument with some examples of respondents' views on economic dependency, before moving on to explore ways that finances were organized between women.

The importance of financial independence

An emphasis on 'co-independence' was an important feature of lesbian partnerships amongst respondents interviewed. My respondents valued their financial independence and were very unwilling to become dependent on a partner for the maintenance of their standard of living. Respondents felt that economic dependency would tip the balance of power to an intolerable degree. As we will see, they thought that financial dependency would set up undesirable relations of reciprocity, for example sexual and/or domestic, and would lead to difficulties in terminating a relationship.

Nicola discusses the way she associates financial dependency with inequality and the need to repay in kind through sexual services:

> I couldn't handle [being financially dependent on a partner] at all . . . I just think that I really like to be autonomous and have my own money to spend as I want. And if the person I was with was supporting me, I really wouldn't like that . . . I'd feel too dependent . . . I think that I would feel that I owed them something, either sexually or I don't think it would be an equal partnership and I am not into that sort of thing. I would want it to be equal. (19)

For Elaine economic dependence was seen to foster an unequal division of labour:

> I think the price might be intellectual stagnation . . . and to, in fact, become the very kind of housewife that I have no wish to become. Because by virtue of being at home all day, it's very easy to slip into the old role models: 'You're at home all day, I am going out to work, where's my tea? Why isn't the house clean?' (37)

Even when a woman hated her job, she did not wish to exchange her economic independence for dependency. This was the case for Lillian, who worked all her life in a series of low-paid clerical jobs:

> [Once a woman offered to keep me] I was horrified that some person would keep me. I mean, I don't like work, but there is no way I would let any one keep me. [*What do you think it would mean to be kept by someone?*] It would mean you would have to be there for them sort of, you know what I mean, you'd feel obliged to do things for them – whether it's doing washing up, or, you know, dropping your knickers. (45)

Importantly, financial dependency was seen to trap individuals in their relationship. Henrietta explains this:

> I would hate it, absolutely hate [being economically dependent on a partner]. [*Why?*] I really think it would affect the power

balance in the relationship, if I was spending somebody else's money. I would hate not to have my own money, or my means for leaving a relationship. Because I think a relationship can only be truly equal if both people can know they can get out of it. And it would be very difficult to get out of it if I was dependent financially on somebody. So I always have to be able to be alone in order to be happy with someone else. (35)

A similar feeling comes from Jocelyn, a professional woman, who has been in a relationship for five years with a partner in a manual occupation:

[Financial independence is important]: I wouldn't give up my own bank account and I wouldn't want [my partner] to do that. And I also wouldn't want [my partner] to not work, and I wouldn't want me to not work. I think if ever it happens that either of us didn't work, say if we decided to have children or something like that, then I would think it was important that we would both get back to it. Largely because of economic independence, but also to do with have a feeling of contributing . . . My fear is – and it's not just for me, but from [my partner's] point of view too – I would hate to see one of us in a situation where I have seen a lot of [married] women, where they can't make the break and do what they really want to do because they don't have economic independence. (27)

Respondents who had been married were often the most fervent in their rejection of economic dependency, as is illustrated by Isabelle, a divorced clerical worker:

[*Do you see yourself as a lifelong worker?*] Yes, I never want, I never ever want to be kept. I don't want to be a kept woman at all, no way! (29)

Overall, respondents believed that being totally or partially dependent on a partner for their standard of living would be difficult. Some had experienced this in their relationships with men and were unwilling to reproduce this kind of power dynamic unintentionally into their relationships with women. Importantly, respondents' sensitivity to the power derived from differences in income allowed many to anticipate this problem and develop strategies to mediate its impact. We now move on to explore ways in which respondents viewed and approached the tensions arising out of economic imbalances, and extend the discussion to include another source of tension, unilateral home ownership.

The organization of finances in lesbian households

Twenty-eight women in my sample were in long-term relationships ranging from one year to 19 years. Of these, 22 were living with their partners. Partnerships tended to be between women of similar ages and all but one respondent, who had given up waged work for health reasons, were in 'dual earner' relationships. It must also be remembered that none of my respondents was currently responsible for children under school age.[6] Commuting at weekends to be with a partner because of job commitments was a quite common accurance, with 16 respondents having experienced this in the past or at the time of interview. We now turn to respondents' accounts of the way household finances were organized in past and present relationships.

Cohabiting respondents usually held separate bank accounts. This seems to be a common practice amongst cohabiting couples who do not intend to marry (Blumstein and Schwartz, 1985:97; Pahl, 1989:106). The holding of separate accounts by respondents may have been motivated, at one level, by a desire to pre-empt haggling over money in the event of the relationship breaking up. It was also motivated by the desire to retain some control over their own income, so that, within reason, they could spend their money as they wished. Kathleen explains why this was important to her:

> Well, as you are handling your own money, that economic power is something, when you are deciding what you are spending your money on. If you are in a relationship, you are both earning equal wages, it's more equal. Whereas I think, when a woman goes out to work, when she is married, that money goes into the family, it's not really for her. They wouldn't think of going out and buying themselves a stereo system ... The husband will buy that for the family, but he will have major use of it. (41)

This respondent has identified a problem faced by many married women. Pahl's (1989, 1991) British study exploring the links between money and power in marriage suggest that it is rare to find wives viewing their own earnings as personal spending money (p.129). Eileen, a childless divorced woman, like most previously married respondents, found that her earnings had a different symbolic meaning during her marriage. Although she had pursued a career in a female profession, her salary was considerably lower than her husband's:

I didn't realize how I felt about it, about being dependent, until I wasn't. And I realized now that I used to feel guilty about buying things for me, clothes and things, because it wasn't my money. It was our money, and therefore I ought to be buying things for the house. (45)

The most common way for respondents to organize household finances was to divide up household bills, rent or mortgage payments, and put this money into a joint account specifically for household bills. The paying of bills and keeping of accounts was usually carried out together, or taken in turns. None of the sample reported problems with this arrangement. An example of how this worked comes from May, a divorced woman with a teenage daughter:

It was easy really, we divided the rent up and I paid more because I had [my daughter]. We just had a tin. It was really great, if either of us did shopping we just chucked the receipts in the tin and wrote our name on the back. And every month we did the accounts, and I paid a certain proportion and [my partner] paid the other, and we put so much into an account every month for bills. It was really good and it worked very well, it was never any problem. (49)

There was, however, one woman who delegated financial management to her partner. Veronica is a professional woman who has been living for almost three years with a previously married partner who had an administrative job. She earns more than her partner, and admits to being a poor manager of money:

I am earning much more than [my partner] does. I don't think that is important. I am useless with money, I have been overdrawn since the age of 13. . . I am a financial liability. I came [into the relationship] with £6000 of debts, just for starters. She manages the money and she does it brilliantly. It's the only way to cope. I can't be trusted with money, I want to spend it . . . We have single bank accounts and we have a joint bank account, and [my partner] manages them

all and balances the money between them; all I just do is
sign the cheques. (37)

Coping with income differentials

Given the constraints on women's earnings and respondents'
efforts to achieve living wages, the couples in my sample did
not experienced the large income differentials which appear
to contribute to imbalances in power in heterosexual couples
(Blumstein and Schwartz, 1985:146; Pahl, 1989:169). Most of
the ten couples where I know each partner's salary had income
differentials of less than 20 per cent, and the highest was 44
per cent. In contrast, Pahl (1989) found substantial income
differentials between wives and husbands, with 79 per cent of
the men earning more than the highest earning wife in the
sample (p.65). Pahl concludes:

> Many couples wanted their marriage to be a relationship
> between equals and tried to express this equality in their
> financial arrangements. However, the results of this study
> showed that the greater earning power of husbands continues
> to be associated with greater control over finances and greater
> power in decision making within the family. (p.169)

Pahl's conclusion reminds us that, despite the contrary inten-
tions of individual actors, structural inequalities between women
and men intervene to place limitations on the extent to which
they may conduct 'equal' relationships. Couples who attempt
'equal' relationships usually do not take into account inequality
of conditions, such as the lower earning power of women.
Consequently, the pursuit of 'equality' which ignores the social
and economic processes which construct women and men to
be different serve to maintain the status quo.[7] For example,
when each partner in a heterosexual relationship believes that
s/he should contribute an equal share to the household finances
this usually means that women contribute a greater proportion of their salaries than their male partners. When female
partners fall short of parity in financial contribution (which
they often do), they generally feel compelled to pay in kind,
by taking on a greater share of domestic chores (Pahl, 1989:170;
Blumstein and Schwartz, 1985:86).

As was noted earlier, although differentials in income were
usually fairly narrow amongst my couples, larger differentials

did sometimes exist. Many respondents appeared to be very sensitive to the potential power discrepancies generated by this situation. Although I was unable to pursue this in any great depth, some of the different strategies they followed in an attempt to neutralize the effects of economic imbalance are worth looking at. When partners' financial conditions where markedly unequal, many took this into account so that feelings of dependency could be limited. In some cases, inequality of income was reflected in household contributions. Here, contributions were agreed according to the means of the respective partners, and this was perceived as the fair way of doing it. An example of this kind of financial arrangement comes from Theodora, a professional woman in a nine-year relationship:

> [The house is owned jointly] . . . she pays half the mortgage, as far as day-to-day things we split it down the middle, but for big purchases we split it according to our respective salaries; it works out at 12/17th or something silly like that [laughter]. (45)

A similar arrangement is reported by Suzanna who is in a 19-year relationship. Both she and her partner worked in female-dominated professions:

> [My partner] has always resented the fact that I have [earned] slightly more and she tends to think that I should pay for slightly more. So I pay slightly more of the mortgage, but it hasn't made a lot of difference . . . The salary difference has never been that important to me. (44)

Many respondents felt uncomfortable with the idea of living beyond their means. A solution offered by some couples was to live at the level of the lower earning partner. Lotty, a professional woman, explains:

> [*Do you think there would be a problem if you had a partner who was earning a lot less than you?*] I would be very careful about [that] . . . Say someone was earning half my salary, I would choose things to do that she could afford, so that she could pay her half, rather than always pay for her – because I think that's 'yuckie'. Nobody likes to be bought, not too obviously anyway. (24)

The experience of being married to a higher earning partner often provided empathy towards a partner in this situation. Heidi, a previously married woman in a senior administration job, explains how this experience has motivated her approaches to lesbian relationships. Her discussion also illustrates the contrasting options she saw as available for dealing with economic imbalances in heterosexual and lesbian relationships:

> [*You are in a well paid job. What if your partner wasn't as well paid as you?*] Some have been better paid and some have been worse paid, but I have never found it to be a problem. [*How do you avoid the problem?*] Well possibly because I have been aware of the implications of it being a problem when I was married, I have actually worked hard at it not being a problem in relationships with women. [*How do you sort it out?*] We negotiate it. [*How do you sort out joint ventures like going on holidays that she can't afford?*] If she can't afford it we don't do it. That was never an acceptable option while I was married: we have to do it, we have the money. [*You wouldn't think of saying let's use some of my money?*] No, partly because I have been in the situation with a woman who earned more money than me and having to work quite hard at saying, 'Look, we are going to live within my means not yours.' And having to work quite hard to achieve that. (33)

Those respondents in well-paid employment often spoke of the power derived from their greater earnings as playing a negative role when it came to negotiating relationships with someone earning less. Norma, who has a high professional salary, describes this:

> Well, speaking for myself, I can only say that sometimes I have been quite embarrassed about earning more than my partner. It's been an encumbrance rather than anything else. (52)

The examples above illustrate some of the strategies adopted by respondents for counteracting the effects of economic imbalances. My material is limited. The examples I have presented represent successful and thoughtful approaches to the problem. I do not suggest that all my sample utilized such diligence in approaching inequalities in income. Perhaps those who had abused their financial power were less willing to discuss the problem. However, although some did report situations where they had experienced power imbalances derived from money, none suggested that either they or a partner intentionally

abused this power. None of the respondents was in a relationship at the point of interview which was seen as problematic
in terms of economic imbalance. This may be because, when
partners recognize an imbalance of economic power and are
unable, or unwilling, to take steps to counter the problem, the
relationship is short-lived.

Power and unilateral home ownership

Another potential source of power imbalance related to income
is unilateral house ownership. Often respondents suggested an
awareness of difficulties associated with living in a house that
was owned by a partner. This situation was understood to 'set
the agenda' at a fundamental level of the decision-making
process. In these situations, neither partner seemed particularly
happy with the unintended power dynamics that resulted, because
it constrained autonomy and supported feelings of dependency.
However, with the best will in the world, some respondents
experienced the unintentional power imbalances associated with
unilateral home ownership and felt uneasy with this situation.
Madelaine, a professional woman, describes how she felt that
unilateral home ownership 'set the agenda' of decision making
in a previous relationship. In this case there was also an inequality
in income and occupational status between herself and her
partner:

> [The relationship] didn't involve role playing, but unfortu-
> nately it also wasn't equal, because I had a better job and
> more money and the property was mine, which didn't lead
> to an equal relationship . . . I controlled where we lived, and
> that is never equal if you own a house and the other person
> doesn't. [*Did you abuse that power?*] Never! No. I didn't feel
> it to be a power, right, but had I been the other person I
> would have felt it as an unequal power, and ultimately it is,
> isn't it? But obviously it is, because if you fall out and part,
> that person's going to be the person who has to leave, hasn't
> she? [*What about decision making?*] Decisions at a leisure level,
> definitely equal, but decision making on what house and where
> we lived, where there were no choices. (45)

In this next extract from Charlotte we can see how it felt to be
in the situation of living in a partner's home. Again imbalances
came also from income differences and occupational status.

She was employed at the time in factory work and her partner was a professional woman. Like the previous respondent, she experienced inequalities in power as the unintentional outcome of economic differentials:

> [*When you were involved with [this partner], you followed her job; did you feel that because she earned more money it allowed her to make more decisions?*] Yes, yes. Well, I suppose the fact that it was her house and, as you say, the fact that she earned the biggest proportion of money, yes. I suppose towards the end, I suppose that was a lot of it, I felt that I was perhaps living in her shadow . . . [*Did you feel she was insisting on getting her way because she made more money?*] No, no there was never any pressure, it was just something I felt. (49)

I suggested to her that she may have been in a similar position to many married women. She did not agree:

> No I don't think so, not the same. Because I think men want women to feel that way, whereas this was just something that happened. I know in fact, I know [she] didn't think that way. It was just what I felt, but I think men want women to feel sort of beholden to them.

In this next extract, we can see how the discomfort of being dependent on a partner for housing can lead to a speedy renegotiation of the conditions of the relationship. This was the case for Michelle who had recently ended her marriage and had experienced a period of homelessness when she first left her husband. Despite earning a similar income to her female partner, she felt that living in her partner's house conflicted with her ardent desire never to be economically dependent again. As her partner was unwilling to sell the house and to co-own a home, Michelle decided to buy her own mobile home and move out. She works in a clerical occupation:

> [*Do you feel that you would be dependent on someone financially again?*] No! This is the trauma I am having with [my partner] now. This is why I can't remain living here. I can't actually stand the thought that if our relationship ends I am out on the street with nothing. I was given that choice before – I wasn't given a choice – but I walked away from it. This time I will not allow myself to even be given that choice, because I will own that mobile home, it will be mine. It doesn't

matter who it is, but whenever you go into a relationship, even if it is shared, at the end of the day you end up with nothing. If I look at what I am getting from [my ex-husband], I have earned about £1000 a year in 11 years of marriage. (29)

For those respondents who decided to remain in their lover's house, various strategies were developed to pre-empt feelings of alienation and dependency. Loraine has been living in her lover's house for four years. She is in management and earns a similar salary to her partner. She had just managed to achieve her ambition of buying her own flat when they met. Her partner did not wish to co-own a property as she had suffered financial loss in the break-up of a previous relationship. Rather than feel overly dependent in the relationship, Loraine decided to keep on her own flat and rent it out:

I have [a flat] but I rent it. I feel secure because I have that place, but I have been renting it out for three years. I don't intend to give it up and pool my resources with [my partner]. I want to keep my financial independence if nothing else. [*Why do you think that's important to you?*] I suppose because – having said I don't look to the future – I have begun in the last five or six years thinking about when I get older. And I know that relationships don't seem to last: the ideal is that you are going to be with someone for the rest of your life, but it doesn't work that way, with the best will in the world it doesn't always work that way. I am frightened of ending up on the street, or ending up in accommodation that I can't afford to pay for, so at least I know it's an investment. (32)

Even with having her own home to go to in the event of the relationship breaking up, Loraine still felt uncomfortable with the situation. The house furnishings and decor reflected the identity of her partner; living surrounded by her lover's choice of decor symbolically signified her externality. The solution she arrived at was to claim her own territory. She took over a room in the house, furnished and redecorated it to reflect her own identity:

[*Do you ever feel it a problem living in someone else's house?*] I did at one stage. There are very few things in this house on display that are actually mine. The house shows [my partner's] personality rather than mine. She had just bought the house when I started to see her, and I got frustrated because nothing in the house is mine. When I moved in, a lot of my things were in my flat; whatever I brought over didn't seem to match or [my partner] didn't like, and that really worried me. I thought this is not going to work, I feel like a permanent lodger. It suddenly dawned on me one day, all I needed was one room to call my own, so I decorated it and put my things in it. And I don't ever really use it, but I know that I can. I like the garden too and a lot of that represents me.

Again decor represented a problem for Tierl, who has been living in her lover's home for the past year. In this case, a partial solution to the problem of feeling external in the relationship was to redecorate the whole house:

[*You didn't experience power in the relationship in terms of your partner owning the house?*] No, we talked about that a lot. I expressed it was something I couldn't cope with, and it was something she didn't want. What we actually did, after a settling period of about six months, we redecorated, and we made it our house rather than her house, and we felt that was the way round it. That is one of the ideas behind moving, which we are considering ... that was our way of overcoming the potential power – that neither of us wanted us to have – that was obviously there. So that was the way around it, to claim it for us. (27)

Respondents were usually uncomfortable with unilateral house ownership. They considered that this situation would under-mine their own or their partner's sense of independence. Again, their discussions reflect their recognition of the unintentional consequences of power and, as a result, some attempted to construct strategies to defuse or avoid the situation. Co-ownership was the preferred option, for those respondents who could afford it. At the time of interview, 15 respondents were co-owners of their homes, and only three were in a unilateral home ownership situation.

Intimate strangers versus intimate friendships

People's experience of emotions is slowly becoming an area of interest to sociologists. Studies of couples in North America (Hochschild, 1983, 1989) and Britain (Duncombe and Marsden,

1993; Brannen and Moss, 1991; Mansfield and Collard, 1988) suggest that the gender division of labour includes 'emotional labour'. Women tend to do the bulk of this emotion work as they attempt to keep themselves and their families happy. Women and men appear to have very different understanding about emotional expression. Processes which construct gender difference seem also to place women and men in different *emotional cultures* (Duncombe and Marsden, 1993). Mansfield and Collard (1988:178–9) suggest that wives and husbands come together as *intimate strangers*, with very different emotional goals in marriage. Women desire intimacy and empathy, while most of the male partners interviewed wanted 'home life, a physical and psychological base'. Duncombe and Marsden (1993), whose study specifically explores the emotional worlds of heterosexual couples, suggest that men appear to find it difficult to articulate and express their emotions and feel threatened if encouraged to do so, while women feel disappointed and frustrated by the unwillingness of their male partners to participate emotionally in relationships with themselves or their children. They point out that women in long-term relationships with men usually have to work hard at constructing coping strategies to deal with their disappointment about the lack of partner intimacy and sharing they experience. They argue that the inequalities of women and men's perceived emotional needs should be seen as a form of intentional or unintentional power:

> Men's withholding from women the emotional validation which they seek through intimacy may become a source of male power, and indeed some women reported that they experienced men's unusual 'remoteness' as a form of power. In a mysterious way, the giving or withholding of emotion and intimacy thus becomes one kind of 'carrier' of gender power. (p.236)

Given the gendered nature of emotional expression, it is not surprising that my respondents did not usually experience their partners as *intimate strangers*. In fact, those who had had heterosexual experience as a reference point usually (*n* = 27) volunteered that the emotional content and quality of their relationships with women was a major differentiating feature. They commented on the high levels of intimacy and communication which characterized their lesbian relationships. Ginny describes her feelings about her partnership of two years:

I think what I've got is a total trust, total understanding, and just a communication that I never thought I would ever have ... It's almost like ESP ... It's like strange things, like understanding, in the sense that I know what she is thinking, what she's feeling at certain moments, which is very important ... there are so many traits that are attributed as being particularly female, but are nice, wonderful traits – softer, the kinder generosity – whether that's something that men try to hide about themselves that's really there or not, I don't know. (24)

Another example comes from Andrea, who has been in a lesbian relationship for the past eight years:

[My relationship is] very much more in-depth as far as communication is concerned, and communication as distinct from chat. It's very much more fulfilling in that I feel a person in my own right. I didn't when I was married. (45)

However, lesbians are not immune to the negative operation of 'emotional power'. The research on lesbian couples discussed earlier suggests that, of all possible sources of power, differences in emotional involvement are the greatest source of inequality between women. A partner who is less involved in the relationship usually has more power. This may be self-evident and probably holds true for any emotional relationship. However, given that women may feel encouraged to invest greater emotional energy in their relationships with each other and expect this situation to be reciprocal, emotional imbalances may be experienced as a major source of power inequality.

Of all the different possibilities of inequality between women in a relationship, extreme emotional imbalances were reported by my sample as presenting the most difficulty. Imbalances involved different degrees of emotional manipulation. The fear of losing a partner inevitably led to allowing a partner to take greater control over the operation of the relationship. These emotional conflicts often temporarily affected the 'wronged' partner's ability to do her job as usual, and this sometimes led to having to 'come out' to an employer. The achievement of the high degree of closeness, so often described by respondents, generates a corresponding risk of vulnerability. In this situation a thoughtless, immature or cruel partner can effectively wield considerable power (although these kinds of relationships were usually short-lived). Interestingly, none of my respondents admitted to being the 'abuser' in this domain, probably because it is easier to admit being wronged than having wronged. It must be pointed out, however, that these abuses of emotional power were rare: taking all their relationships into account, only nine women reported having experienced this. In most cases women thought fondly of previous lovers. Because friendship is generally an important aspect of lesbian relationships they do not simply end in the conventional sense – they are transformed. In other words, usually after a period of (often very painful) adjustment, ex-lovers retain positions as close friends.[8] As one respondent commented with reference to her ex-lovers, 'as friends, they are the jewels in my life'.

BALANCING HOME AND EMPLOYMENT COMMITMENTS

The division of labour within the home, and between the home and the workplace, has been identified as a major source of inequality between women and men. As lesbian couples do not have gender difference to guide their approach, it is interesting to see how respondents balance domestic and employment commitments in their relationships with women. This section first illustrates examples of their different approaches to household task allocation. We will then focus on the way waged work was negotiated in partnerships and outline some important employment consequences of their more balanced approach.

Gender divisions of household labour

Research clearly demonstrates that, in the overwhelming majority of heterosexual partnerships, women take responsibility for, and perform the bulk of, domestic tasks, even when they are in full-time waged work (Mansfield and Collard, 1988; Hochschild, 1989; Brannen and Moss, 1991). This situation holds for couples without children (Mansfield and Collard, 1988; Blumstein and Schwartz, 1985), for couples where wives have a higher occupational status (McRae, 1986) or the man is unemployed (Morris, 1990), as well as for cohabiting couples (Macklin, 1983; Blumstein and Schwartz, 1985) and those who see themselves as sharing household work (Doucet, 1995). When the analysis is extended to include a broad range of household tasks, the very gendered nature of task allocation becomes clearly apparent

(Pahl, 1984; Seymour, 1992). 'Male' household work includes activities such as car upkeep and house maintenance, improvements and repair, whereas women are responsible for routine and time-consuming housework, domestic production and childcare (Pahl, 1984). Gender boundaries exist between the two areas of responsibility, and change has generally taken the form of a slight increase in male participation in the wife's sphere rather than a rethinking of the boundaries of responsibility.[9] In consequence, it is women who generally find themselves balancing the responsibilities of home and paid work, so that it is their employment schedules that are adjusted to compensate, and it is they who experience the fatigue, strain, guilt and anxiety because they 'choose' to be employed (Doucet, 1991:17).

Lesbian approaches to household task allocation

In the light of the above, it is interesting to look at the way the domestic division of labour is negotiated in households where there are no gender and differentiated guidelines upon which to base the allocation of tasks. The few North American studies that do consider task allocation in non-heterosexual households suggest that, contrary to popular stereotypes, homosexual couples rarely follow a traditional division of labour. Peplau and Cochran's (1990) comparative study of gay, lesbian and heterosexual couples looked at household task allocation. They found that, if there was any specialization in household tasks amongst lesbians, it was usually based on individual skills and interests (p.344). They noted that lesbians were less inclined towards role playing than either gay men or heterosexual couples and it was rare to find one partner in a lesbian relationship performing mostly 'masculine' or mostly 'feminine' tasks. Blumstein and Schwartz's (1985:149) large-scale comparative study of different couple forms found that, of all the couples, lesbians had the most equitable division of household labour. They also found that women in a lesbian relationship spent the least amount of time on household tasks of any of the other women interviewed.[10] Johnson (1990) also noted that, regardless of the job status of a partner, household tasks in lesbian homes were usually shared fairly evenly. Weston's study (1991:149) of gays and lesbians in San Francisco found that both men and women felt that an equitable division of domestic labour was a crucial element in the construction of the egalitarian relationships they desired.

We now turn to my data to explore ways in which the allocation of household tasks were arranged. It must be pointed out, however, that my data are limited because the research did not specifically set out to investigate divisions of labour in lesbian households. The sample was not drawn with this aim in mind. I did not necessarily interview both partners or seek out couples with dependent children. My analysis of task allocation is based on their brief descriptions and in most cases their accounts could not be verified by their partners. However, where both partners were interviewed, I found little contradiction between their descriptions. My current research on the sharing arrangements of lesbian couples with dependent children does, however, suggest that we can be fairly confident about the findings outlined below.[11]

Overall, respondents' descriptions of divisions of household labour in lesbian partnerships past and present suggest that tasks were allocated in an even-handed way. Thirty-seven respondents commented on the importance to them of feeling relatively free from the *expectations* and *responsibilities* associated with a gender division of labour. They were aware of the 'double day' experienced by many of their heterosexual female colleagues and saw no reason to emulate this pattern in their own relationships. Home life was rarely ruled by the tyranny of being houseproud, perhaps because their identity and self-worth were not seen as being derived from a demonstration domestic excellence. Consequently, some may have had low standards of household tidiness. Angela, a professional woman who has been living with her partner for the past three years, sums up a fairly typical approach to housework found amongst respondents:

> I do not consider housework and cooking the 'be all and end all of life'. I will hoover and clear up when friends come round, but I am not a fanatical housewife . . . I would rebel if it were expected of me. I mean, I had no objection this morning to belting around with the hoover, but nobody, neither [my partner] nor I, expects me to have to do it. It would have been impolite to you, I think, to have walked into the house in the mess it was in this morning [laughter]. But neither one of us expected 100 per cent that the house had to look clean and tidy, otherwise the interview could not go ahead. It's that absolute down the line expectation that I cannot understand. So [my partner] said she doesn't

want to do the ironing, as she said just before you came –
fine I'm not bothered. (37)

However, certain tasks ultimately have to be carried out and
we now focus on some of their approaches to the allocation of
these tasks, considering the three main styles of task organization which I have identified. I term these the 'symmetric shared
approach', the 'symmetric specialized approach' and the
'asymmetric approach'.

The 'symmetric shared approach' to household tasks

A 'symmetric shared approach' to task allocation was very common and was particularly favoured amongst feminist respondents.
Here tasks were performed together or taken in turns, and
there was very little specialization. In fact, some went to great
lengths to avoid specialization. Underlying this approach was
a belief that each partner should feel competent in performing both 'male' and 'female' tasks. They generally viewed task
specialization along gender lines, as supporting partner dependency and thus thwarting self-determination. Karen, working in
a male-dominated manual occupation, describes this kind of
approach and explains why she thinks it necessary. The relationship she is referring to began as a 'commuting relationship':

> The domestic thing worked out very well; we shared it. Shared
> the shopping, and the cooking, and the washing up, and all
> of that I really respect, that part of our relationship. I think
> if one of us was more stressed out, the other of us would
> like do it for a week at the most. Later on we lived together,
> because we bought a house together, and we lived together
> for 15 months in that house. [*Why do you think it is a positive
> thing not to have set roles?*] It is much better if you can have
> the confidence to do everything in a relationship. Although
> you might be better at doing something – so you might in
> the end always end up, say, doing the plugs. If you know
> how to mend a plug, then you are not going to give that
> power to someone else all the time. I think it is important
> for both people to know how to do things, like drive a car,
> cope with the running of the house; both people should be
> as competent as possible in all areas – to know that you both
> can do it, and you both know what it is like to do it, I think
> that must be the best way. (35)

In some cases a more formalized arrangement was devised for the allocation of household tasks. A rota would be drawn up to ensure that each did a fair share. In this next example, the rota was developed more as a way of introducing the young son of the respondent's partner to the responsibilities of household labour. Both partners are full-time employees and committed feminists. Rachel works in a 'Women's Movement' organization and has been living with Linda for a year:

> [*How do you work out roles and things?*] [laughter] We made out a rota at the weekend; how do we work it out? We share it, basically, the rota was merely to try and get [Linda's] son involved, rather than us. We both have very, very stressful jobs. We both work with people, we both do very emotionally draining work, so that means we are both very drained at the end of the day, so organization is of the essence to keep sanity, basically. So we are very organized about it. (26)

Usually those following a 'symmetric shared approach' were more flexible. Tasks were performed because they needed to be done, and whoever was available did them. Partners seemed to approach tasks on the basis of perceptions of fairness; they were happy to do more than their fair share at times, so long as this was not an *expectancy*. An example of this comes from Caroline who has been living with her partner for the past three years. She co-owns her house with her partner, and they renovated it together. She is in a male-dominated manual occupation; her partner is training to enter a male-dominated profession:

> No, there's no role play, things get done because they have to get done – if the washing has to be taken out of the washing machine and whoever's there at the time [does it]. The cooking has to be done, whoever is free cooks it. It may turn out that one of us does it three nights on the trot, and then the other one night, and then two nights on the trot, but then we don't really think about it like that, we do it because we want to do it. Generally speaking, we do most of the cooking together anyway, because we do enjoy doing it; we do most things together, quite honestly. It just happens if someone has to study for exams or something one of us covers and does both those sort of things a bit more often than normal. (29)

Importantly, underlying this shared approach was that neither partner held primary responsibility for the overall running of the household. The burden was shared and both partners were competent in performing 'male' and 'female' tasks. Doing tasks together was seen as an expression of love, making a relationship complete. Tasks performed together could become fun, rather than a drain on energy. Furthermore, this was seen to make sense, for two busy women performing tasks together was a speedy way to dispense with routine chores and provide more time for shared leisure.

The 'symmetric specialized approach' to household tasks

A strict sharing of tasks was not to everyone's liking. Dividing up tasks according to particular likes or dislikes was another favoured approach followed by respondents. This was particulary the case for older women, who had perhaps developed skills in previous relationships, or in marriage. It may also be associated with more long-term relationships where certain routines and patterns become established. Importantly, neither partner held overall responsibility for the domestic functioning of the household. Some tasks were shared, while others became the responsibility of one or the other. Sylvia contrasts her approach to household tasks in her current five-year partnership with a 'symmetric shared approach' she had experienced in an earlier lesbian relationship:

> [My ex-lover] was very much a feminist, would make a point of one week I would do the housework and the next week she would do it, and cooking the same. I found this very rigid. The way [Delia] and I work, which is much better – I hate ironing and she does all the ironing, we share the cooking, 'cos we both like cooking. I look after the kitchen, the bathroom and she looks after this room [living room] and the bedroom. She likes this and so do I. I think you should divide it up, and do it equally, but you do things you like, not things you hate. (38)

Her partner Delia describes the arrangements from her point of view:

> [Sylvia] does more of the day-to-day cooking, and I perhaps go mad if someone is coming to dinner, and throw myself into doing that. But we do things together which is very nice, we just seem to enjoy doing things together . . .

They are both enthusiastic gardeners and equally competent
in household maintenance. One partner had been to night
school to learn carpentry and she had made all the fitted
cupboards in the house.

In this next example, we can see a greater degree of specialization in the relationship. Virginia a divorced women in professional management, has been living with her lover in their
co-owned home for the past eight years. She and her partner
mainly share out the tasks. However, as she has had more experience in cooking she tends to do more of that. Since she
has injured her wrist and cannot lift heavy items, her partner
performs more of the heavy work:

> [*Do you feel you have a double day?*] No, not at all. Simple
> things like doing the food shopping, if you do that on your
> own for a household it is really quite hard work on top of
> the day's work, but we do it together, all those sorts of things,
> like the ironing. All the stuff like that, the house the cleaning
> – not that we do very much cleaning [laughter]. No, it's
> much more equal. . . . As far as organizational things are
> concerned we split most things down the middle . . . shopping
> and cooking and housework and stuff, except that I tend to
> cook more because having been married for ten years you
> get very used to cooking, and it's something I can do with
> my eyes closed, whereas [my partner] doesn't feel that she
> is very good at it, but she does from time to time. Other
> things we split down the middle. Except four years ago when
> we were on holiday I had a bike accident, and fractured my
> right wrist badly. It was mishandled here which means that
> my right hand is not good for heavy things like cutting the
> hedge, and mowing the lawn and shifting furniture, and so,
> because of that, a certain amount of the heavy work falls on
> [my partner], but I don't think it's a role thing, it's more
> out of necessity. (45)

Household labour involves tasks that have come to be socially
defined as 'male' and 'female'. Unless women can afford to
employ outside help, 'male' tasks must be learnt and carried
out. If one partner, through developing a skill, or just by superior
strength, performs certain 'male' tasks, is a traditional division
of labour being replicated at some level? Do the gender labels
that are attached to some tasks 'gender' the performance? The
previous example, and the next two, are examples of this kind

of specialization. My view, based on my impressions of these respondents, was that, contrary to examples that we will see later, these tasks were perceived as 'practical' tasks, rather than 'masculine' tasks. The women involved in doing these 'practical' tasks did not see them as expressing the more masculine side to their personality. Nor had they relinquished their more routine domestic responsibilities. This contrasts with the 'egalitarian' men in Pahl's study (1984) who 'helped out' substantially with the domestic routines, yet both partners still held to a gender division of *responsibility* within the two household spheres. This, I think, demonstrates the power of heterosexual gender scripts to impede the momentum of change towards egalitarianism.

Another example of task specialization in 'practical' areas comes from Ruth, who is in a 15-year relationship. She has shared in the care of her partner's two children. Domestic responsibilities and tasks are described as shared.

> No, we have always shared cooking, cleaning. The only thing [my partner] does that I can't do is woodwork, I really can't; I would if I could. Practical things, she does things like that, because I am not very practical. Whoever gets home first [cooks the dinner]. Sometimes both of us get home so late it's not worth starting faffing around, we just muck in together and get something quick and have the rest of the evening free . . . I certainly wouldn't want to fit into a wife role anyway, I don't want to fit into any role really, or have any label attached to me. I think I am just being me. (45)

For this next couple, there is more task specialization and less performing of tasks together. Shelly and Shirl divided up the domestic tasks; one did the cleaning and the other the catering. Again one partner appeared to specialize in the more 'male' areas of tasks that require physical strength. As in the previous example, neither partner saw this as being male/female role play; rather it was the result of one partner's greater strength. They are both in their early fifties, they have lived together for 19 years, and have recently retired from 'female' professions. They co-own a fairly large house, and have spent several years renovating it together. Shelly describes a fairly equitable division of domestic tasks, based on specialization and separate responsibilities:

> I do the housework and she does the cooking. I am a hopeless cook, and she is a very good cook, so it works out fairly evenly. [*And the shopping?*] She does all the catering.

Shirl's description reveals a greater degree of specialization, where she takes on more of the heavy tasks:

> Well, I think there is a great deal more giving and taking . . . in the 'housey' bit really. I don't do much of [the house-work] now, [Maud] does it. There is no great thing about who does what. We tend to do what we are better at, I sup-pose. I am stronger physically, so I have done the stronger things, she is not so strong physically, so I've done things like chopping logs, and gardening and things.

In none of these examples of specialization did one partner appear overburdened by household responsibilities. The division of labour appeared to be equitable and fair, and was per-ceived by each partner as such. It was the freedom from *expectations* regarding responsibility for, and the performance of, tasks that was perceived by respondents as essential. This they usually saw as differentiating their partnerships from past relationships with men or their observations of task allocation in most heterosexual households they knew. The flexibility in task allocation often extended to judgements about task ex-ecution: when both women were tired or busy with other ac-tivities, chores would just be left undone.

The 'asymmetric approach' to household tasks

Not all relationships, however, were free from inequalities in task allocation. When respondents took into account their ex-periences of living with female partners past and present there appeared to be a range of ways that inequalities in task alloca-tion and execution could develop over the duration of a relation-ship. Sixteen respondents reported being familiar with this situation, although only a few were experiencing this in their current relationship. These inequalities were usually quantita-tive, where one partner did considerably more that the other, or they were occasionally gendered, insofar as the gender ideol-ogies which shape task allocation between men and women were mirrored in relationships between women.

Just as some lesbian couples may find a solution to the de-mands of balancing domestic work and paid work by lowering their standard of household tidiness, inequalities can be intro-duced when partners have different dirt threshold levels. As may be very familiar to people who have lived in shared ac-commodation, the one with the lowest 'dirt threshold', tends

to do more of the domestic work. At least five respondents
had experienced this in past relationships. Of these five, two
women spoke of having taken on the main burden of domestic chores for this reason, while the others reported that their
partners had done so. These kinds of relationships were more
often between women with a fairly large age gap, and were
generally short-lived. These inequalities were more usually
understood as being the result of immaturity, or inexperience,
than of adherence to role play.

Sometimes inequalities were related to unemployment or long-
term illness, this was the case for three respondents. Rita explains how she fell into a more traditional division of labour
when she was temporarily unemployed and her partner was in
a well-paid professional occupation:

> I think I became quite a housewife at that point . . . it's so
> easy to fall into that. Someone has to get up in a rush –
> 'That's OK, I'll do the washing up later' – and it just sort of
> goes on until you are no longer offering to do it, but it's
> assumed you will do it. (30)

For others a more traditional approach came about when their
partnerships operated more along the lines of what I would
call a 'mother/daughter' dynamic and, in a few cases, when
their relationships attempted to mirror heterosexual relationship, that is, 'butch/femme'.[12] The 'mother/daughter' division
of labour tended to be more like those with an imbalance of
dirt threshold than those with 'butch/femme' relationships. They
were often between a young woman, who had recently left home,
and an older woman who had been previously married. The
younger woman would be fairly incompetent at caring for herself and the older woman would take charge. Again these relationships tended to be short-lived and transitory.

The household division of labour in 'butch/femme' relationships tended to be fairly traditional, or at least began that way.
Six respondents reported having experienced 'role play' with
regard to household tasks. Bobbie discusses the approach to
domestic work in a previous relationship. She was working in
a supervisory position in the motor trade; her partner was doing
factory work;

> [*In the eight-year relationship, how did you sort out the roles?*] I
> suppose it was very male/female. I was taking the 'male' role
> and she the 'female' role. [*What about in terms of roles around*

the home: were you coming home expecting the meal to be ready?]
No, no, I never ever did that. Very often I used to come
home and cook the meal, especially if we were both working. I sort of mucked in with the housework; she did basically most of it – she complained that I didn't do it as well
as her. I was prepared to muck in. It wasn't a partnership,
certainly, she did probably most of the cooking. [*Were you
earning the same money?*] Yes, about the same; in fact she was
earning a bit more than me. Being a factory job, she was
probably earning more than me.

Dot describes the evolution of the division of household labour
in a previous long-term relationship, which began along the
lines of 'butch/femme'. At that time she was in a management
position in a male-dominated occupation and her partner was
a successful business woman:

In the beginning [my partner] did the cooking, and the bits
and pieces and I did the garden and the painting and the
decorating and things. But over the years, that's evolved round
into us doing it together. The reason being that, if we did it
together, we got the job done twice as quick, which meant
we had more time to spend together. It did occur that I did
the 'male' jobs more than [my partner], mainly because I
was more competent at them than she was, but over the years
I've learnt to cook better, iron . . . and things like this, but
this was only to facilitate spending more free time together.
[*Has [your partner] learnt how to do those more male tasks?*] Yes,
she can decorate now; still can't put a plug on very well, but
she has a bash – as she has tended to leave most of the
male-oriented things to me: you do don't you? If you find
that someone is good at a particular thing, you tend to leave
them to do it, so that's what we tended to do really . . . At
the end of the day, we would both get a meal, just fiddle
around the kitchen, get the meal. She would dish up, I would
wash up as we were going, sit down and eat it, finish up the
washing up, and then go and have a bath together and talk,
and that was the start of our evening. (43)

Interestingly, the women who took on the more 'feminine' tasks
were often in their first lesbian relationship. Some of these
women were described as unsure of their sexuality, and some
had later returned to heterosexual relationships. However, for

Meg, staying firmly within a traditional female role was seen as
her way of affirming her femininity. She describes her reasons
for filling a more traditional role in an earlier relationship.
She reported that, in subsequent relationships, male and female tasks were slightly more shared:

> It was definitely a bit of a – she did the 'male-ish' things,
> but, having said that, I suppose it was a bit like that because
> I suppose I thought of her as in the 'male' role . . . I was
> determined that I was still going to be a woman; there was
> no way I was going to do mannish things. If I was in a situ-
> ation where a 'man's' job needed doing, I'd either get a
> man to do it, or if I was with a woman I'd get the woman: if
> she wanted to do it and wanted to be like a man, let her do
> it. [*What sort of things did you see as a man's job?*] Well, mak-
> ing and mending things and painting, you know, 'men's' jobs.
> I still call it 'men's' jobs, I use it as a parody and I make a
> joke about it; at the same time I am not going to do these
> jobs. I can't, I can't even put a plug on. I am capable, I
> suppose I could do, but I don't want to know if it's a 'man's'
> job. I do gardening and I think that's very manly. (40)

The end result of these more 'butch/femme' divisions of household labour was more reminiscent of examples of Pahl's
(1984:288–308) egalitarian couples. In these cases husbands
shared in the routine domestic tasks, while retaining responsibility for the male household tasks. Wives still viewed the routine domestic tasks as their responsibility, but welcomed the
help given by their spouses. It must be pointed out that most
of the women who had described these unequal divisions of
labour had since developed a more equal approach. None of
those aged under 30 had experienced 'butch/femme' relationships and they had no desire to do so.

Generally, respondents embraced an egalitarian approach to
household labour. Part of the reason for this may be that contemporary lesbians, as has been argued earlier, lack an ideology that legitimizes the domination of one partner over another.
Consequently, domination is more clearly perceived for what
it is. It is probable that, for many, the egalitarian perspectives
they held were a major underlying motivating factor in their
previous dissatisfaction with and rejection of heterosexual relationships and their choosing to follow a lesbian lifestyle. While
some strongly egalitarian women engage in the brave task of

changing their male partners, others have discovered a different place to express these values. As a result, women who choose to share their lives with other women have no desire to subject themselves to the kind of power dynamic that they perceived as underpinning relationships with men.

Employment advantages of lesbian homelife circumstances

Finally, I would like to explore ways that respondents negotiated their careers in lesbian relationships. As we will see, most were aware that their relationships facilitated their ability to participate more fully in their jobs. First of all, the more equitable and flexible division of household labour experienced by most was seen as aiding them in the performance of their jobs. Fifteen women commented on this. This household situation was particularly valued by respondents in demanding and stressful employment. These women believed that they would have great difficulty in performing their jobs if they also had sole responsibility for the smooth running of the home. A second source of advantage, reported by 20 respondents, was the high levels of partner support, encouragement and understanding of their work commitments that they received. These advantages were perceived as contrasting with their experience and/ or understanding of married women's situation.

Importantly, a partner's right to be committed to her job was not challenged. This mutual support of careers is, it is suggested, very much linked with respondents' views on financial dependency, and their jobs represented, if nothing else, their independence. In general they expected mutual respect for the paid work component of life. Krish, who works in a male-dominated profession, illustrates this:

> I think we are both very good at valuing the other one's career and that even if that meant that we would have to work in different towns or we would have to work until 11 o'clock at night every night that would be OK. Her career's as important to me as mine is. (24)

Importantly, respondents did not seem to see themselves in competition with their partners in the way that Blumstein and Schwartz (1985) noted was the case for cohabiting men. Beth discusses ways that the encouragement she feels she receives in lesbian relationships differs from a previous heterosexual relationship. She works in a management position in transport:

> [He] was great . . . he encouraged me . . . He could only, and
> I think most men only encourage so far. If they think they
> are being shown up to be not as good, they don't like it,
> and they will pull back on the encouragement. There isn't
> the same genuine wanting to see you do well. Only if it suits
> them . . . I find that my relationships with women have been
> so different: it's encouragement all the way through, there
> are never any restrictions. (29)

This partner support was very much tied in with the more flexible
roles that constituted relationships between women. There were
no lines of demarcation regarding spheres of achievement. A
woman doing well at work did not undermine her partner's
gender identity, as appears to be the tendency in heterosexual
relationships (see Chapter 4). This held true even amongst
'butch/femme' couples, because employment status was independent of these roles. Poppy has been living with her partner
for four years. She works in a management position in a male-
dominated occupation. Poppy thought that the flexibility in
the division of labour at home together with the understanding she received from her partner greatly facilitated her ability
to do her job:

> [*How much time do you think you could devote to your job if you
> were in a heterosexual relationship?*] Probably not as much . . .
> My impression is that most men come home from work and
> expect things to be done for them, so I wouldn't be able to
> devote myself as much to my work. I would have to cut my-
> self off from it. I would either have to have a less stressful
> job, or I think the relationship might suffer. I think a lot of
> men don't actually like to think that their wives are taken
> up with their jobs; they think it's just a means of getting
> some money. Perhaps I am wrong, because I haven't had
> any relationships with men for 12 years, but that was my
> impression then, and I still sort of get that sort of impres-
> sion now. [*Have you found that in your relationship you have
> found encouragement towards your work?*] Yes, I have. She doesn't
> mind how much time I have spent at home doing work-re-
> lated matters, not at all because any housework to do, you
> either leave it or she'll do it, or it can wait to another day.
> So, yes, I am not expected to do anything, I am not ex-

pected to have dinner on the table. I am not expected to hoover the floor ... There is a certain amount I bring home; she's really good about it; but then she does a very similar thing, she brings home work from time to time, so it works both ways. I am not sure if a man or husband would put up with that; it depends on what sort of husband you have, I suppose. (32)

In this partnership there is 'give and take' between the demands made by a responsible job, the domestic demands and the relationship. Each understood the other's need to bring work home from time to time. Both women are in fairly senior positions at work and they earn similar wages.

The same points are made by Mary-Jane. Her junior management position in agriculture makes considerable demands on her time and energy. Again she does not believe that she could devote as much energy to her job if she were married:

[My sexuality has] enabled me to do the job I do ... [In my line of work] there are a lot of gay people in it ... I guess because the amount of time the job consumes you almost have to be gay. I couldn't hold down a marriage I don't think, to be honest, not if somebody wasn't, unless it was a gay marriage, because I don't think people would put up with it. I couldn't do it. I couldn't run a house, a family and do the job that I do, so it's probably just as well really. [*How does it help being in a gay relationship?*] Well [my partner] has her career and she's very definite what she wants to do ... She actually knows I have to do work, I have to be there; if anyone else is working I want to be there, I want to be in the thick of it, and she understands that it takes a lot of my time, and gives me time to do it, and that then gives her time to do her job, so ... We don't have a conflict with jobs really, she has a job that's very demanding. In the heterosexual relationships that I know, the man wants to be looked after, come home, dinner there. I might work till 10 pm. I need to be able to know that I can, if necessary, work all night. (25)

Again the women in this partnership have jobs which make similar demands on their time and earn similar salaries.

In contrast to her experience of marriage, Mary-Rose was actively encouraged by her partner to move out of low-paid

'women's' work and start her own business. She is now em-
ploying 12 women and is the only woman in the region running such a business. She explains how other women see her
lifestyle:

> Straight career women . . . say I am lucky not to have the
> restrictions of a man, and envy me. [*They see men holding them
> back?*] Yes, yes, but a necessary thing in their lives. I am often
> being told I am lucky, especially by single women in a het-
> erosexual relationship. They say I have the support of some-
> one but not the restrictions. [*It interferes with their careers how?*]
> I can't see how it doesn't, it has more effect. By choosing
> the sexuality I am, has made me more successful, work harder,
> and given me the freedom to work harder. [*What makes the
> difference?*] The role playing. The male should be, in the world's
> opinion, a breadwinner; the woman can be successful pro-
> vided the male is more successful. (35)

Indra felt that, if she were heterosexual, the time and mobility
demands made by her traditionally male profession would pre-
clude a relationship:

> If I was straight, I think it would be very difficult to find a
> man that could fit into my life. [*How so?*] Mainly the travel-
> ling and the hours that you spend at work, and the commit-
> ment you have: you have to work weekends; it's a type of
> thing that if you need to work late you do work late, and if
> you are posted you may be given two weeks' notice, but then
> you have to move, and I haven't yet met a man that would
> ever consider doing that for his girlfriend or wife. (24)

She is at present in a relationship which involves commuting
to be with her partner who is in a similar occupation. This was
seen as the best compromise until they could find satisfactory
employment in the same location.

All these respondents quoted have something interesting in
common. Both they and their partners were in occupations
that are usually filled by men. Only the first and last couples
were professional women. The rest had no further education
and were almost all from intermediate or manual social backgrounds. Their jobs made similar kinds of demands to those
faced by professional people. Their ability to do these demanding
and well paid 'male' jobs was seen as greatly facilitated by the
nature of their relationships. Here lies the great advantage

experienced by many lesbians. They did not feel they had to sacrifice or forgo relationships for the sake of their careers, as may be the case for other women. Conversely, they do not have to subordinate their working lives to a relationship, as is the case for many married or cohabiting single women. It is by considering the experiences of these 'ordinary' working women that we can see the employment constraints imposed by gender dichotomies contained within institutional heterosexuality.

So far we have said very little about the impact of children on shaping respondents' employment circumstances. At the time of interview, few respondents were or had been responsible for dependent children, although they did not necessarily rule out this possibility in the future. We have very few data on lesbian parenting (see, for example, Handscombe and Forster, 1982; Richardson, 1981) and I know of no published research which specifically explores divisions of employment and home life responsibilities between lesbian parents. My current research aims to help fill this gap. The study is in its early stages. I have conducted a series of interviews with 20 couples, have time-diary data on these couples, and background information on a further six couples. Most of these couples have children under five via donor insemination. On the basis of these data, the main trends identified include the absence of a traditional division of household labour, and partner flexibility in relation to paid work. We have yet to find an example where being a biological mother has resulted in loss of employment status. Further partner differentials in salary and/or employment participation levels cannot be predicted on the basis of biological motherhood. These tentative early findings suggest that, in the absence of gender scripts, lesbians may be constructing novel and less oppressive parenting strategies.

The negotiation of career development within lesbian partnerships

As we have seen in earlier chapters, respondents were usually highly committed to their jobs and often saw their occupational advancement as involving geographic mobility. Obviously, this can be a potential source of conflict between partners. Consequently, it is worth looking at the way partners negotiated employment opportunities which required relocation. Of the eight women in relationships of five years or more, five spoke of their career development involving relocation, and said that this had been carefully worked out as a joint venture, often with great difficulty. An example of this comes from Pru. Both she and her partner of 19 years rose to senior positions in female-dominated professions:

> [*Did you ever have a sense that one of your careers had priority?*] Not really, we worked very hard at making sure that we both got equal chances. We only ever looked for a situation where we were both going to get the job we wanted. We once applied to Worcester at one point and [my partner] got the job she wanted and I didn't get mine, so she had to go back and turn hers down. So there was no question of me taking on a lesser job. We have always worked so we could both get what we wanted. [*How easy has that been?*] Fairly difficult – not terribly, because we were prepared to go anywhere in the country as long as we could afford the property. Have been both fairly fortunate. (50)

This type of 'solution' was usually facilitated by the fact that the partners were in similar jobs. A different 'solution' was followed by a couple in a 15-year relationship who had brought up children together. Linda had devoted the early part of her life to the care of their children, and had consequently experienced fairly low-paid part-time employment. When the children were older, she decided to return to full-time education. This involved moving home. Wilhemina, her partner, gave up a senior position by relocating, feeling that it was now Linda's turn to develop her career. Both considered this to be a fair compromise.

By partners not prioritizing one career over another, problems often arose when career opportunities could not be found in the same geographic location. One couple solved this by buying a house half way between their two workplaces. However, commuting was the most common solution. At the time of interview, two respondents were in a commuting relationship because of job commitments and at least 14 had some experience of commuting relationships for this reason. Rather than giving up a good job to be with a partner, respondents spoke of the importance of taking time to find the right kind of job in the right location. This is discussed by Elizabeth, who works in the arts:

> ... it's got to be the career in a way, that is important. [My partner] can never be here just to be here, and I can never

be there just to be there. I am perfectly prepared at this stage to look for a job in London, which would be convenient, because [she's] there, as long as it was the right job, I mean that's the thing. [*How important is work to you?*] It is very important to me but it is not as important as my relationship . . . but I am not just going to just, like, give it up, I've got to have a good reason to, I want to do it properly. (24)

Rebecca speaks of this dilemma. She is in a commuting relationship because she did not wish to jeopardize the career opportunities offered by her male-dominated profession. However, finding a compromise between the demands of her career and her desire to live with her partner was important to her:

[*You said that with your kind of job you didn't think you could handle a relationship with a guy, how does it work out with a woman?*] With a lot of travelling, yes . . . I am going to Northhampton most weekends or she is coming down here. I can see myself changing, changing jobs 'cos a relationship would mean a lot to me. I would not leave the industry, but I would change to a job that still gave me everything I wanted out of a job, but would mean that I wouldn't have to travel so much, so I could turn [the relationship] into a more permanent thing. (24)

As we have seen in the previous chapter, respondents were often fairly ambitious. Unless a respondent was living in a large city such as London, career development often involved relocation. Clearly, the way that workplace opportunity is modelled on a 'traditional masculine model of employment' (one that ignores workers' home life responsibilities and assumes that a woman will follow her partner's career (Brannen and Moss, 1991)) disadvantages women and egalitarian couples. At some point three respondents had followed their partner's career because they felt that they could find a job more easily than their partners could. However, if one partner was settled in one location and unwilling or unable to move home, difficult decisions had to be made. Two respondents placed their relationships above a career move that would have required relocation. These respondents were both in valued relationships and had already established their careers. Unless both partners were highly committed in a relationship, career opportunities could bring a partnership to an untimely end. When faced with the decision whether to move for a career opportunity, or stay with a partner, six respondents chose to move. These women were usually in the early stages of career development. A further five respondents said that they would not relocate for a partner or expect their partner to relocate for them. This was the view expressed by Adrianne, who was a scientist:

> [*How central to you is work?*] It's a large part. I have put in a fair amount of effort to get to this point in my life. I wouldn't consider giving up my job and moving to another part of the country for somebody or anything like that, but equally I wouldn't expect anyone to do the same for me ... I think the secret is to get involved with somebody who is in the right place in the first place – having had a long-distance relationships in the past, I don't think they are good for the sanity, but you can't always control who you fall in love with. (25)

Clearly, inequalities between women in terms of occupational status and/or circumstance can cause problems. Two women spoke of tensions arising when their partner was in a less rewarding job. As one woman commented, 'It is hard for a partner to understand why you work late every day, when they are in a poorly paid, nine-to-five job.' These strains brought a heavy toll and, consequently, these relationships tended to be short-lived. However, it must be remembered that, for a number of reasons, respondents were usually in relationships with women in broadly similar occupational circumstances.

CONCLUSION

There are two important interrelated factors shaping respondents' approaches to the balancing of employment and home commitments. First, lesbian relationships do not have the institutional backing of marriage to encourage longevity. Relationships are rarely entered on the assumption that they will last forever. This is not to say that lesbians do not take their relationships seriously, or that partners are dropped unceremoniously. The second important influence is economic. Respondents did not expect to enter a lifelong relationship with a woman who would be the main breadwinner. Nor did they desire this situation. They were aware of the problems associated with economic dependency. Consequently, respondents recognized

that their lifestyle required that they be economically self-sufficient. As we have seen in previous chapters, this underpinned
a perspective on employment that was lifelong. In many ways,
employment rather than any particular relationship provided
a source of continuity in their lives. This contributed to the
understanding that neither partner had the right to place constraints on her partner's employment participation. Partners
did, however, have to contend with differences relating to, for
example, income, employment status, ethnicity and education.
Because of the absence of 'gender scripts', the intentional or
unintentional operation of power in relationships was more
clearly visible. Where possible they attempted to develop strategies
aimed at neutralizing the effects of power imbalances, because
they claimed to be uneasy about being dominated or dominant. Sometimes imbalances created a gulf that was too great
to breach, which contributed to the break-up of a relationship.

The more balanced approach to domestic and employment
commitments developed by the couples in my sample was,
however, very much assisted by the similarities they experienced
as women. Their relative freedom, in relationships, from op-
erational constraints based on reciprocal gender identities ensured that tasks and achievements were not judged in the context
of appropriate gender behaviour. Although 'butch/femme'
relationships appear to be fairly *uncommon*, their existence does,
in part, complicate this argument. Women in these kinds of
relationships did emulate more polarized heterosexual domestic arrangements. However, as was said earlier, the more polarized division of domestic labour experienced did not extend
to their approaches to employment. It is also worth mentioning that often the more 'masculine' partner earned less than
her partner.

From respondents' accounts of their lesbian relationships it
would appear that one partner's gender identity is not usually
threatened by the employment successes of her lover. Nor is it
contingent on monopolizing any one domain, insofar as neither
partner usually feels the need to take responsibility for domestic tasks or 'breadwinning'. The achievement of more balanced
task allocation at home, together with the emotional and practical support characteristic of lesbian relationships, appears to
be an important aspect of a lesbian's ability to engage in demanding employment. She does not have to sacrifice or forgo
relationships for the sake of her career, as may be the case for

other women. Nor does she have to subordinate her working life to a relationship, as is the case for many married or co-habiting single women.

The flexibility offered in women's relationships with each other, together with the similarities they shared, facilitated the operationalization of egalitarian ideals. This raises questions as to how far these more symmetric arrangements can be achieved by women and men who seek egalitarian relationships within the context of institutional heterosexuality. On the one hand, their efforts to bring about change may be limited by external social, economic, legal and political structures and processes which serve to reproduce differences in the social, symbolic and material conditions of individual women and men. On the other hand, gender inequalities are deeply embedded in the heterosexual gendered identities that these structures and processes constitute. This leads us to two thorny question. First, if heterosexual desire is based on the eroticization of difference, what is so attractive about difference that is not related to the gendered power structures that feminists seek to undermine? Second, once processes supporting these gendered differences are undermined, how probable would a heterosexual outcome be? Unless we challenge and take seriously the role of institutionalized heterosexuality in shaping differences between women and men in most areas of social life, the feminist project will fail to move beyond the glass ceiling.

NOTES

1. Relationships were described as 'exactly equal' by 48 per cent of heterosexual women, 38 per cent gay men and 40 per cent of heterosexual men.
2. See Blackburn (1988) and Chapters 1 and 3 of the present volume for a discussion of the empowering aspects of the questioning which novel situations in people's lives might prompt.
3. For general discussions of power, see Lukes (1974) and his edited volume (1986) and Merquior (1985, ch.8) on Foucault's approach to power. For a feminist consideration of power, see, for example, Griffin and Arnold (1991), Smart (1989), Fraser (1989) on Foucault and the edited volume by Davis *et al.* (1991) on Lukes, Giddens and Bourdieu.
4. As Smart (1989:2) points out, feminists have often placed greater stress on the negative aspects of power, such as men holding all the power, women lacking power and being unable to make choices. This approach tends to obscure women's agency and the degrees

to which power may be distributed unequally within the category 'woman'.

5. Women are more likely than men to take a more egalitarian stance on gender roles. The British Social Attitudes Survey noted that there was a statistically significant difference in male and female perspectives on this issue (Scott *et al.*, 1993). Furthermore, constraints exist on heterosexual partners' ability to put egalitarianism into action. There appears to be a huge gulf between the advocation of egalitarian views and the operationalization of shared household task allocation (Witherspoon, 1988:185). I believe that an important reason for lesbian relationships offering greater possibilities for egalitarian outcomes is that it is in both partners' interests.

6. See note 11 below.

7. For an overview of the feminist debates on 'sameness' and 'difference', see, for example, Gross (1992), Mackinnon (1990), Scott (1990), Barrett (1987) and Phillips (1987).

8. See, for example, Green (1992) and Weston's (1991) research for a discussion of ways that ex-lovers become important in lesbian 'kinship' networks.

9. Research suggests that there is a less strictly gendered approach to domestic labour in African–American households (Miller and Garrison, 1982:242).

10. Sixty-nine per cent of lesbian respondents spent less than ten hours on housework a week, as compared with 58 per cent of full-time employed cohabiting women and 56 per cent of full-time employed wives. In contrast, approximately 80 per cent of both married and cohabiting men spent less than ten hours a week on housework (Blumstein and Schwartz, 1985:139–46).

11. I have recently begun a three-year project looking at divisions of labour between lesbian partners, particularly those with dependent children. I am working with Henrietta Moore, Bob Blackburn and Kim Perren. This research uses a wide range of methodologies, including time-diaries and in-depth interviews. The early findings suggest that lesbians are developing very creative and balanced approaches to the sharing of parenting, household tasks and employment responsibilities. This research is funded by the Economic and Social Research Council, grant no: R00023 4649.

12. The studies of lesbian couples referred to at the beginning of this chapter suggest that butch/femme couples are a very rare occurrence. See also Faderman (1992) and Weston (1991) for a more detailed discussion of the recent history of lesbian culture in the USA.

CHAPTER SEVEN

Concluding discussion

The recognition of the interacting and overlapping nature of the 'public' and 'private' has provided important insights for feminist understandings. We can see ways that the structuring by gender of people's expectations and experience of their domestic, sexual and emotional worlds serves to constrain or enhance their employment circumstances, and vice versa. By charting the complex social and ideological mechanisms which shape taken for granted practices, and by understanding their political nature, we illuminate potential transformatory pathways. However, when we observe the realities of people's everyday worlds we find diversity: for instance, women of African–Caribbean origins different gender self-concepts and experience. In many respects the discovery of diverse standpoints has undermined our theoretical confidence. Instead of drawing on these to illuminate and distinguish among the wide range of social mechanisms which interact to constrain or empower women, difference is often tacked on as an after-thought, at best, dealt with as a self contained case study. Thus the theoretical insights necessary for an integrated analysis remain unincorporated.[1] In Women's Studies courses, for example, specific time is usually set aside to explore lesbian experience with specialized reading to guide discussion.

This separating off of lesbian experience under the rubric of difference has important consequences. Most crucially, it implies that the acquisition of sexual identities is only of interest within the context of difference. When lesbianism is thus treated as 'other', the acquisition of *heterosexual* identities remains unquestioned, preserving the integrity of mainstream feminist theorising and the illusion of heterosexuality as an unproblematic given. The findings of this research suggest that, far from being marginal, an understanding of lesbian experience can tell us a great deal about women's experience more generally. It illuminates the range of different social mechanisms which interact to constrain or enhance women's opportunities. The recognition that sexuality is socially produced through institutional practices and ideological processes cannot be added on or ignored. It is deeply implicated in constructing gender differentiated opportunities, outcomes and identities.

If we acknowledge the socially produced nature of sexual and emotional outcomes we can think about the relationship between 'public' and 'private' in a more enlightened way. This study has provided hitherto unavailable empirical data on the home lives and employment experiences of non-heterosexual women. We have found important material dimensions to the movement beyond heterosexuality: the financial self-reliance this movement *necessitates*. This often led respondents to improve their employment circumstances through the acquisition of skills and qualifications and/or through occupational change. Lesbian experience thus shows that *gender alone* does not explain the differential employment situations that people experience as men and as women. This financial link should also alert us to another insight. The economic disadvantages faced by women serve to constrain their ability to move beyond heterosexuality. It is no accident that women in my sample already were or struggled to become educationally and/or occupationally advantaged. This is emphasized by the fact that such a large proportion of those who came from the most disadvantaged economic backgrounds were educationally privileged. As already mentioned, we cannot understand employment outcomes without consideration of home life circumstances. The exploration of lesbian home lives allows us to consider this relationship in an interesting way. We know that women and men do not usually negotiate the labour market under similar conditions. Men's ability to appropriate the unpaid labour of women is central to understandings of gender inequalities in employment circumstances. This volume has argued that lesbians may represent a different kind of worker for sociological analyses because their employment ambitions and experience are not negotiated within this context. Their approach to employment is neither constrained by being secondary workers nor enhanced by social expectations that they be primary breadwinners. We have seen that the similarities that lesbians share as women, and the more flexible non-gender-differentiated relational scripts

that flow from this, enable the construction of more egalitarian partnerships. By the sharing of household tasks and the
supporting of each other's right to work, lesbian relationships
facilitate partners taking on more challenging employment. Thus
it is not home life per se which can represent a drain on women's
energies, but rather home life *within heterosexual contexts*. All
these differences in the way lesbians negotiate and experience
their interpersonal and material lives demonstrate that interpretations of sexuality are the *medium through which we experience* the overlapping nature of public and private worlds.
Consequently, MacKinnon (1982:515) may be right when she
argues that 'sexuality is to feminism what work is to Marxism'.

The recognition that interpretations of sexuality provide this
connection with 'public' and 'private' interactions and
understandings has been generally obscured in feminist thinking because the *givenness* of heterosexuality has been taken for
granted. A reason for this assumption is the tendency to focus
on heterosexuality as *sexual practice* rather than as *social institution*: we look at what people do, rather than why they do it.
However, social processes are also involved in the shaping of
our desires and emotions. In this way what is essentially *social*
becomes *embodied*: social processes reach that which we perceive to be the most natural and deeply unique aspects of
ourselves. Because the notion of the natural is so powerful,
without the experience of having been and moving beyond
heterosexuality, it is difficult to truly acknowledge a social
constructionist understanding of sexuality. In this way our sexual
and emotional worlds remain private: the problematic nature
of their production only partially explored and their implications left mostly unexamined in feminist analysis. In contrast,
this study has taken as it starting-point the view that heterosexuality is an institution which is deeply implicated in the
production of gender difference and gender hierarchies. In
order to test this hypothesis we have taken as our focus the
experience of those who have moved beyond heterosexuality.
This has enabled the asking of different sorts of questions about
how and why current arrangements come about, and whose
interests are served.

The dominance of heterosexuality has far-reaching consequences. The production of heterosexual coupling rests on dual
processes of differentiation and hierarchization. Central is the
construction of gender-differentiated identities: the idea that

heterosexual desire arises out of the eroticization of difference. Also central is the production of gender-differentiated pay cheques: the poor wages that most women receive deny many the ability to exist as independent persons. The dominance of heterosexual outcomes rests on the generation of hierarchies: the emotions are subordinated to the sexual, and penetrative sex is privileged over other forms of sexual and sensual expression as the basis of primary relationships. The question might be asked, whose interest does this serve? From a woman's perspective the emotional may hold far more importance than the sexual. One also needs to think about what one is left with in a relationship when difference ceases to have erotic power. This privileging serves also to devalue and constrain the construction of alternative interpersonal relationships where the sexual may be limited or have no bearing on their quality. Thus possibilities for building partnerships or parenting arrangements within or across gender on the basis of friendship are generally obscured.

This volume has tried to develop different ways of thinking about the way sexuality is produced. One way has been to focus on factors which may shape desire: in particular, ideas about gender construction. As Rubin (1975) observes, 'gender is a socially imposed division of the sexes. It is a product of the social relations of sexuality . . . [whereby] male and female [are transformed] into "men" and "women", each an incomplete half which can only find wholeness when united with the other' (p.179). According to Connell (1987:246), as these reciprocal differences become eroticized, heterosexuality becomes the attraction of opposites. If we accept these arguments, it would make sense that those who develop broader gender self-concepts and capabilities will be less inclined to desire and seek wholeness through union with members of the opposite sex. This rather reverses the notion that homosexuals are lacking. The study can offer insights in this respect.

The analysis of respondents' girlhood experience suggests they had developed broader gender self-concepts and capabilities. It was tentatively argued that these, together with the more independent early aspirations they usually reported, placed them at odds with the dictates of dominant forms of adolescent femininity. The above discussion would suggest that those whose sense of self is less polarized will be less likely to find relationships with the masculine 'other' an erotic experience, and that the culture of romantic heterosexuality would hold less appeal. This tended to be borne out by the findings of the study. However, regardless of whether this romantic culture holds appeal, the research of others shows that it is difficult for young people to resist incorporation. For many women in the study the existence of 'avenues of escape' was important. For instance, sport, a single-sex schooling environment or being .in an academically inclined sub-culture may have enabled many to resist investment in heterosexual relations.

My respondents' experiences will have resonances amongst many women and therefore it would be wrong to attempt to provide simple predictive explanations of sexual outcomes. The fact that respondents often did not seriously question the appropriateness of heterosexuality until well into their twenties, thirties or even forties suggests that the issues are complex. Why, against all the odds, some women move beyond heterosexuality and others do not will have to remain a mystery, although our understandings of this may be helped by drawing on more general theories of social reproduction. In this way we can explore how it is that people come to evaluate and reassess the legitimacy of dominant accounts of social reality. This alerts us to the importance of experiential knowledge which contradicts an account provided by an ideology. Importantly, it is not enough to know that alternative social arrangements exist, they must also be perceived as *attainable*. The capacity to experience change is linked to personal or group ability to exercise control. Based on the findings of this study, access to higher education and/or employment opportunity appears to be influential both in supporting a questioning perspective on the appropriateness of heterosexuality and in providing the resources to experience life differently. For example, a college environment brings individuals into contact with different ideas and different people and this may enable greater awareness of wider possibilities for living. Further, the resources and alternative sources of validation which flow from educational or occupational advantage seem to generate and sustain a more independent outlook.

When respondents eventually encountered women who powerfully moved them emotionally and/or awakened their desire, the idea of making women central in their lives was appealing. Under these circumstances they could better integrate their emotional worlds with their more independent and egalitarian standpoints on life. However, the fact that lesbianism bears little relationship to dominant representations often slowed down the process of identification. Moving beyond heterosexuality requires undertaking a journey of evaluation. This soul searching is almost inevitably painful. Institutional processes which support the legitimacy of heterosexuality serve also to deny, denaturalized and pervert the meaning of alternative sexual and emotional relationships. My respondents often found this a difficult, unpleasant but ultimately empowering experience. I would suggest that what lesbian and gay men call 'coming out' is really what theorists of social reproduction would call a process of ideological evaluation.

Lesbian women may in many ways represent the vanguard of change. The feminist challenge of the social, ideological and economic processes which constrain women's identities and capabilities, together with changes in the economy, are necessitating and/or facilitating women's independence. This situation appears to be a mixed blessing. As women's expectations grow, increasingly they appear to find relationships with men wanting. At the heart of this is men's apparent inability to take on the equal emotional and practical role that is required to sustain egalitarian partnerships. This study of lesbian lifestyles has shown one way that women appear to resolve this. Crucial to the feminist project is the need to find ways to promote more positive channels through which women may experience both independence and emotional fulfilment. Without widespread positive appraisals of non-heterosexual alternatives and the challenging of institutional practices which preserve men's monopoly of women through heterosexuality, heterosexual lifestyles will remain a source of frustration for women.

NOTE

1. I have found the discussions of *standpoint theory* by Hartsock (1987), Smith (1987), Grant (1987) and Dill (1987) useful. In a modified form, standpoint theory may help us to identify groups whose social location may provide alternative views of social reality. By gearing our research strategies and questions in such a way as might tap different experience, we could generate important insights which can help illuminate and distinguish among the range of constraints and sources of empowerment which shape women's existence.

BOOKS AND ARTICLES

Adams, M. 1976. *Single Blessedness*, New York: Penguin Books.

Addelson, K. Pyne 1981. 'Words and Lives', *Signs*, vol. 7, no. 1 (autumn), pp.187–99.

Adkins, L. 1995. *Gendered Work: Sexuality, Family and the Labour Market*, Buckingham: Open University Press.

Agassi, J.B. 1982. *Comparing the Work Attitudes of Women and Men*, Lexington, Massachusetts: D.C. Heath & Company.

Allen, K.R. 1989. *Single Women Family Ties*, Newbury Park, California: Sage.

Andrews, M. 1991. *Lifetimes of Commitment: Aging, Politics and Psychology*, Cambridge: Cambridge University Press.

Angrist, S.S. and Almquist, E.M. 1975. *Careers and Contingencies: How College Women Juggle with Gender*, New York: Dunellen.

Badgett, M.V., Lee, and Williams M. Rhonda 1992. 'The Economics of Sexual Orientation: Establishing a Research Agenda', *Feminist Studies*, vol. 18, no. 3 (fall), pp.649–57).

Banducci, R. 1967. 'The Effects of Mothers' Employment on the Achievement Aspirations, and Expectations of the Child', *Personnel and Guidance Journal*, no. 46, pp.263–7.

Barrett, M. 1987. 'The Concept of "Difference"', *Feminist Review*, vol. 26 (summer), pp.29–41.

Barrett, M. 1991. *The Politics of Truth: Marx to Foucault*, Cambridge: Polity.

Bartlett, F.C. 1964. *Remembering: A Study in Experimental and Social Psychology*, Cambridge: Cambridge University Press.

Basow, S.A. 1986. *Gender Stereotypes: Traditions and Alternatives*, 2nd edn, Belmont, California: Wadsworth.

Berk, S. 1985. *The Gender Factory: the Apportionment of Work in American Households*, New York: Plenum.

Bernard, J. 1972. *The Future of Marriage*, New York: World.

Bertaux, D. (ed.) 1981. *Biography and Society: The Life History Approach in the Social Sciences*, London: Sage.

Bertaux, D. 1981. 'Life Stories in the Bakers' Trade', in D. Bertaux (ed.).

Blackburn, R.M., Jarman, J. and Siltanen, J. 1993. 'The Analysis of Occupational Gender Segregation Over Time and Place', *Work, Employment and Society*, vol. 7, no. 3, pp.335–62.

Blackburn, R.M. 1988. 'Ideologies of work', in D. Rose (ed.) *Social Stratification and Economic Change*, London: Hutchinson.

Blackwood, E. (ed.) 1986. *Anthropology and Homosexual Behavior*, New York: The Haworth Press.

Blumstein, P. and Schwartz. P. 1990. 'Intimate Relationships and the Creation of Sexuality', in D. McWhirter, D.D. Sanders and J.M.

Reinisch (eds), *Homosexuality/Heterosexuality: Concepts of Sexuality*, Oxford: Oxford University Press.

Blumstein, P. and Schwartz, P. 1985. *American Couples: Money, Work, Sex*, New York: Pocket Books.

Bradley, H. 1989. *Men's Work, Women's Work*, Cambridge: Polity.

Brake, M. 1976. 'I May Be Queer, But At Least I am a Man: Male hegemony and ascribed versus achieved gender', in D. Leonard Barker and S. Allen (eds), *Sexual Divisions and Society: Process and Change*, London: Tavistock.

Brake, M. 1982. 'Sexuality as Praxis – a consideration of the contribution of sexual theory to the process of sexual being', in M. Brake (ed.) *Human Sexual Relations: Towards a Redefinition of Sexual Politics*, Harmondsworth: Penguin.

Brannen, J. and Moss, P. 1991. *Managing Mothers: Dual Earner Households After Maternity Leave*, London: Unwin Hyman.

Breakwell, G.M. 1985. *The Quiet Rebel: Women at Work in a Man's World*, London: Century Publishing.

Brewer, W.F. 1986. 'What is Autobiographical Memory?', in Rubin (ed.).

British Household Panel Survey (computer file G201R134.EXP)/principal investigator. ESRC Research Centre on Micro-social Change. – Colchester: ESRC Data Archive [distributor], 1994. – Data files and associated documentation.

Bruegel, I. 1989. 'Sex and Race in the Labour Market', *Feminist Review*, no. 32 (summer), pp.49–68.

Bryan, B. 1987. 'Learning to Resist: Black Women and Education', in G. Weiner and M. Arnot (eds), *Gender Under Scrutiny: New Inquiries in Education*. Milton Keynes: The Open University.

Bulmer, M. (ed.) 1977. *Sociological Research Methods: An Introduction*, London: Macmillan.

Bunch, C. 1978. 'Lesbian–feminist Theory', in G. Vida (ed.), *Our Right to Love: A Lesbian Resource Book*, Englewood Cliffs, New Jersey: Prentice-Hall.

Bunch, C. 1981. 'Not for Lesbians Only', in C. Bunch (ed.), *Building Feminist Theory: Essays from Quest: A Feminist Quarterly*, New York: Longman.

Burchell, B. and Rubery, J. 1991. 'Divided Women: Labour Market Segmentation and Gender Segregation', in A. Scott (ed.), *Gender and the Labour Market*, Oxford: Oxford University Press.

Burgess, R. 1984. *In the Field: An Introduction to Field Research*, London: George Allen & Unwin.

Butler, J. 1990. *Gender Trouble: Feminism and the Subversion of Identity*, London: Routledge.

Butler, J. 1993. *Bodies That Matter: On the Discursive Limits of 'Sex'*, London: Routledge.

Caldwell, M.A. and Peplau, L.A. 1984. 'The balance of power in lesbian relationships', *Sex Roles*, vol. 10, pp.587–600.

Caplan, P. (ed.) 1987. *The Cultural Construction of Sexuality*, London: Tavistock.

Cavendish, R. 1982. *Women on the Line*. London: Routledge & Kegan Paul.

Chodorow, N.J. 1978. *The Reproduction of Mothering: Psychoanalysis and the Sociology of Gender*, Berkeley: University of California Press.

Christian-Smith, L.K. 1988. 'Romancing the Girl: Adolescent Romance Novels and the Construction of Femininity', in L.G. Roman, L.K. Christian-Smith and E. Ellsworth (eds), *Becoming Feminine: The Politics of Popular Culture*, London: Falmer Press.

Cockburn, C. 1987. *Two-Track Training: Sex Inequalities and the Y.T.S.*, Basingstoke: Macmillan.

Cockburn, C. 1988. 'The Gendering of Jobs: Workplace Relations and the Reproduction of Sex Segregation', in S. Walby (ed.).

Cockburn, C. 1991. *In the Way of Women: Men's Resistance to Sex Equality in Organizations*, Basingstoke: Macmillan.

Cocks, J. 1989. *The Oppositional Imagination: Feminism, Critique, and Political Theory*, New York: Routledge.

Coe, R. 1984. *When the Grass was Taller*, London: Yale University.

Colangelo, N., Rosenthal, D. and Dittman, D.F. 1984. 'Maternal Employment and Job Satisfaction and their Relationship to Children's Perceptions and Behaviors', *Sex Roles*, vol. 10, no. 9/10.

Collins, P. Hill 1989. 'The Social Construction of Black Feminist Thought', *Signs*, vol. 14, no. 4, pp.745–73.

Connell, M. 1981. 'Romance and Sexuality', in A. McRobbie and T. McCrabe (eds), *Feminism For Girls*, London: Routledge & Kegan Paul.

Connell, R.W. 1987. *Gender and Power*, Cambridge: Polity.

Connell, R.W. 1995. *Masculinities*, Cambridge: Polity.

Cook, B. Wiesen 1979a. '"Women Alone Stir My Imagination": Lesbian Cultural Tradition', *Signs*, vol. 4, no.4, pp.718–39.

Cook, B. Wiesen 1979b. 'The Historical Denial of Lesbianism', *Radical History Review*, no. 20 (spring/summer), pp.60–66.

Crompton, R. and Mann, M. (eds) 1986. *Gender and Stratification*, Cambridge: Polity.

Crompton, R. and Sanderson, K. 1990. *Gendered Jobs and Social Change*, London: Unwin Hyman.

Crompton, R., Jones, G. and Reid, S. 1982. 'Contemporary Clerical Work: A Case Study of Local Government', in J. West (ed.), *Work, Women and the Labour Market*, London: Routledge & Kegan Paul.

Crowley, H. and Himmelweit, S. (eds) 1992. *Knowing Women: Feminism and Knowledge*, Cambridge: Polity.

Davis, K. 1991. 'Critical Sociology and Gender Relations', in K. Davis *et al.* (eds).

Davis, K., Leijenaar, M. and Oldersma, J. (eds) 1991. *The Gender of Power*, London: Macmillan.

Davis, M. and Kennedy, E. Lapovsky 1986. 'Oral History and the Study of Sexuality in the Lesbian Community: Buffalo, New York, 1940–1960', *Feminist Studies*, vol. 12, no. 1 (spring), pp.7–26.

Deem, R. 1986. *All Work and No Play? The Sociology of Women and Leisure*, Milton Keynes: Open University Press.

Dex, S. 1987. *Women's Occupational Mobility*, Basingstoke: Macmillan.

Dex, S. 1988. *Women's Attitudes towards Work*, Basingstoke: Macmillan.

Diamond, F. and Quinby, L. (eds) 1988a. *Feminism and Foucault: Reflections on Resistance*, Boston: Northeastern University Press.

Diamond, F. and Quinby, L. 1988b. 'Introduction', in F. Diamond and L. Quinby (eds).

Dill, B. Thornton 1987. 'The Dialectics of Black Womanhood', in S. Harding (ed.).

Dollimore, J. 1991. *Sexual Dissidence: Augustine to Wilde, Freud to Foucault*, Oxford: Clarendon.

Doucet, A. 1991. 'Striking a Balance: Gender Divisions of Labour in Housework, Childcare and Employment', *Sociological Research Group Working Paper Series*, University of Cambridge.

Doucet, A. 1995. 'Gender Equality, Gender Differences and Care', unpublished PhD dissertation, University of Cambridge.

Douvan, E. 1963. 'Employment and the Adolescent', in F. Ivan Nye and L.W. Hoffman (eds), *The Employed Mother in America*, Chicago: Rand McNally.

Droughn, P. 1986. 'Fathers' Supportiveness: Perceptions of Fathers and College Daughters', in R. Lewis (ed.).

Dugger, K. 1991. 'Social Location and Gender-Role Attitudes: A Comparison of Black and White Women', in J. Lorber and S.A. Farrell (eds), *The Social Construction of Gender*, Newbury Park, California: Sage.

Duncombe, J. and Marsden, D. 1993. 'Love and Intimacy: The Gender Division of Emotion and Emotion Work', *Sociology*, vol. 27, no. 2, pp.221–42.

Dunne, G.A. 1986. 'Women Beware Women: The Social Characterization of the Independent Woman', unpublished dissertation.

Dunne, G.A. 1992. 'Difference at Work: Perceptions of Work from a Non-Heterosexual Point of View', in H. Hinds and J. Stacey (eds), *New Directions for Women's Studies in the 1990s*, London: Falmer Press.

Edwards, T. 1990. 'Beyond Sex and Gender: Masculinity and Homosexuality and Social Theory', in J. Hearn and D. Morgan (eds), *Men, Masculinities and Social Theory*, London: Unwin Hyman.

Ettore, E.M. 1980. *Lesbians, Women and Society*. London: Routledge & Kegan Paul.

Faderman, L. 1985. *Surpassing the Love of Men: Romantic Friendship and Love between Women from the Renaissance to the Present*, London: Women's Press.

Faderman, L. 1992. *Odd Girls and Twilight Lovers: A History of Lesbian Life in Twentieth-Century America*, London: Penguin.

Fagot, B.I. 1977. 'Consequences of moderate cross-gender behavior in pre-school children', *Child Development*, vol 48, no. 3, pp.902–7.

Faraday, A. 1981. 'Liberating lesbian research', in K. Plummer (ed.).

Faraday, A. and Plummer, K. 1979. 'Doing Life Histories', *Sociological Review*, vol. 27, no. 4, pp.773–98.

Ferguson, A. 1981. 'Patriarchy, Sexual Identity, and the Sexual Revolution', *Signs*, vol. 7, no. 1 (autumn), pp.158–200.

Ferree, B.B. and Hess, M.M. 1987. 'Introduction', in B.B. Hess and M.M. Ferree (eds).

Finch, J. 1983. *Married to the Job*, London: George Allen & Unwin.

Finch, J. 1984. '"It's great to have someone to talk to": the ethics and politics of interviewing women', in C. Bell and H. Roberts (eds), *Social Researching: Politics, Problems, Practice*. London: Routledge & Kegan Paul.

Finnegan, R. 1992. *Oral Traditions and the Verbal Arts: A Guide to Research Practices*, London: Routledge.

Foucault, M. 1979. *The History of Sexuality*, vol. 1, London: Allen Lane.

Fraser, N. 1989. *Unruly Practices: Power, Discourse and Gender in Contemporary Social Theory*, Cambridge: Polity.

Fuller, M. 1980. 'Black girls in a London comprehensive school', in R. Deem (ed.) *Schooling for Women's Work*, London: Routledge & Kegan Paul.

Gagnon, J. and Simon, W. 1973. *Sexual Conduct*, Chicago: Aldine.

Game, A. and Pringle, R. 1983. *Gender at Work*, Sydney: George Allen & Unwin.

Gaskell, J. 1992. *Gender Matters from School to Work*, Milton Keynes: Open University Press.

Gay, J. 1986. '"Mummies and Babies" and Friends and Lovers in Lesotho', in E. Blackwood (ed.).

Gerson, K. 1985. *Hard Choices: How Women Decide about Work, Career, and Motherhood*, Berkeley, California: University of California Press.

Giddens, A. 1979. *Central Problems in Social Theory: Action, Structure and Contradiction in Social Analysis*, Basingstoke: Macmillan.

Giddens, A. 1991. 'Four Thesis on Ideology', *Canadian Journal of Political and Social Theory*, vol. 15, no.1, pp.1–3.

Glenn, E.N. 1987. 'Gender and the Family', in B.B. Hess and M.M. Ferree (eds).

Goldthorpe, J.H. 1980. *Social Mobility and Class Structure in Modern Britain*, Oxford: Clarendon.

Gordon, T. 1990. *Feminist Mothers*, London: Macmillan.

Gowler, D. and Legge, K. 1982. 'Dual-worker Families', in R.N. Rapoport, M.P. Fogarty and R. Rapoport (eds), *Families in Britain*, London: Routledge & Kegan Paul.

Graham, H. 1984. 'Surveying through Stories', in C. Bell and H. Roberts (eds), *Social Researching: Politics, Problems, Practice*, London: Routledge & Kegan Paul.

Grant, J. 1987. 'I Feel Therefore I Am: A Critique of Female Experience as the Basis for a Feminist Epistemology', in M.J. Falco (ed.), *Feminism And Epistemology: Approaches to Research in Women and Politics*, New York: Haworth Press.

Green, R., Williams, K. and Goodman, M. 1982. 'Ninety-Nine "Tomboys" and "Non-Tomboys": Behavioral Contrasts and Demographic Similarities', *Archives of Sexual Behavior*, vol. 11, no.3, pp.247–67.

Green, S.F. 1992. 'The Politics of Gender, Sexuality and Identity: An Ethnography of Lesbian Feminists in London', unpublished PhD dissertation, University of Cambridge.

Greenberg, D.F. 1988. *The Construction of Homosexuality*, Chicago: University of Chicago Press.

Grellert, E.A., Newcombe, M.D. and Bentler, P.M. 1982. 'Childhood Play Activities of Male and Female Homosexuals and Heterosexuals', *Archives of Sexual Behavior*, vol. 11, no. 6, pp.451–79.

Griffin, C. 1982. 'The Good, the Bad and the Ugly: Images of Young Women in the Labour Market', stencilled occasional paper, University of Birmingham, Centre of Contemporary Cultural Studies.

Griffin, C. 1985. *Typical Girls?: Young Women from School to the Job Market*, London: Routledge & Kegan Paul.

Griffin, C. 1986. 'It's Different for Girls: the Use of Qualitative Methods in a Study of Young Women's Lives', in H. Beloff (ed.), *Getting into Life*, London: Methuen.

Griffin, C. 1989. '"I'm not a Women's Libber, but . . .": Feminism, Consciousness and Identity', in S. Skevington and D. Baker (eds), *The Social Identity of Women*, London: Sage.

Griffin, C. and Arnold, S. 1991. 'Experiencing Power: Dimensions of Gender, "Race" and Class', paper presented at BPS/WIPS Women and Psychology Conference, University of Birmingham.

Gross, E. 1992. 'What is Feminist Theory?', in H. Crowley and S. Himmelweit (eds).

Gutek, B. and Larwood, L. (eds) 1987. *Women's Career Development*, Newbury Park, California: Sage.

Hakim, C. 1991. 'Grateful Slaves and Self-Made Women: Fact and Fantasy in Women's Work Orientations', *European Sociological Review*, vol. 7, no. 2, (September), pp.101–21.

Hall, M. 1992. 'Private Experiences in Public Domains: Lesbians in Organizations', in L. McDowell and R. Pringle (eds).

Hamer, D. and Budge, B. (eds) 1994. *The Good, the Bad and the Gorgeous: popular culture's romance with lesbianism*, London: Pandora.

Handscombe, G. and Forster, J. 1982. *Rocking the Cradle: Lesbian Mothers – a Challenge in Family Living*, London: Sheba Feminist Publishers.

Hankiss, A. 1981. 'Ontologies of the Self: On the Mythological Rearranging of One's Life History', in D. Bertaux (ed.).

Haraway, D. 1988. 'Situated Knowledges: The Science Question in Feminism and the Privilege of Partial Perspective', *Feminist Studies*, vol. 14, no. 3 (fall) pp.575–99.

Harding, S. 1986. *The Science Question in Feminism*, Milton Keynes: Open University Press.

Harding, S. (ed.) 1987. *Feminism and Methodology*, Milton Keynes: Open University Press.

Hargreaves, J. 1986. *Sport, Power and Culture*, Cambridge: Polity.

Harry, J. 1983. 'Gay and Lesbian Relationships', in E. Macklin and R.H. Rubin (eds), *Contemporary Families and Alternative Lifestyles*, Beverly Hills, California: Sage.

Hartley, R.E. 1960. 'Children's Concepts of Male and Female Roles', *Merrill-Palmer Quarterly*, 6, pp.83–91.

Hartmann, H. 1981. 'The Unhappy Marriage of Marxism and Feminism: Towards a More Progressive Union', in L. Sargent (ed.) *Women and Revolution: A discussion of the Unhappy Marriage of Marxism and Feminism*, Boston: South End Press.

Hartsock, C.M. 1983. *Money, Sex and Power: Towards a Feminist Historical Materialism*. Boston: Northeastern University Press.

Hartsock, C.M. 1987. 'The Feminist Standpoint: Developing the Ground for a Specifically Feminist Historical Materialism', in S. Harding (ed.).

Haskey, J. 1995. 'Trends in marriage and cohabitation: the decline in marriage and the changing pattern of living in partnerships', *Population Trends*, no. 80, summer.

Hemmer, J.D. and Kleiber, D.A. 1981. 'Tomboys and Sissies: Androgynous Children?', *Sex Roles*, vol. 7, no. 12, pp.1205–12.

Hendry, L.B. 1983. 'Sex Roles, Pop Culture and Sociability', in *Growing Up and Going Out: Adolescents and Leisure*, Aberdeen: Aberdeen University Press.

Hennig, M. and Jardim, A. 1979. *The Managerial Woman*, London: Pan Books.

Henshall, C. and McGuire, J. 1986. 'Gender Development', in M. Richards and P. Light (eds) *Children of Social Worlds*, Cambridge: Polity.

Herdt, G. 1993. *Ritualized Homosexuality in Melanesia*, Oxford: University of California Press.

Hess, B.B. and Ferree, M.M. (eds) 1987. *Analyzing Gender*, Beverly Hills: Sage.

Hochschild, A. 1983. *The Managed Heart: Commercialization of Human Feeling*, Berkeley, University of California Press.

Hoffman, L.W. 1974. 'Effects on Child', in L.W. Hoffman and F.I. Nye (eds), *Working Mothers*, San Francisco: Jossey-Bass.

Horn, J.C. 1979. 'Does a boy have the right to be effeminate?', *Psychology Today*, vol. 12, no. 11 (April), pp.34–7.

Hubber, J. and Spitze, G. 1983. *Sex Stratification: Children, Housework, and Jobs*, New York: Academic Press.

Hudson, B. 1984. 'Femininity and Adolescence', in A. McRobbie and M. Nava (eds), *Gender and Generation*, London: Macmillan.

Hughes, K. 1990. 'Trading Places: Men and Women in Non-Traditional Occupations, 1971–86', *Perspectives on Labour and Income*, vol. 2, no. 2 (summer), pp.58–68.

Hyde, J.S. and Rosenberg, B.G. 1974. 'What are little girls made of? Puppy dogs' tails too', *Psychology Today* (August).

Hyde, J.S. and Rosenberg, B.G. 1977. 'Tomboyism', *Psychology of Women Quarterly*, vol. 2, no. 1, pp.73–5.

Jackson, M. 1987. '"Facts of Life" or the eroticization of women's oppression?: Sexology and the social construction of heterosexuality' in P. Caplan (ed.).

Jackson, S. 1987. 'Effects of Father Involvement', in M. Lamb (ed.).

Jackson, S. 1995 'Gender and Heterosexuality: A Materialist Feminist Analysis' in M. Maynard and J. Purvis (eds) *(Hetero)Sexual Politics*, Bristol: Taylor and Francis.

Jeffreys, S. 1985. *The Spinster and Her Enemies: Feminism and Sexuality 1880–1930*, London: Pandora.

Jeffreys, S. 1989. 'Does It Matter If They Did It?', in Lesbian History Group (eds).

Johnson, S. 1990. *Staying Power: Long Term Lesbian Couples*, Tallahassee, Florida: The Naiad Press.

Jones, K. 1988. 'Towards a Revision of Politics', in K. Jones and A. Jonasdottir (eds), *The Political Interests of Gender*, London: Sage.

Joseph, G. 1981. 'Black Mothers and Daughters: Their Roles and Functions in American Society', in G. Joseph and J. Lewis (eds), *Common Differences*, Garden City, New York: Doubleday Anchor.

Jowell, R., Witherspoon, S. and Brook, L. (eds) 1988. *The British Social Attitudes: the 5th Report*, Aldershot: Gower.

Jowell, R., Witherspoon, S. and Brook, L. (eds) 1990. *The British Social Attitudes: the 7th Report*, Aldershot: Gower.

Kanter, R. 1977. *Men and Women of the Corporation*, New York, Basic Books.

Kelly, L. 1988. *Surviving Sexual Violence*, Minneapolis: University of Minnesota Press.

Kiernan, K. 1992. 'Men and Women at Home and at Work', in R. Jowell, L. Brook, G. Prior and B. Taylor (eds), *British Social Attitudes: The 9th Report*, Aldershot: Dartmouth.

King, D.K. 1988. 'Multiple Jeopardy, Multiple Consciousness: The Context of Black Feminist Ideology', *Signs*, vol. 14, no. 1, pp.45–59.

Kitzinger, C. 1987. *The Social Construction of Lesbianism*, London: Sage.

Kohli, M. 1981. 'Biography: Account, Text, Method', in D. Bertaux (ed.).

Komter, A. 1991. 'Gender, Power and Feminist Theory', in K. Davis *et al.* (eds).

Lamb, M. 1979. 'The Father–Daughter Relationship: Past, Present and Future', in C. B. Kopp (ed.), *Becoming Female: Perspectives on Development*, New York: Plenum.

Lamb, M. (ed.) 1981a. *The Role of the Father in Child Development*, 2nd edn, Canada: John Wiley and Sons.

Lamb, M. 1981b. 'Father and Child Development: An Integrative Overview', in M. Lamb (ed.).

Lamb, M. (ed.) 1982a. *Nontraditional Families: Parenting and Child Development*, Hillsdale New Jersey: Lawrence Erlbaum Associates.

Lamb, M. 1982b. 'Maternal Employment and Child Development: A Review', in M. Lamb (ed.).

Lamb, M. 1986. 'Effects of Increased Parental Involvement on Children in TwoParent Families', in R. Lewis (ed.).

Lamb, M. (ed.) 1987. *The Father Role: Cross Cultural Perspectives*, Hilldale New Jersey: Lawrence Erlbaum Associates.

Lamb, M., Pleck, J. and Levine, J. 1987. 'Effects of Increased Paternal Involvement on Fathers and Mothers', in C. Lewis and M. O'Brien (eds).

Lazoff, M.M. 1974. 'Fathers and Autonomy in Women', in R.B. Kundsin (ed.), *Women and Success*, New York: Morrow.

Lees, S. 1986. *Losing Out: Sexuality and Adolescent Girls*, London: Hutchinson.

Lees, S. 1989. 'Learning to Love: Sexual Reputation, Morality and the Social Control of Girls', in M. Cain (ed.), *Growing Up Good: Policing the Behaviour of Girls in Europe*, London: Sage.

Leonard, D. 1980. *Sex and Generation: A Study of Courtship and Weddings*. London: Tavistock.

Leonard, D. 1988. 'Women in the Family: Companions or Caregivers?', in V. Beechey and E. Whitelegg (eds), *Women in Britain Today*, Milton Keynes: Open University Press.

Lesbian History Group (eds) 1989. *Not A Passing Phase: Reclaiming Lesbians in History 1840–1985*. London: Women's Press.

Lesbian Oral History Group (ed.) 1989. *Inventing Ourselves: Lesbian Life Stories*, London: Routledge.

Lewis, C. and O'Brien, M. (eds) 1987. *Reassessing Fatherhood: New Observations on Fathers and the Modern Family*, London: Sage.

Lewis, R. (ed.) 1986. *Men in Families*, Beverly Hills, California: Sage.

Lindsey, L. 1990. *Gender Roles: A Sociological Perspective*, Englewood Cliffs, New Jersey: Prentice-Hall.

Lopata, H. 1987. 'Women's Family Roles in Life Course Perspective', in B.B. Hess and M.M. Ferree (eds).

Lorber, J. 1991. 'Principles of Gender Construction', in J. Lorber and S.A. Farrell (eds), *The Social Construction of Gender*, Newbury Park, California: Sage.

Lukes, S. 1974. *Power: A Radical View*, London: Macmillan.

Lukes, S. (ed.) 1986. *Power*, Oxford: Basil Blackwell.

Machung, A. 1989. 'Talking Careers, Thinking Job: Gender Differences in Career and Family Expectations of Berkeley seniors', *Feminist Studies* (spring), no. 1, pp.35–59.

MacKinnon, C.A. 1982. 'Feminism, Marxism, Method and the State: an Agenda for Theory', *Signs*, vol. 7, no. 3, pp.515–44.

MacKinnon, C.A. 1990. 'Legal Perspectives on Sexual Difference', in D. Rhode (ed.), *Theoretical Perspectives on Sexual Difference*, London: Yale University Press.

MacKinnon, C.A. 1992. 'Sexuality', in H. Crowley and S. Himmelweit (eds).

Macklin, E. 1983. 'Non Marital Heterosexual Cohabitation: An Overview', in E. Macklin and R.H. Rubin (eds), *Contemporary Families and Alternative Lifestyles*. Beverly Hills, California: Sage.

Maguire, A. 1992. 'Power: Now You See It, Now You Don't', in L. McDowell and R. Pringle (eds).

Mansfield, P. and Collard, J. 1988. *The Beginning of the Rest of Your Life?: A Portrait of Newly-Wed Marriage*, London: Macmillan.

Marini, M.M. 1978. 'Sex-Differences in the Determination of Adolescent Aspirations: Review of Research', *Sex Roles*, vol. 4, no. 5, pp.723–53.

Marshall, G., Newby, H., Rose, D. and Vogler, C. 1988. *Social Class in Modern Britain*, London: Hutchinson.

Martin, B. 1988. 'Feminism, Criticism and Foucault', in I. Diamond and L. Quinby (eds).

Martin, C.L. 1990. 'Attitudes and Expectations about Children with Nontraditional and Traditional Gender Roles', *Sex Roles*, vol. 22, no. 3/4, pp.151–65.

Martin, D. and Lyon, P. 1972. *Lesbian Women*, New York: Bantam Books.

Martin, J. and Roberts, C. 1984. *Women and Employment: A Lifetime Perspective*, London: HMSO.

McDowell, L. and Pringle, R. (eds) 1992. *Defining Women: Social Institutions and Gender Divisions*, Cambridge: Polity.

McIntosh, M. 1981. 'The homosexual role', in K. Plummer (ed.).

McRae, S. 1986. *Cross-Class Families: A Study of Wives' Occupational Superiority*, Oxford: Clarendon.

McRobbie, A. 1978. 'Working-Class Girls and the Culture of Femininity', in Women's Studies Group (eds), *Women Take Issue*, London: Hutchinson.

McRobbie, A. 1981. 'Just like a Jackie Story', in A. McRobbie and T. McCrabe (eds), *Feminism For Girls*, London: Routledge & Kegan Paul.

McRobbie, A. 1990a. *Feminism and Youth Culture*, London: Macmillan.

McRobbie, A. 1990b. 'Teenage Mothers: A New Social State?', in A. McRobbie.

Merquior, J.G. 1985. *Foucault*, London: Fontana.

Meyer, J. 1991. '"Power and Love": Conflicting Conceptual Schemata', in K. Davis *et al.* (eds).

Middleton, S. 1987. '"Streaming" and the Politics of Female Sexuality: Case Studies in the Schooling of Girls', in G. Weiner and M. Arnot (eds), *Gender Under Scrutiny: New Inquiries in Education*, London: Hutchinson.

Miles, M. 1984. *Qualitative Data Analysis: A sourcebook of new methods*, Beverly Hills, California: Sage.

Miller, E. 1989. 'Through All Changes and Through All Chances: The relationship of Ellen Nussey and Charlotte Brontë', in Lesbian History Group (eds).

Miller, J. and Garrison, H.H. 1982. 'Sex Roles: The Division of Labour at Home and in the Workplace', *Annual Review of Sociology*, vol. 8, pp.237–62.

Miller, N. 1995. *Out of the Past: Gay and Lesbian History from 1869 to the Present*, London: Vintage.

Mitchell, J. 1987. 'Women and Equality', in A. Phillips (ed.).

Moore, H.L. 1988. *Feminism and Anthropology*, Cambridge: Polity.

Morris, L. 1990. *The Workings of the Household*. Cambridge: Polity.

Mortimer, J.J. 1986. *Work, Family, and Personality: Transition to adulthood*, New Jersey: Ablex Publishing Corporation.

Newson, J. and Newson, E. 1976. *Seven Years Old in the Home Environment*, Harmondsworth: Penguin.

Newson, J. and Newson, E. 1986. 'Family and Sex Roles in Middle Childhood', in D.J. Hargreaves and A.M. Colley (eds), *The Psychology of Sex Roles*, London: Harper & Row.

Nichols, M. 1990. 'Lesbian Relationships: Implications for the Study of Sexuality and Gender', in D. McWhirter, D.D. Sanders, and J.M. Reinisch (eds) *Homosexuality/Heterosexuality: Concepts of Sexuality*, Oxford: Oxford University Press.

Nicholson, L. 1990. *Feminism/Postmodernism*, London: Routledge.

Oakley, A. 1981. 'Interviewing Women: a contradiction in terms', in H. Roberts (ed.), *Doing Feminist Research*, London: Routledge & Kegan Paul.

Oldersma, J. and Davis, K. 1991. 'Introduction', in K. Davis *et al.* (eds).

Ortner, S.B. and Whitehead, H. (eds) 1981. *Sexual Meanings: The Cultural Construction of Gender and Sexuality*, Cambridge: Cambridge University Press.

Pahl, J. 1989. *Money and Marriage*, Basingstoke, Macmillan.

Pahl, J. 1991. 'Money and Power in Marriage', in P. Abbott and C. Wallace (eds), *Gender, Sexuality and Power*, Basingstoke: Macmillan.

Pahl, R. 1984. *Divisions of Labour*, Oxford: Basil Blackwell.

Pateman, C. 1988. *The Sexual Contract*, Cambridge: Polity.

Patton, M.Q. 1987. *How To Use Qualitative Methods In Evaluation*, Beverly Hills, California: Sage.

Pearce, F. 1981. 'How to be immoral and ill, pathetic and dangerous, all at the same time', in S. Cohen and J. Young (eds), *The Manufacture of the News: social problems, deviance and the mass media*, London: Constable.

Peplau, L.A. and Cochran, S.D. 1990. 'A Relationship Perspective in Homosexuality', in D. McWhirter, D.D. Sanders and J.M. Reinisch (eds), *Homosexuality/Heterosexuality: Concepts of Sexuality*, Oxford: Oxford University Press.

Peplau, L.A., Cochran, S., Rook, K. and Pandesky, C. 1978. 'Loving Women: attachment and autonomy in lesbian relationships', *Journal of Social Issues*, vol. 34, no. 3, pp.7–28.

Phillips, A. (ed.) 1987a. *Feminism and Equality*, Oxford: Basil Blackwell.

Phillips, A. 1987b. 'Introduction', in A. Phillips (ed.).

Plumb, P. and Cowan, G. 1984. 'A Developmental-Study of Destereotyping and Androgynous Activity Preferences of Tomboys, Nontomboys and Males', *Sex Roles*, vol. 10, no. 9/10, pp.703–12.

Plummer, K. (ed.) 1981. *The Making of the Modern Homosexual*, London: Hutchinson.

Pollert, A. 1981. *Girls, Wives, Factory Lives*, London: Macmillan.

Prandy, K. 1981. 'Alienation and Interests in the Analysis of Social Cognitions', (Sociology Reprint no. 9), *The British Journal of Sociology*, vol. 30, no.4, (December), pp.442–74.

Prandy, K. 1990. 'The Revised Cambridge Scale of Occupations', *Sociology*, vol. 24, no. 4, pp.629–55.

Prendergast, S. 1995. 'The "Come On 'En Boys": Masculinity, School and Bodily Capital', paper presented in the Levi Strauss Masculinities Seminars, University of Cambridge.

Prendergast, S. and Forrest, S. 1996. '"Shorties, Low-Lifers, Hardnuts and Kings": Boys and the Transformation of Emotions in School', in G.A. Bendelow and S.J. Williams (eds), *Emotions in Social Life: Social Theories and Contemporary Issues*, London: Routledge.

Prendergast, S. and Prout, A. 1980. 'What Will I do...? Teenage Girls And The Construction Of Motherhood', *Sociological Review*, vol. 28, no. 3, pp.517–35.

Pringle, R. 1992. 'What is a Secretary?', in L. McDowell and R. Pringle (eds).

Rapoport, R.N. and Rapoport, R. 1982. 'British Families in Transition', in R.N. Rapoport, M.P. Fogarty and R. Rapoport (eds), *Families in Britain*, London: Routledge & Kegan Paul.

Rich, A. 1984. 'On Compulsory heterosexuality and Lesbian Existence', in A. Snitow, C. Stansell and S. Thompson (eds), *Desire: The Politics of Sexuality*, London: Virago.

Richardson, D. 1981. 'Lesbian Mothers', in J. Hart and D. Richardson (eds), *The Theory and Practice of Homosexuality*, London: Routledge & Kegan Paul.

Roberts, A. 1980. *Out to Play: The Middle Years of Childhood*, Aberdeen: Aberdeen University Press.

Robinson, J.A. 1986. 'Autobiographical Memory: A Historical Prologue', in D.C. Rubin (ed.).

Roos, P.A. 1983. 'Marriage and Women's Occupational Attainment in Cross-Cultural Perspective', *American Sociological Review*, vol. 48, no. 6 (December), pp.852–64.

Ross, M. 1980. 'Retrospective Distortion in Homosexual Research', *Archives of Sexual Behavior*, vol. 9, no. 6, pp.523–33.

Rossi, A. 1971. 'Women in Science: Why so Few?', in C.F. Epstein and W.J. Goode (eds), *The Other Half: Roads to Women's Equality*, Englewood Cliffs. New Jersey: Prentice-Hall.

Rubin, D.C. (ed.) 1986a. *Autobiographical Memory*, Cambridge: Cambridge University Press.

Rubin, D.C. 1986b. 'Introduction', in Rubin (ed.).

Rubin, G. 1975. 'The Traffic in Women: Notes on the "Political Economy" of Sex', in R. R. Reiter (ed.) *Towards an Anthropology of Women*, London: Monthly Review Press.

Runyan, W.M. 1984. *Life Histories and Psychobiography: explanations in theory and method*, Oxford: Oxford University Press.

Russell, S. 1986. 'The Hidden Curriculum of School: Reproducing Gender and Class Hierarchies', in R. Hamilton and M. Barrett (eds), *The Politics of Diversity*, London: Verso.

Safilios-Rothschild, C. 1976. 'Dual Linkages between Occupational and Family Systems: a macro sociological analysis', in M. Blaxall and B. Reagan (eds), *Women and the Workplace*, Chicago: University of Chicago Press.

Sahli, N. 1979. '"Smashing": Women's Relationships Before the Fall', *Chrysalis*, vol. 8, pp.17–27.

Sarah, E., Scott, M. and Spender, D. 1980. 'The Education of Feminists: The Case for Single-Sex Schools', in D. Spender and E. Sarah (eds), *Learning To Lose: Sexism and Education*, London: Women's Press.

Sawicki, J. 1988. 'Identity Politics and Sexual Freedom', in F. Diamond and L. Quinby (eds).

Scott, J. 1990. 'Women and the family', in R. Jowell *et al.* (eds).

Scott, J., Braun, M. and Alwin, D. 1993. 'The Family Way' in R. Jowell, L. Brooks and L. Dowds (eds), *International Social Attitudes: The 10th BSA Report*, Aldershot: Dartmouth.

Scott, J.W. 1990. 'Deconstructing Equality-Versus-Difference: Or, the Uses of Poststructuralist Theory for Feminism', in M. Hirsch and E. Fox Keller (eds), *Conflicts in Feminism*, London: Routledge.

Segal, L. 1994. *Straight Sex: The Politics fo Pleasure*, London. Virago.

Seymour, J. 1992. '"Not a manly thing to do?" Gender accountability and the Division of Labour', in G.A. Dunne, R.M. Blackburn and J. Jarman (eds), *Inequalities in Employment Inequalities in Home-Life*, Conference Proceedings for the Cambridge Social Stratification Seminar. University of Cambridge.

Sharpe, S. 1976. *"Just Like a Girl": How Girls Learn to be Women*, London: Penguin.

Shaw, L.B. 1983. *Unplanned Careers: The Working Lives of Middle-Aged Women*, Lexington: Lexington Books.

Shepherd, G. 1987. 'Rank, Gender and Homosexuality: Mombasa as a Key to Understanding Sexual Options', in P. Caplan (ed.).

Siltanen, J. 1991. 'Component-Wages and Low Pay: Conceptualising the Social Adequacy of Wages', paper presented to the Cambridge Social Stratification Seminar, University of Cambridge.

Siltanen, J. 1994. *Locating Gender: Occupational Segregation, Wages and Domestic Responsibilities*, London: UCL Press.

Simmons, C. 1979. 'Companionate Marriage and the Lesbian Threat', *Frontiers*, vol. 4, no. 3, pp.54–9.

Simon, B.L. 1987. *Never Married Women*, Philadelphia: Temple University Press.

Sloboda, J.A. 1991. 'Music Structure and Emotional Response: Some Empirical Findings', in *Psychology of Music*, 19, pp.110–20.

Sloboda, J.A. 1992. 'Empirical Studies of Emotional Response to Music', in M.R. Jones and S. Hulleran (eds), *Cognitive Bases of Musical Communication*, New York American Psychological Society.

Smart, C. 1989. 'Power and the Politics of Child Custody', in C. Smart and S. Sevenhuijsen (eds) *Child Custody and the Politics of Gender*, London: Routledge.

Smith. D. 1987. *The Everyday World As Problematic*, Milton Keynes: Open University Press.

Smith-Rosenberg, C. 1975. '"The Female World of Love and Ritual": Relations between Women in 19th Century America', *Signs*, vol. 1, no. 1, pp.1–30.

Smith-Rosenberg, C. 1986. *Disorderly Conduct: Visions of Gender in Victorian America*, New York: Oxford University Press.

Stanko, E. 1988. 'Keeping Women In and Out of Line: Sexual Harassment and Occupational Segregation', in S. Walby (ed.).

Stanworth, M. 1984. 'Women and Class Analysis: a reply to John Goldthorpe', *Sociology*, vol. 18, no. 2, pp.159–70.

Statham, J. 1986. *Daughters and Sons: Experiences of Non-Sexist Childraising*, Oxford: Basil Blackwell.

Stein, P. 1983. 'Singlehood', in E. Macklin and R.H. Rubin (eds), *Contemporary Families and Alternative Lifestyles*, Beverly Hills, California: Sage.

Stewart, A. and Blackburn, R.M. 1975. 'The Stability of Structural Inequality', *Sociological Review*, vol. 23, no. 3 (August), pp.481–508.

Stewart, A., Prandy, K. and Blackburn, R.M. 1980. *Social Stratification and Occupations*, London: Macmillan.

Stonewall, 1995. *Less Equal than Others*, London: Stonewall.

Strauss, A.L. 1987. *Qualitative Analysis for Social Scientists*, Cambridge: Cambridge University Press.

Taylorson, D.E. 1980. 'Highly Educated Women: A Case Study of Women Ph. D. Candidates', unpublished PhD dissertation, University of Cambridge.

Tesch, R. 1990. *Qualitative Research: Analysis Text and Software Tools*, London: Falmer Press.

Thomas, W.I. and Thomas, D.S. 1928. *The Child in America*, New York: Alfred Knopf.

Thompson, J.B. 1990. *Ideology and Modern Culture: Critical Social Theory in the Era of Mass Communication*, Cambridge: Polity.

Tilly, L.A. and Scott, J.W. 1987. *Women and Work*, London: Methuen.

Treiman, D.J. 1975. 'Sex and the Process of Status Attainment: A Comparison of Working Women and Men', *American Sociological Review*, 40, pp.174–200.

Vicinus, M. 1982. '"One Life to Stand Beside": Emotional Conflicts in First-Generation College Women In England', *Feminist Studies*, vol. 8, no. 3 (fall), pp.603–28.

Vicinus, M. 1985. *Independent Women: Work and Community for Single Women, 1850–1920*, London: Virago.

Walby, S. 1986. *Patriarchy at Work*, Oxford: Basil Blackwell.

Walby, S. (ed.) 1988. *Gender Segregation at Work*, Milton Keynes: Open University Press.

Walby, S. 1990. *Theorizing Patriarchy*, Oxford: Basil Blackwell.

Walkerdine, V. 1990. *School Girl Fictions*, London: Verso.

Warren, C.A.B. 1988. *Gender Issues in Field Research*, Beverly Hills, California: Sage.

Watkins, S. 1987. *Medicine and Labour: The Politics of a Profession*, London: Lawrence & Wishart.

Weeks, J. 1977. *Coming Out: Homosexual Politics in Britain from the Nineteenth Century to the Present*. London: Quartet.

Weeks, J. 1989. *Sex, Politics and Society: The Regulation of Sexuality since 1800*, Harlow, Essex: Longman.

Weston, K. 1991. *Families We Choose: Lesbians, Gays, Kinship*, New York: Columbia University Press.

Whitehead, H. 1981. 'The bow and the burden strap: a new look at institutionalized homosexuality in native North America', in S.B. Ortner and H. Whitehead (eds).

Wilkinson, S. and Kitzinger, C. (eds) 1993 *Heterosexuality: A Feminism and Psychology Reader*, London: Sage.

Williams, C. 1992. 'The Glass Escalator: Hidden Advantages for men in the "female" professions', in *Social Problems*, vol. 39, no. 3, August.

Willis, P. 1977. *Learning to Labour*, Farnborough, Hants: Saxon House.

Wilson, D. 1978. 'Sexual codes and conduct: A study of teenage girls', in C. Smart and B. Smart (eds), *Women, Sexuality and Social Control*, London: Routledge & Kegan Paul.

Witherspoon, S. 1988. 'Interim Report: A Woman's Work', in R. Jowell *et al.*, (eds).

Wolf, D.C. 1980. *The Lesbian Community*, Berkeley, California: University of California Press.

Wolff, C. 1973. *Love Between Women*, 2nd edn, London: Duckworth.

Yeandle, S. 1984. *Women's Working Lives: Patterns and Strategies*, London: Tavistock.

Zita, J.N. 1981. 'Historical Amnesia and the Lesbian Continuum', *Signs*, vol. 7, no. 1 (autumn), pp.172–87.

OFFICIAL AND GOVERNMENT DEPARTMENT PUBLICATIONS

Census: 1991. 1991. 'Economic Activity: Great Britain', Office of Population Censuses and Surveys, London: HMSO.

Census: 1991. 1991. 'Small Area Statistics', Office of Population Censuses and Surveys, London: HMSO.

Employment Gazette. 1988. Department of Employment (October), London: HMSO.

Employment Gazette. 1994. Department of Employment (December), London: HMSO.

General Household Survey: 1993. 1993. G.H.S. no. 19, Office of Population Censuses and Surveys, London: HMSO.

Labour Force Survey. 1991. Office of Population Censuses and Surveys, London: HMSO.

Low Pay Unit, 1991. *New Review,* no, 11 (August/September).

Low Pay Unit, 1991. *New Review,* no. 13 (December/January).

Marriage and Divorce Statistics. 1991. London: HMSO.

New Earnings Survey. 1990. 'Part D. Analysis by Occupation', Department of Employment, London: HMSO.

New Earnings Survey. 1990. 'Part E. Analysis by Region, Analysis by age group', Department of Employment, London: HMSO.

New Earnings Survey. 1991. 'Part D. Analysis by Occupation', Department of Employment, London: HMSO.

New Earnings Survey. 1991. 'Part E. Analysis by Region, Analysis by age group', Department of Employment, London: HMSO.

New Earnings Survey. 1991. 'Part F. Analysis of Earnings and Hours for Part-Time Women Employees', Department of Employment, London: HMSO.

New Earnings Survey. 1994. Department of Employment, London: HMSO.

Regional Trends 24. 1989. Office of Population Censuses and Surveys, London: HMSO.

Regional Trends 25. 1990. Office of Population Censuses and Surveys, London: HMSO.

Social Trends 21. 1991. Office of Population Censuses and Surveys, London: HMSO.

Social Trends 22. 1992. Office of Population Censuses and Surveys, London: HMSO.

'Whiteabbey' District Council, 1988. *'Whiteabbey': A Centre of Excellence,* The 'Whiteabbey' City Council.

'Whiteabbey' City Research Group, 1990. *The 'Whiteabbey' Economy,* The 'Whiteabbey' County Council.

Note: Page numbers in **bold** type indicate references illustrated by respondents' stories and experiences.

qualifications
  levels in sample 139–41, 227
  unrelated to pay 163, 166
  see also education; skill
    development
questionnaires, research 29

relationships
  egalitarianism in 110,
    179–89, **192**, 194, 231
  father–daughter **56–7**, 76
  see also heterosexual
    relationships; lesbian
    relationships; marriage;
    women, relationships
    between
research ('Whiteabbey' lesbian
  community) 21–37
  analysis 36–7
  the community 24–5, 28–30
  effect on researcher 31–2
  fieldwork 24
  interviews 29–32
  life-history approach 23,
    32–6
  secrecy problems 27
  themes 30–1
  see also sample
respondents *see* sample
Rich, A. 1, 11–12, 26
Robinson, J.A. 35
role play
  in heterosexual
    relationships **113–18**,
    181–8, **182–3**
  in lesbian relationships
    207–8, **210**, **212–14**, 223,
    227–8
romantic heterosexuality 18,
  22, 72–8, 229–30
Roos, P.A. 128
Rubin, G. 3, 6, 15, 179, 229

Safilios-Rothschild, C. 109
Sambia (of New Guinea) 4–5
sample 23–9
  ages 23–4, 27–8
  class background 39–40
  education 26–7, 76–7;
    higher 87;

    qualifications 139–41
  employment 82; number
    career-oriented 83–4;
    pattern of maternal 43–4
  ethnic minorities in 28, 40–1
  household division of
    labour 49, 51
  locating respondents 26–9
  occupations 39–40, 132–5;
    numbers in male-
    dominated 139–41;
    perception of gender
    composition of 139–41
  relationships: interaction with
    male carers 54–5; numbers
    in long-term lesbian 192;
    respondents expecting to
    marry 77, 78, 82;
    respondents finding
    marriage desirable 53;
    respondents not expecting
    to marry 83–4
  selection 25–6
  sexuality: questioning in
    adolescence 72;
    respondents' perceptions of
    childhood self 60
  see also research
Sanderson, K. *see* Crompton, R.
  and Sanderson, K.
Schwartz, P. *see* Blumstein, P.
  and Schwartz, P.
'Second Wave' feminism 17,
  20, 49
segregation, labour
  market 132–41
  horizontal 132–5
  and sexuality of
    workers 154–5
  vertical 135, 138
self-employment 175
self-esteem 76, 110
Sex Discrimination Acts (1975
  and 1986) 129
sex education 17–18
sexism, at work **148–52**, **155–6**
sexual identity
  of Black women 16
  and employment 22
  empowerment derived